DIONYSIUS THE AREOPAGITE AND THE NEOPLATONIST TRADITION

'Dionysius the Areopagite' is arguably one of the most mysterious and intriguing figures to emerge from the late antique world. Writing probably around 500 CE, and possibly connected with the circle of Severus of Antioch, Dionysius manipulates a Platonic metaphysics to describe a hierarchical universe: as with the Hellenic Platonists, he arranges the celestial and material cosmos into a series of triadic strata. These strata emanate from one unified being and contain beings that range from superior to inferior, depending on their proximity to God. Not only do all things in the hierarchy participate in God, but also all things are inter-connected, so that the lower hierarchies fully participate in the higher ones. This metaphysics lends itself to a sacramental system similar to that of the Hellenic ritual, theurgy. Theurgy allows humans to reach the divine by examining the divine as it exists in creation.

Although Dionysius' metaphysics and religion are similar to that of Iamblichus and Proclus in many ways, Pseudo-Dionysius differs fundamentally in his use of an ecclesiastical cosmos, rather than that of the Platonic Timaean cosmos of the Hellenes. This book discusses the Christian Platonist's adaptation of Hellenic metaphysics, language, and religious ritual. While Dionysius clearly works within the Hellenic tradition, he innovates to integrate Hellenic and Christian thought.

ASHGATE STUDIES IN PHILOSOPHY & THEOLOGY IN LATE ANTIQUITY

Series Editors

Dr Mark Edwards, Oxford University, UK
Professor Patricia Cox Miller, Syracuse University, USA
Professor Christoph Riedweg, Zurich University, Switzerland

The *Ashgate Studies in Philosophy & Theology in Late Antiquity* series focuses on major theologians, not as representatives of a 'tradition', whether Christian or classical, but as individuals immersed in the intellectual culture of their day. Each book concentrates on the arguments, not merely the opinions, of a single Christian writer or group of writers from the period AD 100–600 and compares and contrasts these arguments with those of pagan contemporaries who addressed similar questions. By study of the political, cultural and social milieu, contributors to the series show what external factors led to the convergence or divergence of Christianity and pagan thought in particular localities or periods. Pagan and Christian teachings are set out in a clear and systematic form making it possible to bring to light the true originality of the author's thought and to estimate the value of his work for modern times. This high profile research series offers an important contribution to areas of contemporary research in the patristic period, as well as providing new links into later periods, particularly the medieval and reformation.

Other titles published in this series:

Origen Against Plato
Mark Julian Edwards

Dionysius the Areopagite and the Neoplatonist Tradition

Despoiling the Hellenes

SARAH KLITENIC WEAR
Franciscan University of Steubenville, USA

and

JOHN DILLON
Trinity College Dublin, Ireland

ASHGATE

Published by
Ashgate Publishing Limited
Gower House
Croft Road
Aldershot
Hampshire GU11 3HR
England

Ashgate Publishing Company
Suite 420
101 Cherry Street
Burlington, VT 05401-4405
USA

Ashgate website: http://www.ashgate.com

British Library Cataloguing in Publication Data
  Dillon, John M.
  Dionysius the Areopagite and the Neoplatonist tradition : despoiling the Hellenes. – (Ashgate studies in philosophy & theology in late antiquity)
  1. Pseudo-Dionysius, the Areopagite 2. Neoplatonism
  I. Title II. Klitenic Wear, Sarah
  270.2'092

  ISBN-13: 9780754603856

Library of Congress Cataloging-in-Publication Data
Dillon, John M.
  Dionysius the Areopagite and the Neoplatonist tradition : despoiling the Hellenes / John Dillon and Sarah Klitenic Wear.
    p. cm. – (Ashgate studies in philosophy & theology in late antiquity)
  Includes bibliographical references (p.   ) and indexes.
  ISBN-13: 978-0-7546-0385-6 (hardcover : alk. paper)
  1. Pseudo-Dionysius, the Areopagite. 2. Neoplatonism.
  I. Klitenic Wear, Sarah. II. Title.
  BR65.D66D55 2007
  230'.14092–dc22

                                                                        2006029283

ISBN 978-0-7546-0385-6

Printed and bound in Great Britain by MPG Books Ltd, Bodmin, Cornwall.

Contents

Acknowledgements   *vii*
List of Abbreviations   *ix*

1   Introduction   1
2   God as Monad in the *Divine Names*   15
3   God as Trinity in the *Divine Names*   33
4   On Hierarchy   51
5   The Problem of Evil   75
6   Scriptural Interpretation [*Theoria*] as Onomastic Theurgy   85
7   *Hierourgia* and *Theourgia* in Sacramental Activity   99
8   Union and Return to God: *The Mystical Theology* and the
     First Hypothesis of the *Parmenides*   117
9   Conclusion   131

Bibliography   *135*
Index   *141*

Acknowledgements

The original idea for this book was conceived by Sarah Lloyd of Ashgate, who some years ago invited JMD to contribute a volume to the series *Ashgate Studies in Philosophy & Theology in Late Antiquity* on the relationship between Dionysius the Areopagite and the Neoplatonic School of Athens. Not being in a position to take up this challenge at the time, JMD passed the task on to SKW, who was at that time completing a doctoral thesis with him on the Neoplatonist Syrianus, a major figure of the Athenian School, and who had previously herself worked on Dionysius. SKW bravely took up the challenge, selected the topics to be dealt with, and composed the great bulk of the text, with JMD merely exercising a supervisory and advisory role, and contributing some sections.

In view of the topic that it was asked to address, this book has a somewhat restricted focus, and it is one that cannot be expected to please all lovers of the Areopagite. The authors are, after all, approaching him from a predominantly Neoplatonic, rather than a Patristic perspective, and will thus tend to view patterns of influence somewhat differently from someone with the latter background. We would be the first to admit that, in most cases (the topic of Evil being a notable exception), Dionysius contrives to make it less than perspicuous just where he is getting his ideas and formulations from, but we feel that we have at least located the broad ambience from which he is drawing his inspiration. His actual identity must always remain a mystery, as he would have wished, but we feel that he can be located with reasonable probability in a certain time and space, and we have expressed our views on that subject in Chapter 1.

The authors are most grateful for the support of their respective spouses, Kenneth Wear and Jean Dillon. Because of the distance between Lincoln, Nebraska and Dublin, Ireland, much of the collaborative work was accomplished during ten very intensive days in January 2006 in Dublin. This 'Dionysius boot camp' would not have been possible without Kenneth Wear, who took a week off work to watch two baby girls, and Jean Dillon, a most hospitable host and wife.

We wish also to record our thanks to the Press's anonymous reader, who made many useful suggestions, and to our ever-patient editor, Sarah Lloyd.

For translations of the works of Dionysius, we have generally made use of the translation of Colm Luibhéid and Paul Rorem, in their *Classics of Western Spirituality* edition (see Bibliography), with minor alterations.

List of Abbreviations

Pseudo-Dionysius

CH	*Celestial Hierarchy*
DN	*Divine Names*
EH	*Ecclesiastical Hierarchy*
Ep.	*Epistulae (Letters)*
MT	*Mystical Theology*

Other Authors

ARISTOTLE
Met.	*Metaphysics*

BASIL OF CAESAREA
Adv. Mac.	*Adversus Macarium*
C. Eunom.	*Contra Eunomium*
De Spir.	*De Spiritu*

Chald. Or.	*Chaldaean Oracles*

CYRIL OF ALEXANDRIA
C. Julian.	*Contra Julianum*

CYRIL OF JERUSALEM
Com. in Joh.	*Commentarius in Johannem*

DAMASCIUS
De Princ.	*De Principiis (On First Principles)*

GREGORY OF NAZIANZUS
Or.	*Orationes*

GREGORY OF NYSSA
De diff. ess. et hyp.	*De differentia essentiae et hypostaseos*
De s. Trin.	*De sancta Trinitate*
Ex comm. not.	*Ad Graecos (ex communibus notionibus)*
Or. cat. m.	*Oratio catechetica magna*

IAMBLICHUS
DM	*De Mysteriis*
De An.	*De Anima (On the Soul)*
In Phaedr.	*In Phaedrum Commentarius*

In Tim.   *In Timaeum Commentarius*

NEMESIUS
De nat. hom.   *De natura hominis (On the Nature of Man)*

ORIGEN
C. Cels.   *Contra Celsum (Against Celsus)*
De Princ.   *De Principiis (On First Principles)*

PLATO
Parm.   *Parmenides*
Soph.   *Sophistes*
Tim.   *Timaeus*

PLOTINUS
Enn.   *Enneads*

PLUTARCH
De Is.   *De Iside et Osiride (On Isis and Osiris)*

PORPHYRIUS
Sent.   *Sententiae ad intelligibilia ducentes*

PROCLUS
DMS   *De Malorum Substantia (On the Real Existence of Evil)*
ET   *Elements of Theology*
PT   *Platonic Theology*
In Alc.   *In Alcibiadem Commentarius*
In Crat.   *In Cratylum Commentarius*
In Eucl.   *In Euclidem Commentarius*
In Parm.   *In Parmenidem Commentarius*
In Remp.   *In Rempublicam Commentarius*
In Tim.   *In Timaeum Commentarius*

PS. JUSTIN
Ad orth. resp.   *Quaestiones et responsiones ad orthodoxes*
Exp. rect. fid.   *Expositio rectae fidei*

SIMPLICIUS
In Cat.   *In Categorias Commentarius*
In Phys.   *In Physica Commentarius*

[SIMPLICIUS] (= PRISCIANUS)
In de An.   *In de Anima*

SYRIANUS
In Met.   *In Metaphysica Commentarius*
In Tim.   *In Timaeum Commentarius*

Chapter 1

Introduction

Identity of the Author; History of Scholarship

'Dionysius the Areopagite'[1] is arguably one of the most mysterious and intriguing figures to emerge from the late antique world. Ever since the mid-sixth century AD, speculation has swirled around the identity of this portentous figure. Was he, as he presents himself, the first Athenian convert of St Paul, living and writing some time in the later first century AD, or was he rather a sophisticated late-fifth-century pseudepigrapher, despoiling the contemporary Athenian school of Neoplatonism in order to forge a new Christian Platonist theology? Fortunately for the purposes of the present work, we can now regard the controversy as having been definitively settled in favour of the latter alternative, but it is still worth surveying, even briefly, the course of the argument over the past centuries, as it constitutes an interesting chapter in the history of ideas.

From the earliest Christian centuries, speculation had centred on the figure of Dionysius, precisely because so little was known about him. All we hear in the NT (Acts 17:34) is that, after Paul addressed the Areopagus, 'some men joined him and believed, among them Dionysius the Areopagite'. Already in the first Christian centuries efforts were made to fill out some details. Eusebius reports (*EH* 3, 4, 11) that a certain Dionysius of Corinth identified the Areopagite as the first bishop of Athens. There is, however, no suggestion in earlier times that he was the author of any writings. Nonetheless, he plainly constituted a figure on which intellectual baggage could be laid. It was not, however, until some time in the very late fifth century or the first decade of the sixth that anything was made of this. Suddenly, however, in this period, there burst upon the intellectual world of late antiquity a remarkable series of works purporting to emanate from his pen. These works reveal a figure thoroughly acquainted with the latest doctrines and formulations of the contemporary Neoplatonic school of Athens, along with a burning concern to impose an intellectual structure on the doctrines of Christianity.

To comprehend why anyone should want to embark on such an enterprise, we have to consider briefly the intellectual environment in the Greek east of the empire in this period. The Christian Church at this time was racked by controversy, in particular as regards the nature (or natures) of Christ. Already back in 451, the Council of Chalcedon had declared it a dogma that Christ had two natures, a human and a divine, but this did not silence dissatisfaction among the more acute

---

1   To be referred to in the following pages as 'Dionysius', rather than 'Pseudo-Dionysius', not by any means to deny his pseudonymity, but simply for reasons of economy.

minds of the Christian intelligentsia. Particularly in Antioch,[2] various forms and modifications of 'monophysitism' (the doctrine that Christ had but a single nature) prevailed, including 'monotheletism' (maintaining that Christ had a single will) and 'monenergism' (declaring that he had a single source of activity).

Into this cauldron of controversy there plunged the highly-intelligent, but ceaselessly combative, figure of Severus of Antioch. Severus was a native of Sozopolis in Pisidia, born in 465 of a wealthy pagan family and sent to study in Alexandria and then Beirut, where he was destined for the law. While at Alexandria in the late 480s he would have had the opportunity to become acquainted with the doctrines of the Neoplatonism of Proclus, who had just died in 484, since connections between the two Neoplatonic schools were at this stage quite close, with much coming and going.[3] Severus, however, when he went to Beirut, fell under the influence of Christian fellow-students and, as a consequence of the study of the Cappadocian Fathers, was baptized into Christianity. No sooner did he become a Christian, however, than he became involved in controversy, gravitating to the extreme wing of the Monophysite persuasion. He abandoned his career as a lawyer and went to become a monk in Jerusalem. Subsequently he moved to a monastery near the town of Maiuma, where he became acquainted with the interesting figure of Peter the Iberian, who was at this time bishop of Maiuma.

To detail the totality of Severus' adventures, physical and intellectual, is beyond the scope of this work. Suffice it to say that, as a monophysite, he was appointed patriarch of Antioch in 512 through the favour of the Emperor Anastasius, but was deposed from this position in 519 on the succession of Justin I. Severus' importance in this narrative stems from the fact that he is the first known figure to have made reference to works of Dionysius the Areopagite. We know this from the record of a conference held in 532 between a group of orthodox followers of the Council of Chalcedon, led by Hypatius of Ephesus, and a group of partisans of Severus,[4] where the Severians, in support of their position, make reference to a number of authorities, including the Alexandrian patriarchs Athanasius and Cyril, Gregory Thaumaturgus, and finally, 'Dionysius the Areopagite', all of whom assert that there is one nature of God the Logos after the union. It is noteworthy that Hypatius himself, in this connection, expresses some scepticism as to the authenticity of the works of Dionysius the Areopagite.

It was the ingenious suggestion of Josef Stiglmayr, whose contribution to Dionysian studies will be mentioned further below, that the true author of the Dionysian corpus was none other than Severus himself. This attractive proposal, however, has been forcefully countered by the great authority on Severus, Joseph Lebon, and it seems

---

2   Though not by any means exclusively – Alexandria had its partisans of Monophysitism as well, and monotheletism was actually at one point adopted by a pope of Rome (Honorius, in the early 7th cent.).

3   Specifically, Isidore the pupil of Proclus was teaching in Alexandria at this time in the Platonic school of Horapollo, where the young Damascius was also a pupil. It would have been natural for Severus too as a young Hellenic intellectual to have attended such a school.

4   This report is given in a document bearing the title 'Epistle of Innocent the Maronite concerning a Conference held with the Severians' (*Innocentii Maronitae epistula de collatione cum Severianis habita*), reprinted in *Acta conciliorum oecumenicorum* 4–II: 172.

best to yield to him in this,[5] but the fact remains that the author of these remarkable works cannot be far removed from the circle of Severus, experienced a course of education similar to that of Severus, and Severus probably knew who he was.

Our next evidence of the existence of the Dionysian corpus comes from the annotations composed upon it no later than 532 by John of Scythopolis. John is much concerned to indicate the orthodoxy of Dionysius,[6] and equally concerned to distance him from any affinity to Neoplatonism, indicating that he was conscious of the dangers of such a connection. He also lets slip, in a number of details, that some doubts had been raised as to the authenticity of the corpus.[7] Specifically, he is at pains to defuse a suggestion that a reference to a formulation by Ignatius of Antioch at *DN* 709B constitutes a serious anachronism – as indeed it does. John makes a valiant effort to argue that Dionysius could have known Ignatius, but what is significant is that the objection had been raised.

John's efforts were successful, and the works of Dionysius escaped the condemnation incurred by Severus in respect of all of his works which resulted from the synod called by the anti-Monophysite Patriarch Menas in Constantinople in 536, ratified reluctantly by Justinian. By the latter part of the century, when Maximus the Confessor composed a commentary on the Dionysian corpus, his authenticity and his orthodoxy were assured. His translation into Latin, first in 838 by Hilduin of the monastery of St Denys near Paris (who also ventured to make an identification between the Areopagite and the Dionysius who was first bishop of Paris), and then by John Scottus Eriugena in 862, established Dionysius likewise in the Western Church as the archetypal Christian theologian. Thereafter, the authenticity and orthodoxy of Dionysius remained substantially unchallenged until the Renaissance, when Lorenzo Valla directed the first shaft of doubt against the authenticity of the corpus in 1457. These doubts were picked up by the great Dutch scholar Erasmus in the next generation (1505), but the full force of their challenge was not widely appreciated until the early nineteenth century, when modern scholarship on the subject of Dionysius may be said to begin with the monograph of Johann G. Engelhardt in his *Dissertatio de Dionysio platonizante* of 1820 and a number of subsequent works. Engelhardt actually asserted that the corpus exhibited clear and numerous traces of Proclus' philosophy, but he failed to produce detailed instances of dependence. At the end of the century, however, a decisive breakthrough was made by Josef Stiglmayr in his essay 'Der Neuplatoniker Proclus als Vorlage des

---

5   However, the claims of Peter of Iberia have also been put forward by Honigmann (1952), with rather less plausibility, in view of Peter's known career. He seems to have gone from life as a hostage in Constantinople for the good behaviour of his father, who was king of Georgia, directly to Jerusalem to become a monk. Furthermore his chronology (*c.* 411–491) makes him less likely to have been a student of Proclus. As Honigmann admits, Peter, in his surviving writings, shows no sign of the characteristic formulations or metaphysical system of Dionysius.

6   On John, cf. the useful study of Rorem and Lamoreaux (1993). A notable example of his procedure is his scholion on *EH* 313, where he is concerned to emphasize (somewhat optimistically) the orthodoxy of Dionysius on the nature of Christ, a topic to which we will return below.

7   John of Scythopolis, *Prologue to the Works of Saint Dionysius, PG*, 4, 20.

sogen. Dionysius Areopagita in der Lehre vom Uebel',[8] in which he demonstrated that Dionysius' excursus on the nature of evil in Chapter 4 of the *Divine Names* is fairly closely dependent on the treatise of Proclus *De Malorum Subsistentia* on the same subject. Once this point had been agreed, there was no further need to search for suitable niches for Dionysius in previous centuries. Stiglmayr's further proposal, alluded to above, in an article of 1928, 'Der sogenannte Dionysius Areopagita und Severus von Antiochien',[9] proved less persuasive, but does serve to emphasize the close relationship between the works of Dionysius and the circle of Severus. Further important contributions to our understanding of the dependence of Dionysius on the Neoplatonic school of Athens have been made by the eminent scholars Salvatore Lilla[10] and Henri-Dominique Saffrey.[11] Among other leading scholars of Dionysius to whom the present work is indebted on various points are Hugo Koch,[12] René Roques,[13] Victor Lossky,[14] Walther Völker,[15] Jean Vanneste,[16] Eugenio Corsini,[17] Endre von Ivanka,[18] Maurice de Gandillac,[19] Bernard Brons,[20] Andrew Louth,[21] Paul Rorem,[22] Stephen Gersh,[23] Ronald Hathaway[24] and Ysabel De Andia.[25]

Dionysius and the Monophysite Controversy

The main features of Dionysius' philosophy will be discussed in the chapters that follow. It seems appropriate here, however, to say something about his Christology, since this feature of his thought is crucial for his relationship to the circle of Severus of Antioch, and may indeed have been one of the stimuli to the creation of the corpus in the first place – the other, of course, being a desire to 'reclaim' the whole edifice of Neoplatonic philosophy for the Christian faith.

Whatever may have appeared the case to later Byzantine and Western commentators, it is fairly clear, particularly from a study of such a document as Dionysius' Letter 4, that his position, although couched in high-flown and convoluted terms, calculated to confuse the dull-witted, is in accordance with the Monophysite

---

8   Stiglmayr (1895).
9   Stiglmayr (1928).
10 Lilla (1997).
11 Saffrey (1982).
12 Koch (1900).
13 Roques (1954).
14 Lossky (1930).
15 Völker (1958).
16 Vanneste (1959).
17 Corsini (1962).
18 Ivanka (1956a, 1956b).
19 Gandillac (1958).
20 Brons (1975, 1976).
21 Louth (1989).
22 Rorem (1984, 1993).
23 Gersh (1978).
24 Hathaway (1969).
25 De Andia (1996).

position – or, more particularly, advances a position which may be described as Monenergism, that is to say, the doctrine that within Christ there is just one source of activity (*energeia*), and that is the activity of the god-man who is Jesus Christ. What may have led more orthodox pro-Chalcedonian thinkers to suppose that Dionysius was on their side is his emphasis on the unmixed and pure Christ in his mortal body. A quotation from Letter 4 may illustrate this:

> You ask how it could be that Jesus, who transcends all, is placed in the same order of being with all men. He is not called a man here in the context of being the cause of man but rather as being himself quite truly a man in all essential respects. But we do not define Jesus in human terms (*ouk anthropikôs*). For he is not simply a man, nor would he be supra-essential (*hyperousios*) if he were only a man. Out of his very great love for humanity, he became quite truly a human, both superhuman and among humans; and, though himself beyond being, he took upon himself the being of humans. Yet he is not less overflowing with supra-essentiality (*hyperousiotês*), always supra-essential as he is, and supra-abundantly so. While truly entering into essence, he was essentialized in a supra-essential way and superior to man though he was, he performed (*enêrgei*) the activities of men. (*Ep.* 4, 1072AB)

This jaw-breaking series of formulations amounts to a statement that God the Son, as a transcendent, supra-essential divinity, entered and manipulated a human body, without himself compromising his full divinity. There is no question here of two natures, since the human body is simply an instrument with which he unites in order to do his work as Jesus Christ. Dionysius goes on to adduce two aspects of his human existence as proof of his special status, the first his virgin birth, the second, remarkably, his walking on the water; in this latter case, he speaks of the water remaining unparted and bearing up his feet because of his supernatural power (*hyperphyês dynamis*).[26] Lilla, with reference to this doctrine,[27] most acutely draws attention to a possible source for Dionysius' position in Porphyry's theory, in his *Symmikta Zêtêmata*,[28] of the mode of union between soul and body in general as being a union without contamination on the part of the soul. Here, there is no question of the body having a conscious 'nature' of its own. It is merely an instrument which the soul vivifies and controls. This doctrine, carefully crafted as it is, seems to have been sufficiently obscure to avoid condemnation with the rest of the Monophysite movement, mainly, we must presume, because of its emphasis on the maintenance of Christ's supra-essential status.

Dionysius ends his letter with a flourish of remarkable complexity:

> Furthermore, it was not by virtue of being God that he did divine things, not by virtue of being a man that he did what was human, but rather, by the fact of being God-made-man

---

26 *Ep. 4*, 1072B.

27 Lilla (1996).

28 Porphyry, fr. 261 Smith, quoted by Nemesius, *De nat. hom.* 3, 137–41 (p. 42, 9–43, 11 Morani).

(*andrôthentos theou*), he accomplished something new in our midst, the activity of the God-man (*theandrikê energeia*).[29]

This final formulation of *theandrikê energeia* seems to encapsulate very well Dionysius' remarkable position, and it plainly was sufficiently devious to satisfy later generations of orthodox theologians, beginning with his first commentator, John of Scythopolis, and continuing with Maximus the Confessor.

The Dionysian Corpus

The full tally of the works which comprise the Dionysian corpus is as follows. The chief and longest treatise is the *Divine Names*, which contains thirteen chapters, discussing the nature of God as both transcendent and creative. Aspects of the divine are discussed in terms of God's many names, the sources for which are both scriptural and Platonic: Chapter 1 introduces the transcendent God; Chapter 2, procession, including Christ as procession; Chapter 3, prayer. In Chapters 4 through 13, Dionysius offers names for God which speak to particular aspects of God, beginning with, in Chapter 4, 'Good', 'Light', 'Beautiful', 'Love', 'Ecstasy', 'Zeal', particularly with respect to God as the source of all things which incites in them a desire to return to God, as well as a long excursus on the nature of evil (ss. 18–35); Chapter 5 discusses the name 'Being' as a procession of God which extends to all existent things; Chapter 6, the name 'Life' as the procession encompassing all living things; Chapter 7, 'Wisdom', 'Mind', 'Word', 'Truth' and 'Faith' as the aspect of God processing downward to rational beings, including angels and human minds; Chapter 8, 'Power', 'Righteousness', 'Salvation', Redemption' and 'Inequality', names which point to God as the power for cosmic harmony, delimitation and arrangement, by which all things are preserved; Chapter 9 treats the following names, the ultimate source of which seems to be Plato's *Sophist*: 'greatness and smallness', 'sameness and difference', 'similarity and dissimilarity', 'rest', 'motion', 'equality' – names applied to God as the cause of everything. Chapter 10, which calls God 'Omnipotent' and 'Ancient of Days', is a discourse on time and eternity. Chapter 11 calls God 'Peace', 'Being Itself', 'Life Itself' and 'Power Itself', all of which present God as monadic cause. In Chapter 12, Dionysius calls God 'Holy of Holies', 'King of Kings', 'Lord of Lords' and 'God of Gods', names which point to God as the source of cosmic harmony and law. Lastly, Chapter 13 offers the most significant names, 'Perfect' and 'The One', which address God as the unified cause of multiplicity. The work can thus be seen – and indeed has been, first by Thomas Aquinas[30] but more

---

29 On this phrase John of Scythopolis has an interesting scholion, adverted to by Saffrey (1966), to the effect that, one should on no account confuse this term *theandrike* with the god Theandrites – as if Dionysius were suggesting a connection between such a god and Jesus Christ. As Saffrey ingeniously suggests, John would hardly have made this bizarre remark had he not had in mind, or heard it suggested, that Dionysius might have been influenced by the fact that Proclus had written a hymn to just such a god, worshipped in Arabia under the name of Theandrios.

30 Aquinas, *In de divinis nominibus*, IV, 1, 261–5.

recently by Hans Urs von Balthasar[31] – as exhibiting a pattern of 'procession and return', entirely suitable to its subject-matter.

The Mystical Theology is Dionysius' shortest work, consisting of five chapters which address God as ineffable, transcendent, and reachable only by the absolute abandonment of everything. It presents negative theology as the only path for the soul's return to God. Chapter 1 begins with a prayer to divine darkness, a hymn to God which has been attributed to Gregory of Nazianzus and to Proclus,[32] but which is doubtless Dionysius' own. Chapter 2 addresses the problem that God, while being cause of all, yet transcends his creation. Chapter 3 places negative theology above positive theology as addressing the true nature of God.[33] Chapters 4 and 5 describe God as imperceptible and non-conceptual, denying of him both positive and negative characteristics. It may be that here Dionysius is influenced by Damascius' characterisation of his absolutely first principle, the Ineffable, in his treatise *On First Principles*, but that is not a necessary supposition.

The Celestial Hierarchy and *The Ecclesiastical Hierarchy* treat the angelic and human realms respectively, the latter of which mirrors the former, both of them being divided into a series of triadic ranks. *The Celestial Hierarchy* discusses the angelic realm in fifteen chapters. The first two chapters discuss the nature of symbol. Chapter 3 addresses the meaning of the word 'hierarchy', which is in fact a coinage of Dionysius. Chapters 4–5 concern the function of angels as intermediaries between the divine and human realm. Chapter 6 outlines the celestial hierarchy itself, which is divided triadically, each rank containing a triad: the first contains the Seraphim, Cherubim and Thrones; the second, the Dominions, Virtues and Powers; and the third, Principalities, Archangels and Angels. Chapters 7–9 address each rank, respectively, with Chapter 10 stating the function of the triadic arrangement. Chapter 11 presents the (Neoplatonic) triad of Being, Power and Activity as the three-fold function within each triad. Chapter 12 connects human hierarchs (as the highest rank of the ecclesiastical hierarchy) with the lowest levels of the celestial realm. Chapter 13 addresses divine light and power, as mediated through the celestial hierarchy, particularly with respect to how the angelic realm purifies and illuminates what is below it. Chapter 14 deals with the number of angels and what that signifies, while Chapter 15 discusses biblical representations of angels and explains that the relationship between triads is that of superior, intermediate, and subordinate.

The Ecclesiastical Hierarchy consists of seven chapters, divided according to liturgical practices (many of which correspond to modern sacraments). It is here, perhaps, that Dionysius allows his persona to slip most manifestly (though this quite failed to bother his readers and commentators for almost a thousand years), in that

---

31 Von Balthasar would even discern the point of turning from procession to return, not without some plausibility, as occurring in the middle of Ch. 7. See Von Balthasar (1962), 192f.

32 This rather complicated problem is discussed by Sicherl (1988). Sicherl concludes that the hymn does not, in fact, come from Gregory of Nazianzus.

33 We also find in Ch. 3 an interesting review of the author's previous works, one of which is extant (*The Divine Names*), two lost – or imaginary, cf. below – *The Theological Representations* and *The Symbolic Theology*.

he assumes the existence of a fully-fledged panoply of ecclesiastical orders, bishops, priest, deacons, monks, and various grades of laity, such as would have been quite impossible for the first generation of the infant church. The first chapter lays out the function of the ecclesiastical hierarchy as the receptacle for divine power, placed into a series of material symbols designed to lift the worshipper up through the hierarchy, to the realm of angels, and beyond to the divine. In the next three chapters, he deals with the three 'sacraments' (*teletai*) which he recognizes, dividing his treatment, interestingly, into three sections: first, an introduction to the rite; then, a description of the procedure (*praxis*); and thirdly, and most discursively, a discussion of the theory underpinning the rite (*theôria*). This seems like an adaptation of the Neoplatonic exegetical distinction between *lexis*, the discussion of details of the text of a given *lemma*, and *theôria*, the discussion of the broader philosophical issues arising from the text – but adapted to a theurgical context, where what is at issue is not the exegesis of a text, but the exposition of a rite. At any rate, Chapter 2 describes the rite of illumination (*phôtisma*), or baptism, which Dionysius also refers to as 'birth into divinity' (*theogenesia*). Chapter 3 concerns the rite of *synaxis*, or the eucharist, which constitutes the most important of the three sacraments; and Chapter 4 treats of the rite of anointing, or chrism (*teletê myrou*). These sacraments are viewed as a triad, conferring respectively purification, illumination and perfection (*katharsis, phôtismos, teleiôsis*, EH 536D). In the next two chapters he turns to the detailing of the personnel of the church. Chapter 5 sets out the clerical orders, again arranged in a triad: the hierarch (bishop) is the highest of the three and is the perfecting element, in so far as he perfects and consecrates the sacred orders; next come the priests, in charge of illumination, followed by the deacons, responsible for purification. Chapter 6 discusses the three orders of laity: those being initiated (catechumens); an intermediate order of those who are have been purified, and are being illuminated, whom Dionysius refers to on occasion as 'the sacred people' (*hieros laos*, e.g. EH 532C); and the highest order, that of monks, who have been uplifted to the highest order because of their sacred understanding. These chapters also have the same tripartite structure outlined above. Chapter 7, concerning the rite for the dead, with an appendix on infant baptism, seems somewhat anomalous, and may in fact be a spurious addition, as suggested by Bernard Brons (1975), added by someone who found it strange that Dionysius gave no attention to the topic of Christian burial in his treatment of sacraments.[34] This author, or another, adds also a section on the question of infant baptism, which no longer makes any pretence of stemming from the first generation of the church, as he refers to ancient *Christian* authorities (*EH* 568A)!

The Dionysian corpus also includes ten letters. The first four are addressed to the monk Gaius. Letter 1 discusses God as the unknown; Letter 2, the transcendent nature of the divine, while Letters 3 and 4 concern the incarnation, Four being of particular interest in this regard, as we have seen. Letter 5, to Dorotheus, the deacon, addresses the topic of the unknowability of God. Letter 6 concerns the denunciation

---

34 It is doubtful that Dionysius himself would have had much enthusiasm for the doctrine of the resurrection of the body, on which the author of this chapter is very insistent, and on quite unphilosophical grounds.

of cults, but with an interesting note of admonition to the priest Sosipater. Letter 7 advises the hierarch Polycarp on how to deal with the 'sophist' Apollophanes, who has been abusing Dionysius, it seems, and accusing him of 'making unholy use of things Greek to attack the Greeks' – a most apposite accusation, which Dionysius is concerned to refute! Letter 8, the longest in the collection, urges kind behaviour to the monk Demophilus, who is being intolerant towards a repentant sinner, and the priest who was prepared to pardon him. This is certainly one letter, like that to Sosipater, where some reference to contemporary tensions and controversies seems to intrude itself. Letter 9, to the hierarch Titus, which makes reference to the author's (probably fictitious) *Symbolic Theology* (on which see below), constitutes an important statement of Dionysius' theory of symbolic interpretation of scripture, securely based as it is on Neoplatonic principles; while Letter 10 is a brief *consolatio* to St John the Evangelist in relation to his exile on Patmos. Even this, however, might be seen as a coded message to one or other contemporary monophysite figure who might have suffered exile after the accession of Justin I; there is mention, not of the Roman authorities as the cause of John's exile, but simply of 'unjust men'.

A special problem arises with a number of works which Dionysius refers to which have not survived: these include, *The Symbolic Theology*,[35] *The Theological Representations*,[36] *The Properties and Ranks of Angels*[37] and a treatise *On the Soul*.[38] It is difficult to decide whether in fact some works have perished or whether this reference to further works is simply part of the literary game being played, in particular the title 'Representations' (*Hypotypôseis*) is characteristic of a number of authors, Christian and otherwise, while a treatise on the soul addresses a fairly basic philosophical topic.[39]

A word should also be said about the other characters whom Dionysius introduces in the course of his works. There is, first of all, his revered master, Paul, who he calls 'my and my teacher's sun' (referred to by name seven times), whose works are quoted copiously throughout the corpus. Then there is his revered mentor Hierotheus (author of an *Elements of Theology*: DN 648B; 681A; and of *Hymns of Yearning*, DN 713A), mentioned by name five times, and as 'our master', twenty-one times, in terms interestingly reminiscent of Proclus' references to his master, Syrianus, at various

---

35 *DN* 597B; *MT* 1033AB, 14–26; *CH* 336A, 3–5; it is looked forward to in the *DN* as to be composed next. Rorem (1987) suggests that it may be summarized in *Ep.* 9, 1104B, 8f., 1113BC, 22–30. Dionysius suggests that the treatise concerns the perceptible divine symbols, including light.

36 *DN* 585B; *CH* 180D; *DN* 593B, 636C, 640B, 644D, 645A, 953B; *MT* 1032D, 1033AB. It is presented as being composed prior to the *DN*. Rorem suggests that *DN* 589D–592B is a summary of the treatise, which is given a fuller treatment in *MT* 1032D. The treatise discusses divine unity, Trinity and incarnation.

37 *DN* 696B. This is also presented as being composed prior to the *DN*.

38 *DN* 696C. In this work he claims that he has dealt with all the levels of soul from the angelic down to the vegetative.

39 Both Porphyry and Iamblichus, among Neoplatonists, composed treatises *On the Soul*.

points in his works.[40] Thirdly, there is the dedicatee of all the works, Dionysius' fellow-presbyter Timothy, no doubt intended as identical with the addressee of two of Paul's epistles, who is treated as being somewhat junior to Dionysius, being addressed at the beginning of the *Ecclesiastical Hierarchy* as 'most sacred of sacred sons (*paidôn hierôtatôn hierôtate*)'. Of the recipients of the Letters, Gaius (recipient of the first four letters) is probably intended as the companion of Paul mentioned at Rom 16:23, 1 Cor 1:14; and Acts 19:29 – though Dionysius oddly addresses him as *therapeutês*, a later term for monk, which the original Gaius can hardly have been. Dorotheus (Letter 5), Sosipater, or Sopater[41] (Letter 6), and the monk (*therapeutês*) Demophilus (Letter 8) may well be simply fictitious, but Polycarp (Letter 7) may be intended to recall the real Polycarp, Bishop of Smyrna, while Titus (Letter 9) will refer to the well-known associate of St Paul, and of course Letter 10 is unequivocally addressed to St John the Evangelist.

Survey of the Topics to be Addressed in this Work

While there is much to say about mystical thought, among other topics, in Dionysius' corpus, this work will concern itself primarily with the Platonist aspects of the Areopagite's thought, specifically the post-Plotinian Platonism of the Athenian School. In particular, Chapters 2 and 3 will explore Dionysius' concept of God as Unity and Trinity respectively, dwelling especially on how his theories of God in the *Divine Names* relate to Platonic interpretations of the One as described in commentaries on the *Parmenides*; and how an appropriation of Porphyry's distinctive theory of the relations between the subjects of the first two hypotheses of the latter part of that dialogue enables Dionysius to justify making his ineffable Unity also a Trinity. Chapter 4 concerns Dionysius' Platonic concept of hierarchy and arrangement of the universe, as seen in his treatises on the celestial and ecclesiastical hierarchies. Chapter 5 turns to a detailed examination of Dionysius' doctrine on evil, and its sources in Proclus – this being the 'smoking gun', so to speak, that provides Dionysius with his *Sitz im Leben*. Chapter 6 treats Dionysius' mode of scriptural interpretation, especially his use of Proclus with respect to symbols and the power of words. Chapter 7 discusses aspects of theurgy, the Platonist ritual of tapping into the divine as it exists in matter, as represented in Dionysius' sacramental theology. The final Chapter, 8, compares Dionysius' mysticism with the doctrines of mystical return found in the Neoplatonists, and in particular in the thought of Damascius.

---

40 *CH* 201A: my famous teacher; *EH* 376D: our famous teachers; *EH* 392A: 'as our favourite teacher said'; *EH* 424C.

41 The manuscripts vary here, but if 'Sosipater' is correct, he may be intended as an figure, mentioned (along with Timothy) at Rom 16:21, whom Paul describes as a kinsman (*syngenês*) of his.

Technical Terminology and Use of Language

One notable feature of the Dionysian corpus is the extravagant and hyperbolic use of language that greets one on every page. It is plainly part of Dionysius' project to outdo the Hellenic philosophers in an area in which they would particularly pride themselves, the use of technical terminology. Dionysius not only adopts much of the characteristic terminology of the fifth-century Platonic Academy of Athens; he repeatedly 'trumps' it by devising new terms and compounds of his own, and, in some notable cases, by employing a philosophical term in a new sense.

It is not possible, in a work of this sort, to enter in any great detail into aspects of Dionysius' style, which tends to involve long runs of parallel words and phrases, as well as elaborate word-play involving alliteration and polyptoton, but we may draw attention in particular to certain characteristic types of neologism, building on Platonist practice, but going far beyond it; and to the significant alteration of meaning which he gives to certain key Platonist terms.

First of all, some details of vocabulary. One very characteristic feature is the proliferation of compounds with *hyper-* ('beyond', 'above', 'supra-'): such terms as *hyperkosmios*, *hyperouranios* or *hyperousios* are perfectly Platonist, but what are we to make of *hyperagathos* (and *hyperagathotês*) – 'super-good(ness)', *hyperarrhêtos*, 'super-ineffable', *hyperdynamos*, 'above power', *hypertheos* (and *hypertheotês*), 'above god(ness)', *hyperphôtos*, 'above light', *hyperplêrotês*, 'supra-fullness', *hyperhyparxis*, 'superessentiality', *hyperônymos*, 'above name' and many more? Again, prefixing *auto-* to a given noun to denote the Form of *x*, or 'the *x* itself' is a time-honoured procedure within Platonism, going back to Plato himself, but no Platonist seems ever to have envisaged such compounds as *autoexousiotês* (*CH* 260C; *EH* 400A), *autoagiotês* (*DN* 969B), *autoousiôsis*, *autozôôsis*, *autotheôsis* and *autotheotês* (*DN* 956A) *autometokhê* (*DN* 972B) or *autohyperagathotês* (*DN* 820C).

Then again, Dionysius has favourite suffixes, such as *–arkhia*, signifying 'the rule or dominance of'. This we find attached to *agathos*, to make *agatharkhia; hen*, to make *henarkhia; exousia*, to make *exousiarkhia; zôê*, to make *zôarkhia; theos*, to make *thearkhia; ousia*, to make *ousiarkhia* – and most notably, *hieros*, to make *hierarkhia*, a coinage of Dionysius which has found its way into every modern language.[42] These compounds properly signify the entity concerned in its ruling capacity, but *thearkhia*, at least, which occurs fully 49 times throughout the corpus, comes to mean little more than God himself (who is, admittedly, always ruling).

Another characteristic Dionysian suffix is *–nymia*, which should signify the possession of a certain kind of name, as in the case of *homônymia*, 'possession of the same name', *pseudonymia*, 'possession of a false name', or *anônymia*, 'namelessness', but which Dionysius uses to denote simply 'the name of *x*', as in the case of *agathônymia* (*DN* 680B), 'the name of "Good"', *dynamônymia* (*DN* 889C), 'the name of "Power"', *ousiônymia*, 'the name of "Essence"', and then, most notably (24 examples) *theônymia*, 'the name of "God"'. This indeed, seems

---

42 There is also, we may note, a whole set of adjectives formed from these nouns, ending in *-arkhikos*.

to constitute an example of misuse of Greek principles of word-formation which, along with his remarkable degree of linguistic exuberance, might lead one to wonder whether Greek was possibly not Dionysius' native language.[43] Other innovations in terminology, however, seem quite conscious, and well calculated to distance him from his Neoplatonic mentors. One notable example is the term *theourgia*, which in Neoplatonic (and Chaldaean) usage means 'action directed towards the gods' (as a description of ritual procedures) – by contrast with *theologia*, 'talk about the gods'. Dionysius employs this term (frequently: 29 times in the corpus) to denote, rather, 'action emanating from God', 'divine action' – even as he uses *theologia* consistently to mean 'the words of God' (denoting the scriptures), rather than theology in the normal sense. His equivalent of the Neoplatonic term *theourgia* is actually *hierourgia*, to describe the administering of the sacraments. This sort of terminological alteration is surely deliberate – a way of suggesting superiority to the Platonist tradition: 'We Christians are concerned with the words and deeds *of* God, not just with actions and words directed towards gods'.[44]

At the same time, however, there is no question but that Dionysius' language is shot through with Platonist terminology. The characterization of God, first of all, as Good and as One, or Henad, is thoroughly Platonic, as is his description of God as the transcendent and ineffable cause of all things, and in this connection he uses well-worn Platonist language, enhanced by fanciful compounds of his own devising. Again, the Trinitarian aspect of the divinity is characterized in terms of the triad of *ousia, zôê/dynamis, nous* (Being, Life/Power, Intellect) – with the judicious substitution of the scripturally-sanctioned term *sophia*, 'Wisdom', for the Platonist *nous* – which, for reasons to be revealed presently, he is able to attach to his First Principle rather than to the secondary realm of Intellect, as was usual in Platonism.

Then, the basic cosmic process of remaining, procession and return (*monê, proodos, epistrophê*), by means of which the universe is held together, and infused with the beneficent influence of God, is taken over without modification from Platonism; while the elaborate system of levels of intermediate divinities, arranged in triads, developed initially by Iamblichus, and postulated by Proclus' teacher Syrianus to correspond to the sequence of individual arguments within the second hypothesis of Plato's *Parmenides*, is transmuted and modified by Dionysius, as

---

43 Other bizarre formations of this sort include *arkhiphôtos* (*DN* 701B; *CH* 121A, etc.), 'ruler or originator of light', *autokallopoios* (*DN* 956B), 'creative of essential Beauty', *eirênokhytos* (*DN* 953A), 'pouring forth peace', *theogenesia* (*CH* 392B, etc.), to denote, not 'birth of a god', but rather 'birth into divinity' (of the sacrament of baptism), *sophodotis* (*DN* 816C), 'wisdom-bestowing (fem.)' – none of the above, we may note, gracing the pages of LSJ.

44 A few other curious transformations of words may be noted here. *Arkhisynagôgos* is used elsewhere only in the sense of 'leader of a synagogue'; Dionysius uses it, with etymological 'correctness', to mean 'originator of unification', of God's goodness (*agathotês*) at *DN* 700A, and of his peace, at 948D. Then, *panktêsia*, used elsewhere only to mean 'full ownership' (in inscriptions, and in Philo), is used by Dionysius (969B and 972A) to describe God's 'universal ownership' – though 'full ownership' is also implied; and *patroparadotos*, used elsewhere to mean 'handed down ancestrally (sc. from one's fathers)' is used by Dionysius in the sense of 'handed down from the Father (sc. God)' (*CH* 121A).

we shall see, into a series of angelic triads within the celestial hierarchy. The basic dichotomy between the sensible and intelligible realms of existence is expressed also in throughly Platonist terms.

Other basic terms of Neoplatonism are either adopted without modification, or in some cases given distinctively Christian connotations, such as *aiôn/ aiônios, anagôgê, analogia, aoratos, apeiros/apeiria, arrhêtos, asômatos, aülos, diakosmêsis/diakosmos, eikôn, ellampsis, energeia, epekeina, epopteuô, henôsis, hyperkosmios, hyperouranios, hyperousios, kruphios* (originally Chaldaean), *logion* (in Neoplatonism referring primarily to the *Chaldaean Oracles*, but for Dionysius referring to the scriptures),[45] *methexis, myeô/mystês/mysterion, noeros, noêtos, peras, pêgê/pêgaios* (also Chaldaean), *phôs* (and various compounds of *phôs*, to denote spiritual light), *pronoia, symbolon, taxis, teleios/teleiotês/teleiôsis, telesiourgos/ telesiourgia, teletê* (referring to Christian rites, rather than Chaldaean), *theôria*.[46] By no means all of these terms, of course, are exclusively Neoplatonic, but in the context of Dionysius' work it may be taken that they are part of his Platonist heritage. The overall effect, if one comes to Dionysius from a Platonist background, is an uncanny mixture of the familiar and the exotic, which is presumably very much the effect that he is concerned to create.

Further aspects of his Platonist background and his judicious adaptations of it will be noted in connection with the various salient features of his doctrine to be discussed in the following chapters, but this will serve by way of introduction.

---

45 It should be specified, however, that this usage is by no means original to Dionysius, but goes back, though various Church Fathers, including Origen, to Philo Judaeus. Dionysius will, however, be particularly conscious of the Neoplatonist use of the term to refer to the *Chaldaean Oracles*.

46 A further characteristic feature of our author is to adopt a term which occurs in Neoplatonic sources in one form (e.g. adjectival), and develop other forms from that. For example, *ekphantorikos*, 'revelatory', is a term favoured by Proclus and Damascius, but only in adjectival form. Dionysius adopts it, but adds a noun, *ekphantoria*, and even an agent noun, *ekphantôr*, either of them otherwise only attested in the lexica of Hesychius and the *Suda* (and thus probably derived from Dionysius himself). One might see as other examples of this tendency *arkhetypia*, from *arkhetypos*, or *noerotês*, from *noeros*.

Chapter 2

God as Monad in the *Divine Names*

Introduction

The Dionysian God is a collection of seeming contradictions: it is a unity without distinction which transcends all of creation, and yet this simple being contains the plurality that is creation; it is ineffable, unknowable, untouchable, and yet it pours itself forth in the form of creation and then brings that creation back to it. This struggle between what can positively be said of God – as creator, archetype of form, and mode of salvation is continuously tempered by what cannot be said or known of the transcendent entity:

> Indeed the inscrutable One is out of the reach of every rational process. Nor can any words come up to the inexpressible Good, this One, this Source of all unity, this supra-existent Being. Mind beyond mind, word beyond speech, it is gathered up by no discourse, by no intuition, by no name. It is as no other being is. Cause of all existence, it alone could give an authoritative account of what really is. (*DN* 588B, trans. Lubhéid)

The One is unified and the cause of all creation, but thoroughly unknowable to that creation because it transcends language and discursive reasoning. A constant struggle thus exists between the One that is beyond its product, and that same One as containing it and drawing it back up to itself.

In his treatise On *Divine Names*, Dionysius attributes the following positive names to God to describe God as a monad: Good, Being, Life, Wisdom, Power, Peace, Greatness and Smallness, Sameness and Difference, Similarity and Dissimilarity, Rest and Motion, Equality, and One. These names are gathered from Plato's *Republic*, *Sophist* and *Parmenides*, the Platonist triad of Being, Life, Intellect (*on, zoê, nous*), being ultimately drawn from Plato's *Sophist* 248E, though more immediately from later Platonist sources extending from Porphyry to Proclus. By using these names, Dionysius discusses the aspects of God by which he is both the very essence of these names and beyond them: in this way, Dionysius attributes both the second hypothesis of Plato's *Parmenides* (that the One is) and the first hypothesis (that the One is not) to God. The *Divine Names* is, then, an exposition of the supremacy of the Godhead, both as to how it encompasses and how it simultaneously surpasses the totality of creation.

The Athenian Platonists, likewise, grappled with the names or characteristics of God, particularly in their commentaries on Plato's *Parmenides*. For the Neoplatonists, such as Plotinus and Iamblichus, assigned the positive characteristics of the second hypothesis to the intelligible and intellectual realms, while applying the negations of the first to the One, Syrianus used the second hypothesis of the *Parmenides* to present an articulated panorama of the realm of Being. Proclus adopted this system whereby whatever is denied of the One in the first hypothesis has a positive correspondence in the second. The positive attributes of the *Parmenides* should, thus, be attributed to the mediating intellectual orders, which are dependent upon the One as its inferiors. The One, then, can be described only with the negations formulated by the *Parmenides*, for, as Proclus says 'negations are the mothers of assertions' (*In Parm.* 1133, 3ff.). There is only one figure among the Neoplatonists, as we shall see more clearly in the next chapter, who does not observe this distinction between the first and second hypotheses as referring to the One and the realm of the Intellect, respectively, and that is Plotinus' pupil Porphyry. Dionysius, like Porphyry, can be seen as applying the first and second hypotheses of the *Parmenides* to the same supreme principle, dividing the hypotheses according to the appropriate functions of the divine: the first hypothesis expresses God in his transcendent state, while the second hypothesis describes God in his creative aspect.

Dionysius seems to combine the first and second hypotheses in his description of God:

> *DN* 596A: 'They praise it by every name and as the nameless One'; (and again) *DN* 596C: 'And so it is that as Cause of all and as transcending all, he is rightly nameless, and yet has the names of everything that is' (*Parm.* 142A, 3, 4–5 (first hypothesis); 155D, 6–E, 1 (second hypothesis))

> *DN* 596C: 'he is all, and he is no thing' (*Parm.* 146C, 1–2, 4–5 (second hypothesis); 141E, 9–10; 142A, 1–2 (first hypothesis))

> *DN* 648C: 'the divinity of Jesus is the fulfilling cause of all, and the parts of that divinity are so related to the whole that it is neither whole nor part, while being at the same time both whole and part' (*Parm.* 137D, 2–3 (first hypothesis); 142D, 8–9 (second hypothesis))

> *DN* 842B: 'Therefore, every attribute may be predicated of him, and yet he is not any one thing' (*Parm.* 141E, 9–10, 12; 142A, 1–2)

> *DN* 842B: 'He has every shape and structure, yet is formless' (*Parm.* 145B, 3–4 (second hypothesis); 139B, 2–3 (first hypothesis))

> *DN* 825B: 'He is at rest and astir, is neither resting nor stirring' (*Parm.* 146A, 7 (second hypothesis); 139B, 2–3, 9 (first hypothesis)) and has neither source, nor middle, nor end (*Parm.* 137D, 4, 7–8 (first hypothesis)), he is nothing (*Parm.* 128B, 5–6 (first hypothesis)), he is no thing (*Parm.* 141E, 9–10, 12; 142A, 1–2 (first hypothesis))

> *DN* 872A: 'Of him there is conception, reason, understanding, touch, perception, opinion, imagination, name, and many other things (*Parm.* 155D, 6–E, 2) (second hypothesis)). On the other hand, he cannot be understood, words cannot contain him and no name can lay hold of him (*Parm.* 142A, 4–5 (first hypothesis)).[1]

---

1   See Lilla (1997), 118ff.

Here we have an alternative: either Dionysius himself makes a creative conjunction of the first and second hypotheses to describe the Christian God; or he has learned this idea from some previous source.

God as the Good

In Chapter 4 of the *Divine Names*, Dionysius groups together the names 'good', 'light', 'beautiful', 'love', 'ecstasy' and 'zeal', although the focus is certainly on the overriding name, Good. Dionysius derives this name from Plato's *Republic* VI, 509B, linking the Good to the Sun, as does Plato in an analogy made a little earlier (508Aff.):

> Think of how it is with our sun. It exercises no rational process, no act of choice, and yet by the very fact of its existence it gives light to whatever is able to partake of its light, in its own way. So it is with the Good. Existing far above the sun, an archetype far superior to its dull image, it sends the rays of its undivided goodness to everything with the capacity, such as this may be, to receive it. These rays are responsible for all intelligible and intelligent beings, for every power and every activity. (*DN* 693B)

> And what of the sun's rays? Light comes from the Good, and light is an image of this archetypal Good. Thus the Good is also praised by the name 'Light', just as an archetype is revealed in its image. The goodness of the transcendent God reaches from the highest and most perfect forms of being to the very lowest. And yet it remains above and beyond them all, superior to the highest and yet stretching out to the lowliest. It gives light to everything capable of receiving it, it creates them, keeps them alive, preserves and perfects them. (*DN* 697C)

> So it is with light, with this visible image of the Good. It draws and returns all things to itself, all the things that see, that have motion, that are receptive of illumination and warmth, that are held together by the spreading rays. That is why it is termed 'sun' (*hêlios*) for it makes all things a 'sum' (*aollê*)[2] and gathers together the scattered. Every perceptible thing seeks it, as they seek to see, to be moved, to receive its light and warmth, to be kept together by it. (700BC)

This connection between the Good, the Beautiful and the sun was used by Platonists based on the passage in the *Republic*.[3] In Philo's *de somn.* I, 13 (I, 631), we find: 'lest you wonder, if the sun according to the standard of allegories, becomes like the father and the ruler of everything'; and in I, 14 (I, 732), he has the sun as that which is 'beyond intellection'. This analogy reappears in Plotinus, *Enn.* I, 7, 1, an influential passage for Dionysius, where the sun is a picture of the divine Good:

> For, again, that only can be named the Good to which all is bound and itself to none: for only thus is it veritably the object of all aspiration. It must be unmoved, while all circles around it, as a circumference around a centre from which all the radii proceed. Another

---

2   This involves a fanciful 'etymology' or word-play between *helios* and *aollês*. Dionysius may even be influenced here by the tradition of Plato's *Cratylus*.

3   For a collection of these passages, see Koch (1900), 236–42.

example would be the sun, central to the light which streams from it and is yet linked to it, or at least is always about it, irremoveably; try all you will to separate the light from the sun, or the sun from its light, for ever the light is in the sun. (trans. MacKenna)

Plotinus links the Good with the sun because the sun's emanating power cannot be separated from its source. This understanding of the Good as sun differs from Dionysius who continually makes the point that, while God is like the sun in so far as it is the source of light, God still transcends this light (*DN* 701A). In this way, Dionysius deviates from the traditional Platonic connection between a thing and its power in an effort to preserve God's transcendence over every conception of it. Dionysius also parallels the circle image in the first half of the above Plotinus quotation, although his use of the circle is to show how all things are united in God:

Every number is united in the monad; it is differentiated and pluralized only in so far as it goes forth from this one. All the radii of a circle are brought together in the unity of the center which contains all the straight lines brought together within itself. (*DN* 821A)

Again, this quotation has more to do with the unity and differentiation of that which originates and emanates from God, while Plotinus used his circle image to show how the One remains unmoved as the point of origin.

In Proclus' *In Parm.* 641, 12 there also appears a connection between the sun and God.[4] Proclus begins his discussion by saying that all things, even the lowest, are the offspring and are dependent upon the One, and by participating in the One, all things become God. Next, he says:

For if God and One are the same because there is nothing greater than God and nothing greater than One, then to be unified is the same as to be deified. Just as, if the Sun and God were the same, to be illumined would be the same as to be deified; for the One gives unity, the sun light.

Here, the sun's illuminating rays are analogous to the unity which the One imparts for deification. Dionysius echoes this in *DN* 697C quoted above, whereby God gives his light, or power, to all beings, in so far as they are able to receive it.[5]

Of all the names for God, the one which Dionysius considers to be the most enduring is that of 'One',[6] for it is God's absolute unity which shapes the universe:[7]

The name 'One' (*hen*) means that God is uniquely all things through the transcendence of one unity and that he is the cause of all without ever departing from that oneness. Nothing in the world lacks its share of the One. Just as every number participates in unity – for we

---

4   See also Proclus, *PT* II, 7, pp. 43–51, where the One is linked to the Good and the sun in the *Republic*.

5   See parallel passages in Proclus, *In Crat.* p. 103 and Dionysius, *Ep.* 9, 2 where both use the analogy of fire to describe God's power. See Koch (1900), 237ff.

6   *Parm.* 144E, 3.

7   This passage has a certain affinity with the opening chapters of Plotinus, *Ennead* VI 9, with which Dionysius may possibly have been acquainted.

refer to one couple, one dozen, one-half, one-third, one-tenth – so everything and part of everything, participates in the One. By being the One it is all things. (*DN* 977C)

God is principally oneness in and of himself, and he exists in a state of remaining within himself (*monê*). Even when God processes outward to create the universe, he remains within himself. This quality of unity is shared with the rest of the universe in so far as everything has some degree of unity which it derives from its participation in the divine oneness:

> One precedes oneness and multiplicity and defines oneness and multiplicity. For multiplicity cannot exist without some participation in the One. That which is many in its parts is one in its entirety. That which is many in its accidental qualities is one in its subject. That which is many in number or capabilities is one in species. That which is numerous in species is one in genus. (*DN* 980A)

While Dionysius is not explicit about the function of the quality of unity as it pervades the universe, Proclus gives a metaphysical description of divine unity. In the *Elements of Theology*, propositions 1–6, Proclus explains that every manifold participates in some unity, because a plurality would be unknowable in its infinite state. Dionysius alludes to this basic premise that the world would unravel in a process of infinite regression without some aspect of unity, in the following description of God:

> When things are said to be unified, this is in accordance with the preconceived form of the one proper to each. In this way the One may be called the underlying element of all things. And if you take away the One, there will survive neither whole nor part nor anything else in creation. (*DN* 977D–980B)

Dionysius takes his argument on unity from Proclus' *Parmenides Commentary*. He first notes how the form of oneness is the underlying form of every species; everything in the universe has a particular form which is necessarily unified. Thus, although there may be a plurality of members of a species, all the members are unified in one category because they share a common trait (the multitude of rabbits in the universe all partake in the Form of rabbit)[8] likewise, all species in the universe are unified in the one underlying genus of divine unity. It is with this proposal in mind that Dionysius made the statement above (977D). The fact that God is principally one and that this divine unity, furthermore, shapes the entire universe, is possible because everything participates in the One itself, as the cause and source of all creation. The language of the above passage of Dionysius reflects a similar notion in Proclus' *Parmenides Commentary*, whereby Proclus explains how the One is not like multiplicity:

> The One is neither genus nor a species; for a genus is a genus of something, but the One is relative to nothing; and a species is always essence and plurality and secondary to its

---

8   See Proclus, *In Tim.* I, 441, 10–14, where he examines why some forms only produce one substantiation (e.g. the Form of Sun produces only one sun), but others a multiplicity (the Form of Rabbit produces many rabbits).

genus, but that unity is above essence, above all plurality and second to nothing at all. (*In Parm.* 763.4–9)

Proclus attributes the One and Many of Plato's *Sophist* (254D) to the level beyond Being, arguing that pure unity and pure plurality are beyond Being. Proclus, instead, places the qualities of One and Many at the level of primary Limit and primary Unlimited, stating that the One must exist beyond both one and many (*In Parm.* 764). Proclus further systematizes his universe in so far as he makes Limit and Unlimitedness the purveyors of One and Multiplicity to the universe, a role which Dionysius reserves for God. Dionysius, likewise, while he discusses unity and multiplicity with respect to God, will say that there is an aspect of the One which exists beyond both these qualities. Proclus' discussion, moreover, is more elaborate in so far as he attributes unity to the intellectual beings, while he says that plurality is for those entities which participate in others (*In Parm.* 765).[9]

Divine unity is the source of all oneness in the universe because everything participates in divine unity – based on this premise, Dionysius describes the dichotomy between One and Many in terms of Part and Whole.[10] God is termed 'partless' (917A, 949A, 980B) because he creates the parts and is the totality of them (705C). In *DN* 648C, Dionysius says that Jesus Christ contains and surpasses wholes and parts:

> The divinity of Jesus is the fulfilling cause of all, and the parts of that divinity are so related to the whole that it is neither whole nor part while being at the same time both whole and part. Within its total unity it contains part and whole, and it transcends these too and is antecedent to them.

Jesus as Logos is described as God in the characteristics of whole and part. Dionysius does not go into a Christological explanation for Jesus as whole and parts, although this is included as part of a discussion of the supernatural nature of Jesus and is followed by a description of God coming to be, out of love for creation, at the level of nature and being.

Dionysius describes God as the source of unity and as the totality of all unity which he created, for, in the process of creation, everything proceeds from God, and as part of the cosmic process, everything returns to God: 'The One cause of all things is not one of the many things in the world but actually precedes oneness and multiplicity and indeed defines oneness and multiplicity' (*DN* 977C).[11]

God as divine unity acts as the totality (*to holon*)[12] of his creation which existed primordially within him: 'All things are contained beforehand in and are embraced

9   Proclus, *In Parm.* 765, 6–9: 'If you inquire how these Ideas – I mean unity and plurality – differ from sameness and difference, you will find that the former belong among the beings that exist in themselves, and the latter belong among things relative to something' (trans. Dillon).

10   *Parm.* 137C, 5–6; 137D, 2–3; 142D, 8–9.

11   A continuation of the passage above, see p. 19.

12   In the *PT* II, 20, Proclus likewise says that the absolute One exists beyond the total (*pan*), since the total relates to the parts that comprise it by encompassing those parts. Instead the Absolute One is better called 'entire' (*holon*), a total entity that is not full of parts. In this

by the One in its capacity as an inherent unity' (980B),[13] or, as Dionysius also states, it encompasses and circumscribes everything (*perileptikê* and *proleptikê*), terms also used by Proclus to describe the One.[14]

> But the transcendent unity defines the existent one itself and every number. For it is the source, and the cause, the number and the order of the one, of number, and of all being. (980D)

Proclus describes the One as transcending parts, making the distinction between the One with reference to itself (as set out in the first hypothesis of the *Parmenides*) and the One with respect to others, portrayed in the second hypothesis. In the case of the former, the One is neither whole nor parts, whereas in the latter he says that the One is wholly and essentially One – in which case, Proclus embraces the definition of the totality as a positive definition of the One.[15] He reports his mentor Syrianus as saying that the One holds the universe together by maintaining those things with beginning, middle, and end, while the One itself transcends parts. In a discussion of Plato's *Parmenides* 137CD, Syrianus notes that:

> The first principle is beginning and middle and end, but he is not himself divided into beginning and middle and end; for he is the beginning of all things because all things are directed towards him; for all pangs of desire and all natural striving are directed towards the One, as the sole Good; and he is the middle because all the centres of existent things, whether intelligible, intellectual, psychic or sensible, are established in the One; so that the One is the beginning, the middle and the end of all things, but in relation to himself he possesses none of these, seeing that he possesses no other type of multiplicity. (ap. Procl., *In Parm*. 1115, 27–1116, 1)

Dionysius echoes this description of God with the Platonic names of beginning, middle and end in *DN* 824A:[16] 'he is the creative source, middle, and end of all

---

way, Proclus makes explicit a distinction which Dionysius certainly implies. While Dionysius says that the One is a totality, and in later sections, argues that it transcends parts, Proclus contrasts the terms *pan* and *holon* to show how the One is a totality, not a sum of disparate parts. *PT* II, 20, p. 68, 7–13; p. 71, 7–10; II, 27, p. 95, 14–16. See Steel (1992), 61.

13 See also *DN* 936D where the Dionysian God is said to hold everything in advance as the cause of creation.

14 *DN* 593D and Proclus, *ET* 150 and 121.

15 *In Parm*. 1104, 6–16:

> And so when he says that the One is not Many, he is not saying that the others besides the One are not the One, as though he were denying those of the One, but he is merely saying that it does not possess multiplicity in itself, and that the One is not, together with being One, also Many, but that it is solely One and essentially One, pure of all multiplicity. For when, in the second hypothesis, he proceeds to assert that the One is Many, denying that it is without multiplicity and solely One and thus neither whole nor having parts, he treats the One there in relation to itself. (trans. Dillon)

16 *Parm*. 145A, 8 –B, 1.

things', qualities later denied in *DN* 825B:[17] 'God has neither source, nor beginning, nor middle, nor end'. As a creative entity, God is the beginning as the source of the universe, the middle, because everything is unified in his centre, and the end, as he draws everything back up into himself. That God has neither beginning, middle nor end draws on the Platonic argument in which a unitary entity – as is the One for the Platonists, or God for Dionysius – cannot be composed of different elements.[18] For this reason, the Platonists prefer to call the One a 'whole' (*holon*), a total entity that is not full of parts. The One and God, moreover, as unlimited entities, cannot contain limit, which is what would be necessitated were the One to actually contain beginning, middle and end: parts which have limits.[19] Both Dionysius and Proclus discuss the divine as containing things like limits and parts as the totality of creation, but, at the same time, surpassing such material designations. Here, the two reflect the first and second hypotheses of the *Parmenides*, whereby the One simultaneously 'is' and 'is not' all things. In his discussion of part and limit in the *Parmenides Commentary*, Proclus (following Syrianus) frequently uses the designation of the One 'with respect to others' (the second hypothesis, describing how the One relates to the universe) and the One 'with respect to itself' (the first hypothesis, showing the transcendent essence of the One) to show how the One contains and transcends all things. Proclus, however, differs from Dionysius in his approach to parts and wholes because he attributes beginning, middle, and end, for instance, to the second triad of the second hypothesis, which concerns the intelligibles.[20] Proclus, when describing the One's relationship to wholes and parts, says that the One is an unlimited entity which has wholes and parts in a transcendent fashion because the One exists beyond the total as an entirety.[21]

With the negation of parts, including beginning, middle and end, for the One, Dionysius adopts the Parmenidean conclusion that the One is without limit (it is governed by Unlimitedness, a trait of the first hypothesis).[22] In so far as the One

---

17 *Parm.* 137D, 4–5.
18 *In Parm.* 1110, 31–1111, 5:

He [Parmenides] now removes from it beginning, middle and end, this being a symbol of a rank inferior to that which is a whole and has parts; and we shall understand how he demonstrates this in turn on the basis of what precedes it, pursuing his canons of proof. For if the One does not have parts it will have neither beginning nor middle nor end; for everything that has beginning and middle and end has parts. (trans. Dillon)

19 *In Parm.* 1112, 26–35, Proclus sets out the three definitions of part: (1) a part is that which contains the same elements as the whole, only in a partial manner; (2) a part makes up a totality; (3) a part is linked with other things for the completion of one entity. See also Euclid's *Elements* VII, def. 3; and Proclus, *PT* III, 25, p. 88, 1–3, which identifies the relation of whole before parts to wholes of parts with genus and species.
20 In Proclus' *In Parm.* 1061, 31–1063, 5, the divine classes are called 'totality', 'multiplicity', so that the properties denied of the One in the first hypothesis are attributed to the divine classes in the second hypothesis. See Saffrey and Westerink, *Proclus* (1978), xlv.
21 Proclus, *In Parm.* 1114, 35ff. and *PT* II, 20.
22 Corsini (1962), 88.

is participated in by being and contains multiplicity, however, it is limited, as the source of all Limit and boundary (a trait of the second hypothesis). The Dionysian God is said to contain Limit (*peras*), in that it contains the boundaries of every natural knowledge and energy; at the same time, God is established by an unlimited power which exists beyond the celestial minds (*DN* 593A).[23] In *DN* 825B, God is said to be 'the boundary (*peras*) to all things and is the unbounded infinity (*apeiria*) about them in a fashion which rises above the contradiction between finite (*peras*) and infinite (*apeiria*)'. The Dionysian God is the Limit of all things; when Dionysius wishes to express God as Unlimit itself (909C, 912B), he frequently uses *apeiria* as a basis for compound adjectives: hence, God is unlimited in his knowledge (*apeirognostos, CH* 321A); unlimited in giving (*apeirodôros, DN* 817B, 909C); unlimited in name (*apeirônymos, DN* 969A); and God is unlimited with respect to power (*apeirodynamos, DN* 889D, 681D, 892B).[24]

Dionysius thus places Limit and Unlimitedness within God as the 'boundary of all things', but an unlimited source itself. By positing *peras* and *apeiria* within the One as a description of boundary and infinity, Dionysius differs sharply from the Platonists, who made the *peras* and *apeiria* pervasive, generative qualities in the universe. Proclus draws on *Philebus* 24B for his discussion of Limit and Unlimitedness in both *PT* III, 8, p. 30, 19ff. and *In Parm.* 1118, 22ff.[25] First and foremost, Proclus denies Limit of the One because it has no beginning, middle, and end, and Unlimitedness, as well, because the One surpasses it. Instead, Proclus, following Syrianus on the subject, places Limit and Unlimitedness in the henadic realm as characteristics which pervade the universe. In terms of the structure of the universe, this means that Limit and Unlimitedness exist after the One, and hence, the One transcends them. Iamblichus placed both after the second One,[26] whereas Syrianus places Limit as a monad after the One, followed by Unlimitedness (as a dyad). Syrianus[27] and Proclus make Limit the source of unity and Unlimitedness the source of plurality in the cosmos, so that Limit and Unlimitedness express two aspects of the One in relation to creation. The Athenian Platonists, thus, use *peras* and *apeiria* as the source of intelligible multiplicity, to explain multiplicity in the universe without subjecting the One to lesser principles – Proclus, unlike Syrianus,

---

23　*Parm.* 145A, 1ff.: the One contains the Limit of the all things; *Parm.* 137D, 6–8, the One is Unlimited.

24　For a discussion of God as unlimited power, see Corsini (1962), 89–90.

25　See also Proclus, *In Tim.* II, p. 159.23–160.7 for a discussion of Limit and Unlimitedness in the forms as the ultimate elements of things.

26　Proclus, *In Tim.* I, 82, 11ff. (=Iamblichus, *In Tim.* fr. 7 Dillon):

For since all things derive both from the One and from the Dyad after the One and are united in a way with each other, and have been allotted an antithetical nature, so also in the major categories of Being there is a certain antithesis of the Same as against the Other, and of Motion as opposed to Rest, and all things that are in the cosmos partake of these classes, it would indeed be suitable to consider the conflict as extending through all things. (trans. Dillon)

27　Syrianus, *In Met.* 112, 14ff.

moreover, takes this a step further and makes the two principles generative of the universe itself. In *In Parm.* 1118, 31–1124, 15, Proclus lists ten levels of Limit and Unlimitedness which exist in the universe to show how everything in the universe contains a mixture of Limit and Unlimitedness (with the exception of primal Limit and Unlimitedness and the One).[28] With respect to the One, however, Limit in itself (*autoperas*) is said to be superior to Unlimitedness in itself (*autoapeiria*) because it has unitary properties similar to the One's, and the principle of unity supersedes that of plurality in the Platonic world.[29] Proclus says that Limit maintains the universe, while Unlimitedness oversees the progression from the One which comprises the universe.[30] Dionysius, by placing Limit and Unlimitedness in God, makes a substantial change from the Platonists, in so far as he places henadic principles and causal principles within the first principle of the universe. This move is significant, both in that it makes God directly responsible for creation, and because it means that the pervasive qualities which mark the henadic realm are now the business of God, who directly pervades the universe, something which had been in Neoplatonism the job of the Forms (located in the Intellect).

God as Being, Life, Wisdom[31]

The Platonic triad of Being, Life and Intellect plays a central function in the Dionysian system,[32] and their description occupies Chapters 5–7 of the *Divine Names*; Dionysius' descriptions of these three 'names' parallels the role of these entities introduced by Plotinus[33] and adopted by his successors from Porphyry onwards. These moments served to stratify intelligible reality as developed by Proclus and the later Platonists.[34] Plotinus first, albeit in an informal way, introduced the triad of Being, Life and Intellect, describing the One as 'source of Life, Intellection and Being' in *Enn.* I, 6, 7. Plotinus' One is a self-contained entity which does not produce entities as much as it is said to overflow itself. Its first principle is Intellect (*nous*), which is produced when the One contemplates itself. Intelligence contemplates both the One and itself (its content being the Forms) (V, 1, 7). The self-reflection of Intellect, moreover, results in the order known as Being (V, 9, 8).[35] Thus, Intellect

---

28 The ranks include matter, unqualified body, qualities, realm of generation, circuits of heaven, soul, time, intellect, eternity, infinity/essential limit.

29 *ET*, prop. 132; *ET*, prop. 92.

30 *PT* III, 8, p. 32, 13ff.

31 For strategic reasons, Dionysius prefers to use the term 'Wisdom' (*sophia*) rather than Intellect, as this latter term is too distinctively Neoplatonic, and *sophia* is a term sanctified by biblical usage.

32 For a description of the role of Being, Life and Intellect, see Corsini (1962), 156ff.

33 Hadot (1960), 107–157, 108ff.

34 These are three moments of the intelligible realm, not to be confused with the three hypostases, One, Intellect and Soul.

35 'If the Intellectual-Principle were envisaged as preceding Being, it would at once become a principle whose expression, its intellectual Act, achieves and engenders the Beings; but, since we are compelled to think of existence as preceding that which knows it, we can but think that the Beings are the actual content of the knowing principle and that the very act,

and Being for Plotinus are identical, so that the content of Intellect is the Forms, but the thought of Intellect is Being. Being is responsible for causal generation in so far as all entities are contained within it as the result of the contemplation of Intellect – thus, while Intellect contains the forms as a totality, Being differentiates the Forms, making them productive. Being's function, then, is to differentiate the Forms and then return the divided Forms to the One. The process by which Forms are differentiated and then re-unified is Life. For Porphyry, the triad of Being, Life and Intellect is manifested in the One in its 'outer-related' aspect, so that the One-Being is at once the Father of the noetic realm and a constituent of the henadic realm.

Being, Life and Intellect as known among the later Platonists becomes a much-differentiated, elaborate complex coming from the One and the product of Limit and the Unlimited. Iamblichus established the One-Being as a principle substantially identical with *Nous*. Syrianus and Proclus created Being, Life and Intellect as a trinity appearing at the beginning of the second hypostasis, so that after the realm of the One, the One-Being (or Intellect) exists, followed by Life and Intellect.[36] In this noetic realm, each member relies upon and is contained in the one which precedes it. Within Being, Life and Intellect, moreover, there exists a triad. Syrianus relates the structure of the noetic realm to *Parmenides* 144E, 8–148D, 4. The noetic world thus appears as follows:[37]

The intelligible realm: Being
1st intelligible triad: One-Being
2nd intelligible triad: Eternity
3rd intelligible triad: Intelligible Intellect

The intelligible-intellective realm: Life
1st intelligible-intellective triad
2nd intelligible-intellective triad
3rd intelligible-intellective triad

The intellective gods: Intellect
1st intellective triad: Kronos, Rhea, Zeus
2nd intellective triad: The Connective Gods (*synokheis*)
and the membrane (*hypezôkôs*).

With this structure, Syrianus and Proclus elaborate upon and systematize the universe that Plotinus was advancing. While Plotinus seemed concerned with connecting

---

the intellection, is inherent to the Beings, as fire stands equipped from the beginning with fire-act; in this conception, the Beings contain the Intellectual-Principle as one and the same with themselves, as their own activity. But Being is itself an activity; there is one activity, then, in both or, rather, both are one thing.

Being, therefore and the Intellectual-Principle are one Nature: the Beings, and the Act of that which is, and the Intellectual-Principle thus constituted, all are one; and the resultant Intellections are the Idea of Being and its shape and its act.' (Plotinus, *Enn.* V, 9,8, trans. MacKenna)

36 See *ET*, prop. 103 and *PT* IV, i–iii.
37 Opsomer (2000).

levels through contemplation, Syrianus and Proclus, following Iamblichus, connect levels through a hierarchical structure, whereby the lowest item in one level is the highest of the one which follows. The point of this structure for the Platonists was to reserve unity and transcendence for the One, positing multiplicity and creation to its immediate follower, known collectively as the second hypostasis. Iamblichus and the Athenian Platonists thus mark a strong break from the system created by Porphyry, whereby the One is its creative aspect is assimilated to the One, the first element of the intelligible realm.

Unlike the Athenian Platonists, but like Porphyry, Dionysius places Being, Life and Wisdom within the One as its attributes. Regarding Being, Dionysius places this name above Life and Wisdom so that Life and Wisdom participate in Being. Absolute Being is the foundation of all existence and everything which exists is said to do so because it participates in Being. God is not Being, but acts as the source of Being, containing it as its foundation, but surpassing it by not participating in Being:

> [God] is the being immanent in and underlying the things which are, however they are. For God is not some kind of being. No. In a way that is simple and indefinable, he gathers into himself and anticipates every existence. (817D)

All things, thus, exist because they participate in Being, with the exception of God, who, as the source of Being, surpasses it (824B). Dionysius uses the triad of Being, Life and Intellect (replacing Intellect with Wisdom, as noted above, to Christianize the Neoplatonic triad), so that it refers to God himself, not to an aspect of the second hypostasis.

Life is the source of all living beings, those which have movement, from plants to souls:

> All animals and plants receive life and warmth from it. And whether you talk of the life of intelligence, of reason, of perception, of nourishment, of growth or whatever, if you talk of life, or the source of life or the essence of life, it lives and grants life out of that Life surpassing all life and it preexists in it as the single Cause of life. The transcendently originating Life is the cause of all life, produces it, brings it to completion, gives it specific form. When we speak in praise of it our words must be drawn from all of life, for we have to remember that it teems with every kind of life. It may be contemplated and praised amid every manifestation of life, for it lacks nothing or, rather, it is overflowing with life. It is absolute Life and working far beyond life it transcendently fashions all life, or however else one might humanly praise the ineffable Life. (*DN* 857B)

God, known as Life, is the source of all life and the principle which enforms life.

Regarding Wisdom, Dionysius says that God is the principle of Wisdom, the subsistence of Wisdom:

> Divine Wisdom is the source, the cause, the substance, the perfection, the protector, and the goal of Wisdom itself, of mind, of reason, and of all sense perception. (868C)

This Wisdom, moreover, is described in terms of providence, whereby God's knowledge is a foreknowledge of the providence of existent things:

The divine Mind, therefore, takes in all things in a total knowledge which is transcendent. Because it is the cause of all things it has a foreknowledge of everything. (869A)

Still, these are attributes of the divine as we know them, and hence the names must be transcended in order to express the divine accurately.

The *Megista Gene* of the *Sophist*

In Chapter 9 of the *Divine Names*, Dionysius attributes the following names to God: greatness and smallness, sameness and difference, similarity and dissimilarity, rest, motion, and equality (909B), names which he says are revealed to us in scripture. Dionysius attributes these opposing names to God in two ways: (1) by assuming that God, as the sum total and cause of everything, contains everything; and (2) by attributing some terms to God as immanent creator and other terms as referring to God as transcendent. For instance, the name 'similarity' refers to God because 'his similarity is adverted to in the context of the fact that he is the subsistence of things similar and is responsible for this similarity of theirs' (909B). Such a name can be attributed to God as the source and totality of all things which contain similarity; however, God, in so far as he is transcendent, also bears the name 'dissimilarity'.

The names in Chapter 9 of the *Divine Names*, apart from the first two: 'great' and 'small',[38] were used throughout the Platonic tradition to characterize the realm of true Being, because they comprise the genera of Being in Plato's *Sophist* 256ff. Dionysius, however, differs from his Platonist predecessors in so far as they deny the categories of Being to the One. While Porphyry[39] claims that these genera exist at every level, Iamblichus limits them to the intellective realm, and Syrianus places them in both the intelligible and intellectual realms. In *In Parm.* 1173, 7ff., Proclus gives a summary of the philosophical history of the *megista gene*: Porphyry, while he denies the names of the *megista gene* to the One, attributes them instead to the Primally Existent (*to protôs on*), a level which proceeds from the supra-essential to become Being. Porphyry describes the Primally Existent as having these categories of being in its relation to the One (it is *similar* to the One, because the One created it, but *other*, because it is different from it; it has motion because it proceeds from the One, and stability, because it is established in the One). Iamblichus (ap. *In Parm.* 1174, 3ff.), places the *megista gene* in the intellectual realm at the level of Being, attributing, as he often does, characteristics denied of the One to the noetic realm. Syrianus places the genera of being at the intelligible and intellectual levels, so that the genera exist intelligibly at the intelligible realm and intellectually in the intellectual realm. Proclus agrees with Syrianus, and elaborates his opinion, saying

---

38 These two epithets constitute a problem, since they have no role either in the *Sophist* or the *Parmenides*. If anything, 'great and small' is an epithet of the Indefinite Dyad in accounts (by Aristotle, e.g. *Met.* A6) of Plato's Unwritten Doctrines. However, being greater or smaller than itself or another is attributed to the One at 149D 8ff., and Dionysius could be cognisant of that.

39 Dillon (1988), 39.

that the genera are properties which exist throughout all the different orders of the intelligible universe.[40]

Dionysius thus presents an innovation in the Platonic tradition by applying the categories of being to God himself, using the opposite terms to stress the simultaneous presence and transcendence of God. Still, aspects of his predecessors' thought inhere in the treatise, and his innovation results from attributing both the first and the second hypotheses of the *Parmenides* to the One – as we have seen. Regarding, then, the title 'great', Dionysius says that God has a 'characteristic greatness which gives of itself to everything great' (909C). This vague definition is contrasted with God's other name, 'smallness', which is attributed to God (912A) because he transcends all bulk and extension (*ongkos kai diastêma*), and has the capacity of permeating everything. This designation refers to God as having no extension or shape, as a being without parts, a possible reference to *Parmenides* 137D–138A.[41] Proclus, similarly says in *In Parm.* 1129, 11–16:

> Wherefore it is reasonable that he should say that the One partakes of no shape. For the intelligible cause of shapes and the 'shape' of intellect is inferior to the One. It is not therefore the same to be shapeless as to have no shape, even as it is not the same to be partless as to have no part.

Here, Proclus links shape with intellect and places the cause of shape in the intelligible realm, separating the One from shape altogether. His differentiation between 'shapelessness' and 'having no shape' further separates the One from the lower realms which are marked by appearance and form, even if that form is lack of structure itself.

God is also described as eternally and unalterably 'the same', without change or alteration and 'difference', since he becomes all things for the sake of salvation (912B–913A). For the definition of 'the same', Dionysius uses the Platonic description that the divine lacks change or variation. The Platonists explain the One's eternity as due to its metaphysical position; the One exists beyond time. Proclus, in *In Parm.* 1217, 13–1219, 9, places time in the realm of Soul, which, in turn, keeps the One from partaking in Time as it does not partake in Soul. This was based on Syrianus' non-temporal explanation of Time as the causal principle of the intellectual order. Dionysius, likewise, defines God's sameness as an aspect of his eternity in Chapter 10 of the *Divine Names*, where he treats the names of God, 'Omnipotent', 'Ancient of Days', and 'time' and 'eternity':

> They call him Ancient of Days because he is the eternity and time of everything, and because he precedes day and eternity and time. And an appropriate sense is required too for those other names of his, 'Time', 'Day', 'Season', 'Eternity', all of which refer to someone totally free of change or movement, someone who in his everlasting movement

---

40 Steel (1992), 63. See also *PT* III, 18, where Proclus describes where the genera are situated in the three intelligible triads.

41 See also *DN* 825B: 'He is the boundary to all things and is unbounded infinity'. Interestingly, Dionysius derives this epithet from 1 Kings 19:12, where God is described as appearing as 'a still small voice'.

remains nonetheless in himself, someone who is the cause of eternity, of time and of days. (937C)

Here, Dionysius places God transcendently above Time and uses the Platonic definition of eternity as the measure of being (973C). Metaphysically, eternity exists at the level of being, while time is said to exist at the level of becoming (940A). Based on this placement, God, who exists beyond being, precedes both, but both time and eternity can be considered predicates of God as their source. Still, there is no systematic explanation of the levels of time, as seen in Iamblichus and Proclus, including a description of the application of time at the lower levels of the universe, for the angelic minds or matter.

As the universal cause of this sameness, moreover, God contains all the opposites in a totality. Dionysius ties God's difference to the perception of others, so that he appears in a different manner, appropriate to the person 'seeing' or receiving him. Variation, then, in God has to do with the perception of those other than God rather than any fault or difference within God. This distinction between what God is to himself and what he is to others is a notable one, as well, in the history of the commentary on the *Parmenides*. Proclus, again, makes the point that the One transcends sameness and difference, and that sameness and difference as characteristics can only be applied to the realm of the One Being.[42] In his commentary on *Parmenides* 139BE, Proclus applies the first hypothesis of the *Parmenides* to the One, and the second to One-Being.

God is also called 'rest' and 'motion' by Dionysius in *DN* 916B, referring to *Parmenides* 145E, 7ff. and 'not rest' and 'not motion', a reference to *Parm.* 139B, 1–3. The activities of resting and moving allude to the creative states of *monê* and *proodos*. With respect to resting:

> God remains what he is in himself, that he is established alone in his unmoveable sameness and definitive grounding, that his actions are forever in the same mould and with the same objective and from the same unchanging centre, that his stability begins totally from within himself, that he is absolutely immutable and immobile, and that all these qualities are his in a transcendent manner.

This mode of 'resting' is clearly a reference to God's *monê*, or status as remaining in himself at the time of creation, despite his procession which creates the universe. This coincides with the description of God as eternal and unchanging – God never changes his quantity or position in any way. These positive aspects of God's stability

---

42 'The One, itself, then established above One Being, must be shown to be in no way the same and far less, other; for Sameness is more akin to the One. But he denies both this and Otherness of the One in order that it may be shown to transcend One Being, in which Sameness is placed by Parmenides in his Poem, and Otherness as well – not that these facts are disproved; rather these are added because of the acceptance of the former. For if that which partakes of Sameness and Otherness is not yet One in the true sense, if it is necessary that the truly One should exist prior to these as being pure of these, or else in its participation in these it will not be solely One, being filled with what is alien to the One, for whatever you add to the One by its addition causes oneness to vanish, since it rejects the addition of everything that is alien to it.' (*In Parm.* 1177, 6–23, trans. Dillon)

and motion refer throughout the *Divine Names*[43] to the Platonist doctrine of emanation while 'remaining'.

Dionysius describes the motion of God using three kinds of movement: linear (indicating God's movement at the time of creation), spiral (the continuing procession from him with the 'remaining' aspect of his *monê*) and circular (providence, or the reversion of all creation to its source) (916CD). In this way, the activity of God parallels that of the divine intelligences (704D) and the soul (705A), entities which move in response to God, while mimicking God's providential care in their relationship with other entities; i.e. intelligences move in a circle when they emerge from God, a straight line when they relate to those entities below them, and in a spiral when, providing for those below, they return to God; soul moves in a circle when it turns within itself; in a straight line when it proceeds to those around it, and in a spiral when it reverts and is uplifted from external things. Divine motion, thus, mirrors activity which, in turn, shapes the activities of those which participate in it.

The three types of motion appear also in the thought of Proclus and Syrianus. In his commentary on Euclid's *Elements*, Proclus describes the circle and straight line as shapes governed by Limit and the Unlimited respectively (*In Eucl.* 103, 21), while the spiral is a mixture of both principles (*In Eucl.* 104, 7ff.). Based on the fact that Limit and the Unlimited are said to exist in some capacity at every level of the universe, these basic shapes must also pervade the universe. Proclus, moreover, roughly correlates the three activities of the One with the three shapes, whereby the point is most akin to remaining,[44] the line to procession,[45] and the circle to reversion:[46]

> One may also see on the level of generation these two qualities (sc. linearity and circularity). One may view in the cycle of existence here (for generation returns to itself cyclically, as is written in the *Phaedo* [70Cff.] the circular; while the straight one may see in the processions of each thing from its birth to its decline, and the middle here, which is in front of the extremes, as its peaks of development. (*In Parm.* 1131, 21–35)

While Proclus and Dionysius use the three motions to discuss the First Principle's activity (with minor variations for the point and spiral), we may observe some distinctions between Proclus' discussion of the triple activity of the soul and that of Dionysius. For one thing, Proclus has the soul reverting to *nous*, rather than to the One (*In Eucl.* 147, 12), although the soul is still described as engaging in activity in response to the other entities around it.[47]

---

43 *DN* 825B, 909B, 949A. Stasis as permanence occurs in 916B, where God is said to remain in himself, while motion is described as creative procession in 977AB; 916C, where God moves and creates all things.

44 Proclus, *In Eucl.* 88, 2ff.; 91, 1ff.

45 Iamblichus, *In Tim.* fr. 49 Dillon; Proclus, *In Eucl.* 108, 10–13; 164, 8–11.

46 Gersh outlines these activities in (1978), 73.

47 'The demiurgic *nous* has set up these two principles in himself, the straight and circular, and produced out of himself two monads, the one acting in a circular fashion to perfect all intelligible essences, the other moving in a straight line to bring all perceptible things to birth. Since the soul is intermediate between sensibles and intelligibles, she moves

Dionysius clearly wishes to show that God has the qualities of motion and stability in a transcendent manner, lest we find him similar to the stable things of the material order. Still, the process of creation is a type of motion instigated by God, which Dionysius presents as the equivalent of the *Parmenides* category of 'motion' in *DN* 916C:

> What is signified, rather, is that God brings all things into being, that he sustains them, that he exercises all manner of providence over them, that he is present to all of them, that he embraces all of them in a way which no mind can grasp, and that from him, providing for everything, arise countless processions and activities.

Dionysius, nevertheless, specifies that God's motion does not indicate a change of place or movement in space, nor does it take place in the mind or soul of God (916C), nor does it signify a linear, circular or spiral movement, rather, his 'motion' consists in his bringing everything into existence and his providential care for it.

Proclus, on the other hand, limits these characteristics to the realm of Being, as he correlates motion with Intellection. In *In Parm.* 1153, 1ff., Proclus says that intellection cannot be conceived without motion, so that if there is intellection in the One Being, there is also motion. Motion, moreover, is attributed to lower orders, such as the hypercosmic gods (*In Parm.* 1154, 9–24; *PT* II, 12), while the One is situated beyond rest and motion (*In Parm.* 1154, 2). Because the One is beyond rest and motion, it will also be beyond power and potentiality, which are connected to motion (*In Parm.* 1153, 29–1154, 3). These traits also, however, are attributed to the One by Dionysius (see the section on *peras* and *apeiria* above). Motion and rest for Proclus are the hallmark of being, in so far as motion is the motion of procession and rest is the stability of remaining in a primary cause; as the One neither processes nor remains in anything other than itself, it is said to transcend these categories. The One cannot be self-moved, moreover, because the self-moved is mover and moved, traits which would detract from the essential unity of the One. Clearly, Proclus does not consider the divine motions of remaining, procession and return as types of physical motion or stability.

Dionysius shows the same inclination towards applying Parmenidean categories to God under the auspices of the first and second hypotheses. On the one hand, God can be described according to the categories, on the other hand, he transcends all language and categories. The traits of the Same and Other,[48] similarity and dissimilarity,[49] follow this pattern as well. For the Same and Other, Dionysius discusses the One's relation to its creation. The epithet 'Same' is connected to the One in its state of remaining because it is eternally without change or decline (*DN* 912BC); 'difference' can be attributed to the One in its state of procession, because it is available to all according to their own capacity. Different members of the universe thus partake of the divine to a different degree, depending on how well they can receive the divine. This difference is thus in the eyes of beings other than

---

in a circular fashion in so far as she is allied to intelligible nature, but in so far as she presides over sensibles, exercises her providence in a straight line.' (*In Eucl.* 108, 13ff.)

48 *Parm.* 139E, 1–5 and *Parm.* 147B, 6–8.

49 *Parm.* 139E, 7–140B, 5 and *Parm.* 147C, 1–148D, 4.

God, rather than indicating any multiplicity or change in God himself (*DN* 913AB). This affirmation of the transcendence of God as 'the Same' recurs in the *Mystical Theology*.

Similarity and dissimilarity, although close in meaning to Same and Other, point to God's ability to return his creation to himself, as beings return to those which they resemble. Dionysius restricts the definition of similarity and dissimilarity to creation's similarity to the divine, specifying that God is not similar to anything (913C). In *DN* 9, 6, Dionysius uses the definition of *Parm*. 139E, 7–140A, 4, that the 'One is neither similar nor dissimiliar to another or itself': God is thus neither similar to his creation, nor to 'his own portrait' (913C).[50] While Dionysius is not explicit in this treatise about God encompassing the traits of his creation as a totality, it may be reasonable to assume, based on other descriptions, that the One can be called Same and Other, or similar and dissimilar, because he imparts such qualities to his creation:

> From it derives the existence of everything as beings, what they have in common and what differentiates them, their identicalness and differences, their similarities and dissimilarities. (*DN* 704B)

In Proclus' *Platonic Theology* II, 11, p. 64–5 S–W, the attributes are allotted to the encosmic beings, and in *In Parm*. VII, 1192, 1ff., the One is superior to all the classes and the ten categories which mark those classes, including same and other, like and unlike, equal and unequal, and older and younger, because these categories concern the world of sense, and not the supracosmic orders of being.[51]

The traits of being in another and in oneself,[52] equal and unequal,[53] greater and smaller,[54] younger and older[55] further show the relationship between God and creation, particularly the presence of all things in God and God's ability to maintain transcendence. The same holds true for Dionysius' other names for God, including 'power' and 'peace', which have no clear Neoplatonic analogues.[56]

We see in this chapter the results of Dionysius' argument with the Platonic tradition of negative theology as it arises in the first hypothesis of the *Parmenides* and an impulse derived from his Christian background to attribute positive epithets to God.[57] The most significant of the positive epithets proper to the Christian tradition is the characterization of God as a Trinity of Father, Son and Holy Spirit, and it is to this that we will turn in the next chapter.

---

50 See also *MT* 1048A; *DN* 820B, 909B, 912BC.

51 See Corsini (1962), 98, note 22.

52 *Parm*. 138A, 2–3 and *Parm*. 145C, 1; and *DN* 649C, 693B, 956A, 981A.

53 *Parm*. 140B, 6–140D, 8 and 149D, 81–151E, 1 and 2; MT 1048A; *DN* 897B, 910A, 705C.

54 *Parm*. 140D, 4ff. and 149D, 8–151 and DN 909C, 912A, 588A, Ep. 9, *In Parm*. 1112C, *DN* 648C, 825B, 916A.

55 *Parm*. 140E, 1–141E, 7–14 and 151E, 3–155E, 3.

56 These epithets are dealt with in *DN* Ch. 11.

57 More will be said on Dionysius' negative theology, with particular reference to his *Mystical Theology*, in Chapter 8 below.

Chapter 3

God as Trinity in the *Divine Names*

Introduction

The question of how something simple and unified gives rise to the procession that makes up the cosmos was one with which the Platonists grappled. The Neoplatonists, from Plotinus on, as we have seen, used the first and second hypotheses of the *Parmenides* to describe the unity and plurality of the universe, represented respectively by the One and Intellect, and one of the central mysteries of the Neoplatonic universe is how Intellect, or indeed anything else at all, derives from the One. Dionysius, likewise, used language from the *Parmenides* to describe how a unified, simple God could give rise to a complex universe, but with a very significant difference. The first hypothesis of the *Parmenides*, which draws negative conclusions from the proposition 'the One is', Dionysius applied to God, as transcendent First Principle, and he used this text to express the inexpressibility of God through a series of negations. With respect to his use of the second hypothesis of the *Parmenides*, however, which draws positive conclusions from the same proposition, Dionysius, as has been suggested in the last chapter, differs dramatically from most later Platonists, such as Plotinus, Iamblichus, Syrianus and Proclus. While Proclus attributes the second hypothesis of the *Parmenides* to the realm of Being, with the One transcending Being and everything associated with it, Dionysius attributed the second hypothesis also to God. By attributing both hypotheses to God, Dionysius is able to describe God as simultaneously unified and complex, as both containing creation and transcending it. The ramifications of this scheme, particularly how they shape his Trinitarian theology, however, were not entirely alien to the Platonic Academy. In fact, they bear a significant resemblance to the interpretation of the *Parmenides* put forward by Plotinus' pupil Porphyry.

At *In Parm.* 1142, 10–15, Proclus attributes the following reading of the *Parmenides* to Syrianus:

> Better then, following the lead of my own Father, to proceed along that most safe and sensible course and say that he is denying of the One here just what is asserted of the One-Being in the second hypothesis and he is denying it in the same way as it is asserted there.

Syrianus is here credited with the scheme whereby whatever is denied of the One in the first hypothesis has a positive corollary in the second hypothesis, and thus fully fourteen separate levels of divine entity are proposed to reflect the fourteen identified propositions into which the hypothesis may be divided. However, in all this there is a major difficulty, from the Christian perspective. All this complexity, beginning with the initial triad of One, Being, and the relationship (*skhesis*) between them – viewed as an element of potency (*dynamis*) or 'life' (*zoê*) – is related by the general run of Neoplatonists, not to the First Principle itself, but to a secondary principle, Intellect. For Porphyry, however, the first two hypotheses actually refer to the same entity, God or the One, but in different aspects. The first hypothesis portrays the One in itself, as totally transcendent First Principle; the second describes the One in its active, creative wholeness, as generator of the universe. As such, its nature, from being rigidly monadic, becomes triadic; it develops into a 'trinity' of Unity, Potency/Life and Being/Intellection.

This position of Porphyry's was one of considerable subtlety, since it seems to have largely escaped the comprehension of his successors, or certainly found no sympathetic echo in their thoughts. However, in the first decades of the fourth century, which is the period crucial for the formation of the Christian doctrine of the Trinity in its developed form, in particular at the hands of the Cappadocian Fathers, Basil and the two Gregories (of Nyssa and of Nazianzus), Porphyry was the dominant figure in the Platonist tradition. For thinkers such as Marius Victorinus on the Latin side, and Gregory of Nazianzus or Basil the Great, he was the intellectual opponent to be reckoned with—and one can learn from one's opponents as well as opposing them.

The great advantage of Porphyry's position, from the Christian perspective, is that this triadic structure of Being, Life and Intellect is applied, as we have said, not to a secondary principle, but rather to the supreme principle itself in its creative aspect. We have ample evidence that Porphyry accepted Plotinus' doctrine of the supra-noetic, supra-essential One, but we also have sufficient evidence that he postulated that the One, in its creative, outgoing aspect, could be seen, in the words of the later Neoplatonist Damascius[1], reporting his views, as the 'Father of the Intelligible Triad', that is to say, as the ruling monad of the intelligible world. It is this position of Porphyry's that makes him so useful to Christian intellectuals who were struggling with the problem of a God who is manifested in a complex of three 'persons', all of whom must be co-ordinate and interactive with one another, if one is not to fall into some variety or other of Arianism.

Dionysius clearly borrows from this reading of the *Parmenides* (whether directly or through the intermediacy of the Cappadocians, it is not clear), giving it a greater complexity: For him, what is denied of the One as transcendent Godhead is attributed to it as creator who contains the distinctions of creation, and as Trinity, in so far as it contains the three Persons. God, thus, is represented by both the first and second hypotheses.[2] Dionysius considers God simultaneously as simple unity and as a complex plurality, involving a cosmogonic process of remaining, procession and return (*monê, proodos, epistrophê*).

While Dionysius does appear to be using Proclus' *Commentary on the Parmenides*, therefore, to describe God and his relationship to creation, he deviates from Proclus by applying both the first and second hypotheses of the *Parmenides* to the Godhead, rather than separating God from everything lower than it, beginning with the principle of Being. Thus, God is unity with distinction, distinction within unity. This chapter

---

1   Damascius, *De Princ.* §43, I, p. 86 Ruelle.
2   Lilla (1997), 118.

will explore these two roles of the Dionysian God and its foundation in the thought of Proclus and Porphyry. The importance of where Dionysius steers away from Proclus' representation of the One underscores the peculiarity of the Dionysian One. As was shown in the last chapter, for Dionysius, the One is the transcendent cause of everything, the unified source of all creation which exists beyond creation. This chapter will show how the One is immanent, as a series of unions and distinctions, a unity and a trinity.

Trinity as Unity; Trinity as Distinction

While God is a unified, transcendent entity, he is also a unified multiplicity, both with respect to his creation and with respect to himself. Dionysius returns to the Neoplatonic interpretation of the *Parmenides* in stating that the One is not-being, in so far as it is beyond being, and not-one, in so far as it is beyond one. In the shadow of the *Parmenides*, Dionysius gives his description of God as both one and three. When discussing the entire Godhead, Dionysius describes it as a monad; the divine names as explored in the previous chapter are those applied to God as One:

> The unified names (*hênômena*) apply to the entire Godhead, as I showed at length and by way of scriptural examples in my *Theological Representations*.[3] Hence, titles such as the following – the transcendently Good, the transcendently divine, the transcendently existing, the transcendently living, the transcendently wise.[4] These and similar terms concern a denial in the sense of superabundance. Likewise, the names which have a causal sense, names like good, beautiful, existent, life-giving, wise, and so forth, are ascribed to the Cause of all good things because of all the good gifts it has dispersed. (*DN* 640B)

Dionysius applies names which concern God as transcendent to the entire Godhead, which one can take to mean God as Trinity, based on the discussion of Trinity that immediately follows. The names, moreover, which discuss causal aspects of God also apply to the entire Godhead rather than one person of the Trinity. Thus, the most definitive function of the Godhead, as transcendent cause, is an activity which no member of the Trinity can claim for itself, but in which all members have an equal share.

Still, God is described through the divine names as a sum of distinctions which express the Trinity:

> Then there are the names expressing distinctions (*diakekrimena*), the transcendent name and proper activity of the Father, of the Son, of the Spirit. Here the titles cannot be interchanged, nor are they held in common. Also said to be differentiated is the perfect and unchangeable being of Jesus among us, and the mysteries of his existence and his love for humanity which are manifested here. (*DN* 640C)

---

3 This 'lost' work, as suggested above in Ch. 1, probably being a fabrication.

4 All these titles involve the characteristic prefix *hyper-*: *to hyperagathon*, *to hypertheon*, *to hyperousion*, etc.

The question of how multiplicity arises from a perfect unity in the cosmos, thus, has another element for Dionysius, who draws a distinction between the unity of God as creator and the multiplicity of God's creation, contrasting the unity of the Godhead itself with the multiplicity which arises within it, known as the Trinity. Dionysius is careful to maintain the distinctions of the Persons of the Trinity, while making it clear that the unity of the Godhead supersedes any variation within the three hypostases, as they are all of one essence.

Unity of the Trinity

Dionysius describes God as consisting of a series of divine unities, which form the hidden and permanent aspect of God, as well as differentiations, which are the processions or revelations of God (*DN* 641A). This distinction between the *henosis* and *diakrisis* of the divine Trinity is at the heart of Dionysius' doctrine of Trinitarian theology and the theology of the divine names.[5] In the *Divine Names* Chapter 2, Dionysius considers union and distinction in God as an aspect of God's unity and multiplicity, with respect to creation. God's differentiation, however, is also seen in light of the Godhead's relationship to the Trinity. In descriptions which are rooted in Cappadocian theology, God is called a triadic henad (*DN* 593B)[6] and an henadic triad (*DN* 641A)[7] – above all, it is a trihypostatic henad (*CH* 212C), one in three persons.

When Dionysius describes God as distinction, or a series of processions, these can take place both as emanating from God, as creation, and they can occur within God, as the Trinity. The Trinity is thus described as follows:

> Thus, regarding the divine unity beyond being, they assert that the indivisible Trinity holds within a shared undifferentiated unity its supra-essential subsistence, its supra-divine divinity, its supra-excellent goodness, its supremely individual identity beyond all that is, its oneness beyond the source of oneness, its ineffability, its many names, its unknowability, its wholly belonging to the conceptual realm, the assertion of all things, the denial of all things, that which is beyond every assertion and denial, and finally, if one may put it so, the abiding and foundation of the divine persons who are the source of oneness as a unity which is totally undifferentiated and transcendent. (*DN* 641A)

The superessential unity of God transcends all the distinctions within him even when those distinctions are elements of the Godhead. By explaining how the members of the Trinity are equally mixed and united, Dionysius reproduces the thought

---

5   De Andia (1996), 30.

6   Gregory of Nyssa, *Ex comm. not.* 21, 16; Gregory Naz., *Or.* 25, 17; 31, 9; 39, 11; *Chald. Or.* fr. 26 des Places.

7   Gregory of Nyssa, *Ex comm. not.* 21, 19; Gregory Naz., *Or.* 25, 17; 31, 9; 39, 11.

of the Cappadocian Fathers,[8] as well as the Platonic concept of the unity of the intelligibles.[9]

Proclus uses this doctrine of mixture which retains distinct elements when he discusses the relationship between Forms and Ideas in the Intellect, the faculties of the soul, and the relationship between henads.[10] In *Elements of Theology* prop. 176, Proclus says:

> For if every intelligence is indivisible, and through this intellectual indivisibility its manifold content is also unified, then all the Forms, being contained in a single intelligence devoid of parts, are united with one another, and all interpenetrate all; but if all exist immaterially and without bodies, there is no confusion among them, but each remains itself, keeping its pure distinctness uncontaminated. (trans. Dodds)

The intellectual Forms are unconfused, Proclus adds, because the lower principles are able to participate in each separately and distinctly; nonetheless, they are unified, as evidenced by the fact that a single, unitary existence embraces them. Because the Forms exist without bodies, they are able to maintain a unity and distinctness which members of the sensible world do not know. In another passage, in his *Commentary on the Parmenides*, he discusses the mixture of intelligible species despite the fact that the divine things also exist 'simultaneously without confusion and in a distinction without separation':

> Socrates has reached the final hypothesis regarding communion of Forms in saying that they all undergo separation and combination. For the joint presence of these characteristics in them provides both unconfused unity and inseparable distinctness to these divine objects, so that while they are in one another each may preserve its purity. Consequently, he admires the man who can show that the intelligible Forms can be both unified and distinct, that they do not lose their unmixed purity through union and nor their divine communion through separation, but are both distinguished and combined simultaneously by the bond of 'that wonderful god, Eros,' who, according to the Oracle:
>
> > *Sprang forth first out of Intellect,*
> > *His unifying fire clothed with fire, to mix the mixing-bowls*
> > *From the Source, directing towards them the bloom of his fire.*
> > (*Or. Chald.* fr. 42, DP)
>
> It is this joint mingling and distinctness that Socrates wants to see among the partless intelligible realities; to this he invites his companions' attention, applauding this insight which unites while it distinguishes the intellectual powers governing the sense world – ideal Likeness and Unlikeness, Plurality of that realm and Unity, divine Rest and Motion. (*In Parm.* 768.34–769.22, trans. Dillon)

---

8   See Basil, *De Spir.* 18, 45; *Or.* 24, 4 (*PG* 31, 609A 11–B4); Gregory of Nyssa, *de diff. ess. et hyp.* 4 (=Basil, *Ep.* 38, 86, 76–87, 91); Basil, *Adv. Mac.* 89, 25–90, 4, Mueller, *C. Eunom.* (ii, 315, 2–3 Jaeger); Gregory Naz., *Or.* 28, 1.

9   Lilla (1997), 125.

10 Lilla (1997), 125.

Intelligible species here can mix and still retain their identity,[11] unlike sensible objects which cannot be mixed without losing their distinction.[12]

Dionysius and the Cappadocians use 1 Cor 8:5–6 to show how each hypostasis is a monad, with its unity holding a higher place than its differentiation, thus functioning much like a Procline henad:[13]

> For although there may be so-called gods in heaven or on earth – as indeed there are many 'gods' and many 'lords' – yet for us there is one God, the Father, from whom are all things and for whom we exist, and one Lord, Jesus Christ, through whom are all things and through whom we exist. (*DN* 649D–652A)

That union has the predominant place in the doctrine of 'union in distinction' appears in a number of other places, including his statement in *DN* 652A that every name of God, when applied to any one of the divine persons, must be taken as belonging, without distinction, to the entire Godhead. This concept of union and distinction also appears in Proclus' doctrine of the henads, particularly in book 6 of his *Commentary on the Parmenides*:

> For these henads are supra-essential and, to use technical terms, are 'flowers' and 'summits'. Since then, as we have said, there is within them both unity and distinctness, it is to this that Parmenides is addressing himself, that he may make clear their whole progression, right from the summit of the transcendent henad, and he thus takes for his hypothesis his own One, that is the One which is seen at the level of Being, and he considers this now as one, now as participated. The antecedent he preserves always the same by taking it in various senses, while the consequent he keeps changing, so that through the identity of the antecedent he may demonstrate the unity of the divine henads; for whichever of these you take, you can assume the same for the rest because all are in each other and are rooted in the One; for even as trees by their 'topmost' parts are fixed in the earth and are earthly in virtue of that, so in the same way the divine entities also are by their summits rooted in the One, and each of them is a henad and one through its unmixed unity with the One. Through the changing of the consequent, on the other hand, taking it now as a 'whole', now as a 'shape', now as something else again, and this both affirmatively and negatively, he seeks to demonstrate their distinctness and the particular characteristics of each of the divine orders. By means of the whole syllogism, in turn, he seeks to show both the communion of the divine entities and the unmixed purity of each. (*In Parm.* 1049, 37–1050, 25)

Dionysius also uses the language of light to show how the Father, Son and Holy Spirit relate to one another. In *DN* 645B, he says that 'the Father is the originating source of the Godhead and that the Son and the Spirit are, so to speak, divine offshoots, the flowering and transcending lights of the divinity'. As 'flowers' and 'superessential light', the three persons interrelate such that the Father is the source and the Son and

---

11 See Plotinus, *Enn.* VI, 4, 14 and V, 8, 4 for the intelligible world as unity in distinction, and Dodds (1992), 292.

12 See Proclus, *In Tim.* II, 253, 31–255, 8.

13 Lilla (1997), 125.

Spirit flow out from him. The terminology of 'flower' and 'superessential light' were derived from Proclus who applied it to unity in *De Malorum Subsistentia*, 2, 11.[14]

One of the most important examples of unity in distinction is that of a series of lamps which produce one light:

> In a house the light from all the lamps is completely interpenetrating, yet distinct. There is distinction in unity and there is unity in distinction. When there are many lamps in a house there is nevertheless a single undifferentiated light and from all of them comes the one undivided brightness. I do not think that anyone would mark off the light of one lamp from another in the atmosphere which contains them all, nor could one light be seen separately from the others since all of them are completely mingled while being at the same time quite distinctive. Indeed if somebody were to carry one of the lamps out of the house its own particular light would leave without diminishing the light of the other lamps or supplementing their brightness. As I have already explained, the total union of light, this light that is in the air and that emerges from the material substance of fire, involved no confusion or jumbling of any parts. (*DN* 641BC)

This example of the distinction of many lights formed into a unity of brightness when seen by the eye was used by Proclus in a discussion of the unity of genera. Proclus remarks how Syrianus shows that the immaterial nature of genera renders it possible for them to be combined without loss of power or confusion of essences:

> It is, in effect, the property of immaterial mixture that the components rest indistinct, both mixed and unmixed, but of material mixture that the mixed elements are not distinct one from the other: since the mixture comes about in virtue of simultaneous destruction. And the possibility that immaterial mixtures, such as the ones we speak of, exist is easily appreciated by consideration of the sciences, the creative physical principles, the light that is constituted by a great quantity of lamps. For these multiple lamps, although they produce a single light, yet remain distinct, one from the other, and the multiple creative principles, although they make up one totality, are not less separate one from the other according to the physical property of each of them, and the multiple sciences, despite their compenetration, do not remain mixed one to the other. (*In Tim.* II, 254, 11–17)[15]

A similar analogy between light and the unity of the Trinity occurs in the thought of Basil, who argues that the content of one member of the Trinity is the same as the other; for instance, if the Father possesses the content of light, the being of the Son is also light. Similarly, Basil's argument makes a distinction between the divine and material worlds as regards generic similarity and difference. He says that while men may have different names, they all belong to the same genus because they share

---

14 On this passage, see Lilla (1973), 609; Koch (1900), 162–3; Boese (1960), 192.

15 This metaphor of the unity and distinction of light coming from lamps also appears in Gregory of Nyssa's writing *De differentia essentiae et hypostaseôs*, published in Basil, *Ep.* 38 (*PG* 32, 333A). Basil, *C. Eunom.* 2, 4, also gives as an example that any differentiation in names does not imply a difference in *ousia*, just as Peter and Paul have different names, although there is only one name for mankind. The Cappadocian Fathers expressed the unity of the Godhead in terms of the singularity of essence or *ousia*.

common being (*ousia*).[16] Still, this unity of *ousia* does not imply an identity between men, such as exists between members of the Trinity.

Differentiation of Trinity

The three hypostases of the Trinity represent the distinction which exists within the superior unity of God (*henôsis*) – in this way, the divine henad is triadic because it contains the three hypostases.[17] Dionysius is keen to point out that the names which express distinctions indicate that the hypostases maintain a principle of distinction and are not interchangeable, despite existing in the mode of union (*kath' henôsin*), because they also exist according to their own personal properties:

> Theology, in dealing with what is beyond being, resorts also to differentiation. I am not referring solely to the fact that, within a unity, each of the indivisible persons is grounded in an unconfused and unmixed way.[18] I mean also that the attributes of the transcendently divine generation are not interchangeable. The Father is the only source of that Godhead which in fact is beyond being, and the Father is not a Son nor is the Son a Father. Each of the divine persons continues to possess his own praiseworthy characteristics, so that one has here examples of unions and differentiations in the inexpressible unity and subsistence of God. (*DN* 641D)

There is no convertibility between these properties, as each of the hypostases maintains its own properties (*DN* 641D).[19] The properties, moreover, are also connected to particular functions of members of the Trinity (*DN* 640C).[20]

---

16 Basil, *C. Eunom.* 2, 4, discussed in Prestige (1952), 243.

17 Lilla (1997), 122, makes this point, connecting this concept of the three hypostases as divine distinctions to Gregory of Nyssa.

18 For parallels in Cappadocian theology, see Gregory of Nyssa *Or. cat. m.* 3 (*PG* 45, 17D 5, 8; 20A, 6–7), *De diff. ess. et hyp.* 4 (=[Basil], *Ep.* 38, 85, 42–3 (87, 84 Courtonne)).

19 De Andia (1996), 35.

20 In his *Fourth Theological Oration*, Gregory of Nazianzus gives the following explanation of distinction within the Trinity:

> For how could there be a god of him who is properly God? In the same way he is Father not of the visible, but of the Word; for our Lord was of two natures: so that one expression is used properly, the other improperly in each of the two cases; but exactly the opposite way to their use in respect of us. For with respect to himself God is properly our God, but not properly our father. And this is the cause of the error of the heretics, namely the joining of these two names, which are interchanged because of the union of the natures. And an indication of this is found in the fact that wherever the natures are distinguished in our thoughts from one another, the names are also distinguished; 'The God of our Lord Jesus Christ, the father of glory.' The god of Christ, but the father of glory. For although these two terms express but one person, yet this is not by a unity of nature, but by a union of the two. (Section VIII, trans. Schaff–Wace)

The divine persons, moreover, each have a role which corresponds to their personal properties:[21]

> The procession of our intellectual activity can at least go this far, that all fatherhood and all sonship are gifts bestowed by that supreme source of Fatherhood and Sonship on us and on the celestial powers. This is why godlike minds come to be and to be named 'gods' or 'sons of gods' or 'fathers of gods.' Fatherhood and sonship of this kind are brought to perfection in a spiritual fashion, that is incorporeally, immaterially, and in the domain of mind, and this is the work of the divine Spirit, which is located beyond all conceptual immateriality and all divinization, and it is the work too of the Father and of the Son who supremely transcend all divine Fatherhood and Sonship. (*DN* 645C)

When discussing human intellection, Dionysius identifies fatherhood and sonship as divine gifts, which are realized through the work of the supreme Father, Son and Spirit, located beyond intellection and beyond fatherhood and sonship. The divine works are implemented by the three divine persons, each of whom performs a specific task, while the Godhead oversees the production. The properties of the divine persons appear to be: Father: paternity; Son: sonship; and the Holy Spirit: sanctification or divinization.

An analysis of the vocabulary used by Dionysius situates his Trinitarian theology in the Christology of the fifth and sixth centuries.[22] In particular, Dionysius' use of *ousia*, *hypostasis* and *physis* indicates his adherence to orthodox doctrine.[23] The Trinity is referred to as the *trishypostatos* (*CH* 212C; *DN* 589D, 592A), a term celebrating the monadic and triadic nature of the Trinity. It seems that Dionysius follows the Cappadocian tradition of defence against tritheism in light of the objective triplicity of God. The Cappadocians were, on the one hand, building from Athanasius' emphasis on the unity of God, coupled with an argument against extreme Arians, such as the Eunomians, who emphasized the distinction in nature or essence between the hypostases.[24] Thus, the Cappadocians preserved the unity of God, while maintaining the distinction of the Trinity, by saying that because the three distinct hypostases were equivalent to one another, they formed one *ousia*.[25] In addition to expressing the unity of the Trinity in terms of *ousia*, or shared essence, the Cappadocians also speak of a shared *physis*, or nature. The term *hyparxis* in Cappadocian theology refers to the existence of God, or the mode in which the being of God is expressed and related. Pseudo-Justin, for instance, says that phrases such as *genêtos* and *agenêtos* express modes of *hyparxis*, rather than *ousia*,[26] and he

---

21 Cf. De Andia (1996), 48.

22 Roques (1954), 307.

23 Roques (1954), 309.

24 Prestige (1952), 242.

25 Basil, *Ep*. 236, 6, 'Substance and hypostasis bear the same relation of common and particular as do animal and John Doe: we maintain one *ousia* in the godhead in order to avoid giving a different rationale of the Persons'. For a history of the 'three hypostases' and 'one *ousia*' formula, see Lienhard (1999).

26 Pseudo-Justin, *Exp. rect. fid.* 3; see Prestige (1952), 247.

explains that members of the Trinity, while unified in *ousia*, differ in their modes of *hyparxis*.[27]

When discussing the Godhead, Dionysius employs the terms and concepts of orthodox Christianity: God is one with respect to his substance, but three when concerning the hypostases.[28] Dionysius uses *hyparxis* to refer to the Godhead as it relates to the Trinity. In *DN* 636C, the entire Godhead is called *hyparxis*: 'the entire divine *hyparxis* is praised by the scriptures', while in *DN* 641A, *hyparxis* refers to the essence beyond being which is the unity of the Trinity, or the transcendent aspect of the Trinity:

> And, following sacred scripture, they also say that there are certain specific unities and differentiations within the unity and differentiation, as discussed above. Thus, regarding the divine unity beyond being, they assert that the indivisible Trinity holds within a shared undifferentiated unity its supra-essential *hyparxis*, its supra-divinity, its supra-excellent goodness ... the abiding and foundation of the divine persons who are the sources of oneness as a unity which is totally undifferentiated and transcendent.

Hyparxis, for Dionysius, refers to the unity of the Godhead which holds the Trinity together, despite any differentiations within its members. Thus, the pre-eminent quality of the Trinity is its unity as one God. In *DN* 641D, Dionysius also states that 'each of the divine persons continues to possess his own praiseworthy characteristics, so that one has here examples of unions and differentiations in the inexpressible unity and *hyparxis* of God'. Again, *hyparxis* refers to the unity of the Godhead, as it maintains the unity of its own differentiations expressed through Trinity. *Hyparxis* can also refer to creation:

> And yet, since it is the substantiation (*hyparxis*) of goodness, and by merely being there is the cause of everything to praise this divinely beneficent providence you must turn to all of creation. It is there at the center of everything and everything has it for a destiny. It is there 'before all things and in it all things hold together.' Because it is there the creation and the hypostasis of all things has come about and is established. (*DN* 593D)

Here, God is the *hyparxis* as transcendent cause, but his own creation is his *hypostasis*, which is most likely the universe, rather than the Trinity, which is not referred to as God's creation elsewhere in the text. In his discussion of the passage, Jean Pépin states the importance of Dionysius' distinction as *hyparxis* relates to the Aristotelian question *an sit*, while *hypostasis* refers to the question *quid sit*.[29] *Hypostasis* regularly refers to the Trinity; in *DN* 592A, he refers to the Trinity as a 'trihypostatic manifestation of his supraessential productivity', meaning the three

---

27 Pseudo-Justin, *ad. orth. resp.*

28 Lilla (1997), 121, connects this distinction to Dionysius' application of the first and second hypothesis of the *Parmenides* to God: that God is not being because he is beyond being and not one, because he is beyond One. The concept that God is one with respect to substance and three with respect to the hypostases occurs in a number of the Cappadocians: cf. Basil, *Ep.* 236, 6 (53, 3–4, 5–7 Courtonne); Gregory of Nyssa, *De s. Trin.* 5, 17–20 Mueller; *Ex comm. not.* 21, 6–7, 14–15 Mueller; *Or. Cat. m.* 3 (*PG* 45, 17D, 8–9); Greg. Naz., *Or.* 20, 7.

29 Pépin (1994), 73.

hypostases of the transcendent *ousia* of God. *Hypostasis*, however, is not employed with respect to Christ as the incarnation, in which case Dionysius speaks of Christ's assuming human *physis* (*DN* 648D). In Letter 4, Dionysius describes Christ, using, in particular, variations of the term *ousia*.

Ousia, hyparxis and *hypostasis* are important technical terms in later Neoplatonism. Porphyry uses *hyparxis* to refer to the first member of the intelligible triad. In fragment XVIII of the *Philosophical History*, a passage which comes from Cyril,[30] he describes the relationship between Intellect (*Nous*) and the One as a contrast between the *hyparxis* of the One and the *hypostasis* of Intellect.[31] Just as was seen in the passage cited above, *DN* 641A, both Porphyry and Proclus use the phrase *hyperousios hyparxis* to mean the divine existence beyond being.[32] Often, it appears that Proclus uses *hyparxis* and *hypostasis* as synonyms to indicate something existing in a nature.[33] In his commentary on the *Alcibiades*, Proclus says that the 'three hypostases are in the intelligible gods' (*In Alc.* 51, 9). In his *Commentary on the Parmenides, hypostasis* is a term used by Proclus to indicate the three principles of One, Intellect and Soul.[34] Still, this is not to say that *hypostasis* can stand in for *hyparxis* in Proclus' thought. In his article on Proclus' use of *hyparxis*, Carlos Steel explains that *hypostasis* and *hyparxis* have a variety of uses for Proclus, but that the two are not interchangeable: *hyparxis* generally equals *ousia* for Proclus and is often used to indicate the intelligible forms.[35] It seems that *hyparxis* is a more general term indicating mode of being, as it is used by the Cappadocians and Dionysius. Thus, in a passage in *In Parm* 1054, 27–8, Proclus says that principles do not have a *hypostasis* in thought, but a mode of being according to *hyparxis*. *Hyparxis* for Proclus, as with Dionysius, may indicate the general concept in which the specific takes part. In a discussion on participation in *Elements of Theology*, proposition 65, Proclus says that *hyparxis* denotes a participation in an essence of being: 'All that subsists in any fashion has its being either in its cause (*kath' hyparxin*), as an originative potency; or as a substantial predicate; or by participation, after the manner of an image'. Thus, an effect participates in a cause according to a mode of being proper to the thing participating – *hyparxis*, rather than meaning being itself, thus designates the distinctive way each thing participates in the essence of its cause.[36] The term *ousia* has great complexity for the Platonists, particularly Porphyry, who makes the distinction that the One is not substance (*ousia*) but being (*to einai*). In this way, the One transcends *energeia*, but is *energein*.[37]

---

30 Cyril of Jerusalem, *c. Julian*, p. 32 CD.

31 Smith (1994), 39.

32 Porphyry, *In Parm.* XIV, 15–16; XIV, 18–19, 23; Proclus, *PT* III, 24 (84, 8). Proclus, in the *Platonic Theology* passage, presents God as the *hyperousios hyparxis*.

33 Steel (1994), 80.

34 *In Parm.* 1058, 29–30; 1118, 31–32; 1135, 21; 1213, 8. See Steel (1994), 79.

35 Steel (1994), 81. He cites *In Remp.* I, 270, 13ff., where Proclus distinguishes two sorts of Forms: (1) Essence, Same and Other and (2) Good, Beautiful and Just, with the former relating to *hyparxis*, but not the latter.

36 On this concept, see Steel (1994), 83–4.

37 *Anonymous Commentary*, XII, 22ff.: 'Consider now if Plato does not sound as if he is propounding a riddle; for the One, which is "beyond substance and being" is neither being,

With this, there seems to be some parallel between Dionysius and Proclus' use of *ousia*, *hyparxis* and *hypostasis*. While Proclus speaks generically about the three terms in connection with the phenomenon of participation, especially with respect to the intelligible Forms, Dionysius uses them to describe how members of the Trinity partake in the Godhead. The major difference, however, between the use of the terms is that while Proclus uses them to discuss how a lesser being can participate in a higher one, Dionysius discusses the relationship among equal members of the Trinity, although this parallel could indicate another instance where the Godhead seems to be prioritized in his thought.

In addition to *hypostasis* to indicate the members of the Trinity, Dionysius also employs the technical term *idiotês*. The Cappadocians used the term *idiotêtes* (or 'properties') and *prosôpa* (persons),[38] which is not used by Dionysius, to show how the members of the Trinity differed with respect to how *ousia* presented itself in each person.[39] 'Property' designates what each member possesses, as opposed to unity between the three.[40] Thus, Basil argues that the persons differ based on their particularities, although everything which characterizes the Father, characterizes the Son, as the Son abides in the Father.[41] Particularities, according to Basil, include being *gennêtos* and being *agênnetos*, as modes of being.[42] Dionysius uses *idiotêtes* in a number of ways to mean properties. The properties can be assigned to the heavenly realm: in *CH* 196D he says, 'let us look with a clear eye on the holy attributes (*idiotêtes*) of each of the heavenly ranks'; and in *CH* 208B, the first beings around God are said to 'have as their own godlike property (*idiotês*) an eternally unfailing, unmoved, and completely uncontaminated foundation'.

Dionysius, then, does not have an explicit theory of the Trinity which uses the 'one *ousia*, three hypostases' formula, nor does he systematically describe the relationship between members of the Trinity using the technical vocabulary of the Cappadocian or Platonic schools. Still, he does describe the Trinity in terms of *hypostasis*, and also uses *idiotêtes*, to a lesser degree,[43] with *oikeiotês* acting as his principal term for indicating the particularities of the members of the Trinity. For Dionysius, the properties were not interchangeable. Unlike the Cappadocian Fathers, however, as mentioned above, he does not employ the term *prosôpon* ('person') to refer to the three members of the Trinity.

---

nor substance, nor act but rather is in act and is itself pure action which is prior to being.' See Dillon (1992), 363, on the importance of this distinction.

38 *Prosôpon* in Dionysius designates the anthropomorphisms humans attribute to the divine. On this point see Roques (1954), 307.

39 Prestige (1952), 244.

40 Pépin (1994), 64.

41 Basil, *C. Eunom.* I, 19, Prestige (1952), 244.

42 Basil calls these *gnoristikai idiotêtes*, or 'identifying particularities' (*Ep.* 38, 5; *C. Eunom.* 2, 29) while later theologians, such as Pseudo-Cyril, called them *idiotêtes hypostatikai* (hypostatic particularities) as indicating the different modes in which the divine substance is transmitted. See Prestige (1952), 245.

43 *CH* 144CD, 196D, 205BC, 208B, 237C, 240B, 260A, 284CD, 285A, 293A, 304AB, 305C, 329AC, 337B; *EH* 476D, 480D, 481A; *DN* 641A, 696B, 937C, 952BC; *Ep.* 9, 1105A.

We can here observe Dionysius weaving his way carefully through the technical terminology that had accumulated over the previous few centuries in relation to the Trinity. *Ousia*, *hypostasis*, *hyparxis*, *idiotês* and *prosôpon* all had become burdened by his time with a considerable weight of controversy. Dionysius, though, by virtue of his prestigious pseudonym, manages to upstage all this activity by presenting himself as a source of it.

Dionysius and Porphyry

Perhaps the most significant parallel between Dionysius' discourse on the Trinity and Platonism, as suggested at the beginning of the chapter, is to be found in Porphyry's connecting of the second hypothesis with the One. It may be worth dwelling on it in somewhat more detail here, as it is not a connection that is as yet generally accepted.

The evidence for this distinctive position of Porphyry's is as follows. The later Neoplatonist Damascius, while discussing in his *De Principiis* whether there is one or two principles prior to the intelligible triad, shows how Porphyry differs from the tradition of the Athenian School, which places one principle (the One) before the intelligible triad. Damascius states Porphyry's position as follows:

> After this let us bring up the following point for consideration, whether the first principles before the first intelligible triad are two in number, the completely ineffable, and that which is unconnected to the triad, as is the view of the great Iamblichus in Book 28 of his excellent *Chaldean Theology*, or, as the great majority of those after him preferred to believe, that the first triad of the intelligible beings follows directly on the ineffable first principle; or shall we descend from this hypothesis and say with Porphyry that the first principle of all things is the Father of the intelligible triad? (*De Princ.* §43, I, p. 86, 8ff. Ruelle, trans. Dillon)

Damascius here contrasts Iamblichus' positioning even of his second principle as presiding transcendently over the primary triad of the intelligible realm with Porphyry's doctrine. He claims that Porphyry equates his first principle (the One) with the Father of the intelligible triad. This system is contrasted with Iamblichus', which allows the first One to remain totally transcendent and ineffable by making a second One the creator of all existence – this second principle, moreover, is presented as unconnected to the intelligible realm. Porphyry's position is starkly distinguished by Damascius in this passage from even the general consensus of Platonists: 'Or shall we descend from this hypothesis also, and say, with Porphyry, that the single principle of all things is the Father of the intelligible triad?' What in effect Porphyry is doing, according to Damascius, is to conflate the ruling triad of the second hypostasis with the first principle of all, so that the One is brought into a direct relationship with the intelligible realm.

Damascius, moreover, was not the only one to note this peculiarity of Porphyry's universe. Proclus describes Porphyry's 'Father' as follows:

> We shall, therefore, be very far from making the primal god the summit of the intelligible world, as I observe to be the practice of some leading authorities on divine matters

(*theologoi*), and making the father of that realm the same as the cause of all things. For this entity is a participated henad. After all, he is called an intelligible father and the summit of the intelligible world, and even if he is the principle of coherence for the whole intelligible world, yet it is as its father that he is so. The primal god, however, who is celebrated in the first hypothesis, is not even a father, but is superior also to all paternal divinity. The former entity is set over against its Power and its Intellect, of whom it is said to be the Father, and with those it makes up a single triad, whereas this truly primal god transcends all contrast and relationship with anything, so *a fortiori* is not an intelligible father. (*In Parm.* 1070, 15ff., trans. Dillon)

While Proclus does not mention Porphyry's name here, as is his custom in his criticisms of other philosophers in his *Parmenides Commentary*, this passage is most certainly a critique of Porphyry. As does Damascius later, Proclus complains that Porphyry's system makes the first principle the Father of the intelligible triad. Still, Proclus makes the point that Porphyry shows how this first principle remains transcendent.[44]

The bulk of the evidence from Porphyry on this topic, however, comes by way of the *Anonymous Commentary on the Parmenides*, the author of which has been convincingly identified as Porphyry by Pierre Hadot.[45] Porphyry makes it clear that the One remains transcendent over the intelligible triad, while still possessing *dynamis* which allows it a creative aspect. This view of the One, moreover, is not an arbitrary innovation by Porphyry, but seems to be provoked by Plotinus' doctrine of the One as both totally transcendent, and at the same time the source of all creation, as Dillon argues.[46] For Plotinus, the One exists as source of creative outpouring and as the first member of that outpouring, which is only actualized as *Nous* once it reverts to the One. Dillon points to a passage in *Enneads* V, 6, 2, 8ff., where Plotinus describes the One in itself and as object of intellection (*noêton*):

The intellect which has the object of thought would not exist if there was not a reality (*ousia*) which is pure object of thought; it will be an object of thought to the intellect, but in itself it will be neither thinker nor object of thought in the proper, authentic sense.

Plotinus' doctrine of the One views the One, while conceptually the same, in two different ways, as in itself superior to thought and as an object of thought to Intellect. Basing himself on this concept, Porphyry seems to derive his notion of the One as the first member of the intelligible triad, from the fact that it contains a creative aspect. While Dionysius does not use this language of Being contemplating the One, he does at once identify God with Being, while simultaneously showing how the One surpasses Being as its source.

Still, the One is identified with the intelligible triad in so far as subject and object of intellection can be identical, or in so far as the first and second hypotheses can both be attributed to the One – the first, as the One in itself, the second, as the One as primary object of intellection, the first element of the intelligible triad.[47] In the

44 Dillon (1973), 358.
45 Hadot (1961), 410–38 and (1968).
46 Dillon (1973), 360.
47 Dillon (1973), 363.

Anonymous Commentary, Porphyry shows how the One participates in substance, in light of the fact that it is not substance, but being:[48]

> Consider now if Plato does not sound as if he is propounding a riddle; for the One, which is 'beyond substance and being', is neither being, nor substance, nor act (*energeia*), but rather is in act (*energei*) and is itself pure action (*energein*), which is prior to being. (XII, 22ff.)

For Dionysius, God contains Being, Life and Wisdom (his scripturally-based equivalent of the Neoplatonic Intellect), considered by all other Neoplatonists but Porphyry to comprise the second hypostasis:

> The first gift, therefore, of the absolutely transcendent Goodness is the gift of Being, and that Goodness is praised from those that first and principally have a share in Being. From it and in it are Being itself, the source of beings, all beings and whatever else has a portion of existence. (*DN* 820CD)

God remains pre-eminently above Being, and yet Being is contained within him:

> He is not a facet of Being. Rather, Being is a facet of him. He is not contained in Being, but Being is contained in him. He does not possess Being, but Being possesses him. He is the eternity of Being, the source and the measure of Being. (*DN* 824A)

Thus, while Proclus and others would assert that all positive claims made about the One in the second hypothesis of the *Parmenides* actually address the second hypostasis of Being, Dionysius equates God with Being – thus, Dionysius attributes both the first and second hypotheses of the *Parmenides* to the first principle, condensing Proclus' universe which had separated the first principle from the second. God, moreover, contains all three principles of the second hypostasis – Being, Life and Wisdom. On the one hand, these function as differentiations of God; on the other hand, they are identified with the Godhead:

> What I have to say is concerned with the benevolent Providence made known to us, and my speech of praise is for the transcendentally good cause of all good things, for that Being and Life and Wisdom, for that Cause of existence and life and wisdom among those creatures with their own share in being, life, intelligence, expression, and perception. I do not think of the Good as one thing, Being as another, Life and Wisdom as yet other, and I do not claim that there are numerous causes and different Godheads, all differently ranked, superior and inferior, and all producing different effects. No; but I hold that there is one God for all these good processions and that he is the possessor of the divine names of which I speak and that the first name tells of the universal Providence of the one God, while the other names reveal general or specific ways in which he acts providentially. (*DN* 816C–817A)

The names Being, Life and Wisdom are processions of the Godhead, all of which refer equally to God. For Dionysius, the intelligible triad of Being, Life and Wisdom exists in God and, I think, can arguably identified with the Trinity as God's processions.

---

48 See Dillon (1992), 363.

Still, the Godhead remains transcendently above the names of Being, Life and Wisdom, as shown earlier in this chapter. In this way, Dionysius parallels the description of the Trinity as being, life and wisdom presented by the fourth-century Roman theologian Marius Victorinus, who was deeply influenced by Porphyry. For Marius Victorinus, the Father is being, the Son life, and the Holy Spirit wisdom, with the Father and the Son only differing in terms of their acts – the Father acts internally, the Son, externally:

> Indeed, since these three [Father, Son, Holy Spirit] are living and intelligent existences, we must consider that these three, 'to be', 'to live', and 'to understand', are three so that they are always one and contained in 'to be' but in that 'to be', I say, which on high is 'to be'. In this 'to be', therefore, is this 'to live', this 'to understand', all as to substance, subsisting as one. For 'to live' itself is 'to be'. For in God it is not such as it is in us, where that which lives is one thing, and the life which makes it live is another thing. Indeed, if we suppose and admit that life itself is and exists, and that which is its own power is identical with its 'to be'. (*Against Arius*, III 1, trans. Clark)

Marius Victorinus attaches the persons of the Trinity to members of the intelligible triad, underscoring that the three members are contained and unified in 'to be'. The distinction he makes here between the Godhead and Being is between being and substance, one which also occupied the thinking of Plotinus on the One.[49]

Nonetheless, although God is said to contain all three elements of Being, Life and Wisdom equally, Being seems to have a greater status among the three processions, in so far as whatever participates in Life and Wisdom also participates in Being (*DN* 820B). However, Dionysius never discusses Being proceeding from the One at any particular moment in time, as opposed to Porphyry, who says that *Nous* proceeds forth from the Good 'pre-eternally', so that the Good exists prior to eternity, with Being subsisting in eternity.[50] Dionysius does discuss God as being pre-eternal (*DN* 937D), but does not discuss the manner of procession of either members of the Trinity or of Being, Life and Wisdom. In this way, Dionysius' concept of Being (possibly the Father) may have some kind of ontological priority over the other two names of God, Life and Wisdom, although Dionysius makes the explicit point in a number of passages that all three members of the Trinity are equal.[51]

---

49 See Plotinus, *Enn.* VI, 8, 20, 9ff., on the self-generation of the One:

> Nor should we be afraid that the primal activity is without substance, but posit this very fact as its, so to speak, existence. But if one were to posit existence of it without activity, the first principle would be defective, and the most perfect of all imperfect; while if one adds activity, one does not preserve its oneness. If, then, activity is more perfect than substance, and the first is most perfect, the first will be activity. (trans. Armstrong)

50 Porphyry, Book IV of *History of Philosophy*, about Plato's doctrine of the good (Cyril of Alexandria, *C. Julian.* I, 32CD = fr. XVIII Nauck).

51 This was rather the point of the Cappadocians, who argue that because the members of the Trinity have the same *ousia*, they may differ in operations, but never in essence, or, one may assume, power.

Jesus as the Embodiment of the Son[52]

Dionysius discusses Jesus Christ both as a hypostatic member of the Trinity and as a human entity in the flesh. Although he uses both the names Jesus and Christ, the names do not seem to be restricted to any particular function of Jesus Christ.[53] Dionysius' Christology accommodates the double reality of the divine: while the Godhead is one and many, Jesus is superessential and human. De Andia calls this the opposition between hyper-essentiality and existence according to us.[54] She points out that the divine nature (*physis*) of Jesus is never couched in terms of human nature, but, when Dionysius wishes to express the human side of Jesus, he discusses 'the nature according to us' (*ousia kath' hêmas*). Thus, in *DN* 644C, when Dionysius discusses the incarnation, he says that the 'superessential Word is entirely and truly of an essence which conforms to us' (*ousiôthênai kath' hêmas*). The verb *ousioumai* is quite popular in Neoplatonic circles, not least in the surviving works of Porphyry himself.[55]

In most of his utterances on the subject, Dionysius appears to be in concord with the orthodox doctrine on Christology in his description of Christ as fully man and fully God, to the extent that he was accepted from the period of his earliest commentator, John of Scythopolis, as pillar of orthodox theology. For Dionysius, Jesus possesses the same attributes as God, in so far as he is universal causality (*Ep.* 1, 1065A; *DN* 648CD); the measure of everything (*DN* 648C); creator of good (*Ep.* 7, 1085C); source of peace to men (*DN* 953A); model and reward for all Christians (*EH* 401D, 553BC; 484D; *DN* 980B, 652A).[56] The incarnation is described in Chapter 3 of the *EH*, where Christ takes on humanity with the exception of sin (*EH* 441A), and thus the Word is fully man.[57] Christ is thus human according to our own nature (*DN* 648D). When one probes a little deeper, however, his position becomes more ambiguous. One passage which has attracted notice occurs in *EH* 4, 477C–480A, in the course of the *theôria* of the sacrament of anointing (*teletê myrou*), where the myrrh, as a perfect blend of fragrant substances, is presented as a symbol of Jesus. This has been seen to suggest that Jesus, in his descent into embodiment, retained a single nature. More striking, however, is the contents of Letter 4, which we set out in

---

52 We have included a note on Dionysius' possible monotheistic stance in Chapter 1, pp. 4–6, in connection with our discussion of his motivations in composing the corpus. This section is complementary to what is said there.

53 *Christos*: *CH* 145B; *EH* 396B, 401D, 404A, 437C, 440B, 444A, 484A, 553B, 556D, 560A; *DN* 652A, 712A, 953A, 980B; *Ep.* 3, 1069B; *Ep.* 7, 1081B; *Ep.* 8, 1085C; *Ep.* 10, 1117A. *Iêsous*: *CH* 121A, 124A, 181B, 208C, 209B; *EH* 372A, 373B, 404B, 428C, 429CD, 432B, 441C, 444AC, 477C, 480AB, 484A, 485A, 505B, 512A, 557A; *DN* 592A, 640A, 645B, 648A, 652A, 953B, 980B; *MT* 10336A; *Ep.* 3, 1069B; *Ep.* 4, 1072A; *Ep.* 8, 1089C, 1096C, 1100AC, *Ep.* 9, 1108A, 1113A.

54 De Andia (1996), 42.

55 Cf. De Andia (1996), 43, and Hadot (1971), II, 103, n. 5. From Porphyry, we may quote *Sent.* 39, 8 (*ousiôsthai*); 41, 2, 3, 8 (*ousiômenon, ousiôtai, ousiôsthai*), and *In Parm.* XII, 6 (*ousiôsthai*).

56 Roques (1954), 303.

57 *Ep.* 4, 1072AB; *DN* 648A, 648D; *EH* 444B.

the first chapter, and to which we refer the reader. Carefully weighed, it seems with reasonable clarity to convey the message that the god-man Jesus has after all only one nature, though blended in a truly marvellous manner.

Chapter 4

On Hierarchy

Introduction

God relates to his creation through the medium of hierarchy – the structure of the universe and result of God's deliberation. Hierarchy, especially the principles of analogy and symmetry which govern it, allow God to express his love for creation and for creation to find its way back to God. Through the interconnecting levels of the universe, parallel to those set forth by Proclus in the *Elements of Theology* and *Platonic Theology*, creation relates both to other levels of creation and to the divine. Entities, moreover, partake in the divine based on their ability to receive divine power; an ability proportionately given to them corresponding to their rank in the cosmic hierarchy, and their will for reception.

Divine Activity as Procession

In the Dionysian concept of creation, God extends himself out to form the universe, motivated by benevolence, or love of his own creation:

> For the blessed divinity, which transcends all being, while proceeding gradually outward because of goodness to commune with those who partake of him, never actually departs from his essential stability and immobility. While enlightening all those conforming to God to a degree analogous to their capacity (*analogôs*),[1] the Deity nevertheless maintains utterly and unshakably its inherent identity. (*EH* 429A)

Dionysius' God engages in the Platonist tri-fold motion of remaining, procession and reversion, whereby a self-constituted entity processes downward in a cycle of creation, radiates itself to form a multitude, while simultaneously drawing this multitude back to itself in a process of reversion. This diffusion and its reversion, however, do not affect the source of the multitude, which remains unified in a singular state of 'remaining' (*monê*). Dionysius describes this process of creation through procession using Proclus' language of 'bubbling over':[2] 'it permeates the whole world without ever departing from its own identity. It goes out to all things ... and it overflows in a surplus of its peaceful fecundity' (*DN* 952A).[3] Dionysius, moreover, also speaks of creation as an 'an effusion of wisdom', particularly with reference to

---

1   For a detailed discussion of the concept of *analogia* for Dionysius, see Lossky and Puech (1930).

2   *Hyperbluzô* (8 times), *ekbluzô* (3 times), *anabluzô* (twice).

3   See also *CH* 177C: 'Everything in some way partakes of the providence flowing out (*ekbluzomenês*) of this transcendent Deity who is the originator of all that is'.

the effusion from the intelligences known as the cherubim,[4] and, more generally, the creative process is an 'outpouring'.[5] For Dionysius, God creates through emanating love, and he loves through an excess of goodness (*DN* 708A), in apparent distinction from Proclus' presentation of the process, whereby the Good, though beneficent (*agathourgos*), creates rather from an overflow of power (*ET*, prop. 133). It thus becomes difficult to deduce whether Dionysian divine love is purely a description of beneficence, or whether love is Dionysius' term for power.

Causality as emanation, especially as part of the triad which includes remaining and reversion, is one of the hallmarks of later Platonism. In *Ennead* III, 8 (30) 10, 5ff., Plotinus describes causality in terms of the One's diffusion of itself without any diminishment. Its creation, specifically creation as the formation of Intellection, desires to return to the divine through contemplation. Creation desires a return to its source because the source resides in it and its principles create a desire in the subject for such a return.[6] With respect to the freedom of the One in creation, it has been debated whether the Plotinian One produces out of necessity as a mechanism.[7] In *Ennead* VI, 8, however, Plotinus defends the freedom of the One, in a manner of speaking, in so far as he argues that the One surpasses freedom and necessity. The One wills itself and its creation because it is beyond restraint.[8] For Dionysius,

---

4   *CH* 205B: the name 'cherubim' means 'fullness of knowledge' or 'outpouring of wisdom'.

5   *DN* 649B: the Godhead 'flows over in shares of goodness to all'.

6   Plotinus, *Enn*. III, 8, 7, 15–25:

> That it was necessary, since the first principles were engaged in contemplation, for all other things to aspire to this state, granted that their originative principle is, for all things, the goal. For when living things, too, produce, it is the rational principles within which move them, and this is an activity of contemplation, the birthpain of creating many forms and many things to contemplate and filling all things with rational principles, and a kind of endless contemplation, for creating is bringing a form into being, and this is filling all things with contemplation. (trans. Armstrong)

7   O'Meara (1993), 68.

8   *Enn*. VI, 8, 13 and 18. In *Enn*. VI, 8. 13, 5ff.:

> For if we should grant activity to it – and its activities, in a way, are its will, for it does not act unwillingly, and its activities are, in a way, its essence – its will and its essence will be the same. But if this is so, then as it is willed, thus it is. Therefore, no more does it will and act as it is natural for it than is its essence as it wills and acts. Therefore, it is in every way in charge of itself, since it also has in itself its own being.

And in ll, 50ff.:

> If, then, the Good has been established as existing, and choice and will together make it exist – for it will not be without these, but it is necessary that the Good not be many – its will and its essence must be brought together into one. But if its wanting is from itself, it is necessary that its being also be from itself, so that the argument has discovered that it has made itself, for if the will is from itself – and, in a way, its function and its will is the same

everything is unified in the monad, but proceeds forth in a manner which merely distinguishes what already exists within the divine (*DN* 820D, 640D; *CH* 121A).

Divine Activity as Reversion and Remaining

The state of reversion is one of perfection (*teleiôsis*): Dionysius describes how God perfects and renews all things (*DN* 700A). Iamblichus, in his description of creation and the One in his *Letter to Macedonius on Fate*, states that the One is cause of all being and the source of its reversion. As the source of all plurality, moreover, the One holds multiplicity together, organizing the universe. In this passage, Fate is the organizing principle of the universe, which arranges everything produced through the One:

> All things that exist, exist by virtue of the One, and indeed the primal level of Being itself is produced in the beginning from the One, and, in a very special way, the general causal principles receive their power of action from the One and are held together by it in a single embrace and are borne back together to the first principle of multiplicity, as preexisting in it. And in accordance with this, the multitude of causal principles in nature, which are multiform and fragmented and dependent on a number of [immediate] sources, also derive from one general causal principle, and all are interwoven with each other according to a single principle of combination and this combination of many causal principles relates back to one source – the most comprehensive controlling principle of causality. Neither is this single chain a mere jumble put together from multiplicity, nor does it constitute a unity formed simply as a result of such combination, nor is it dissipated into individual entities; but, rather, in accordance with the guiding and prearranged simple combination of the causal principles themselves, it brings all things to completion and binds them within itself and leads them upwards unitarily to itself. (*Letter to Macedonius*, fr. 1 Dillon)[9]

Not only does the One as creative principle have its creation organized harmoniously, but its emanative creation, moreover, possibly has the mark of benevolence, at least in respect to superior classes towards inferior.[10]

The clearest parallel to Dionysian creation is most certainly Proclus' account, in which he describes creation as a process during which all things proceed from a

---

as its existence – it would, in this way, make itself exist so that it is not what happened to be by luck but what is willed itself. (trans. Gerson)

See O'Meara (1993), 69 for a discussion of this issue.

9   Included in Dillon and Gerson (2004).

10 Iamblichus, *In Tim.* fr. 24 Dillon:

But if one, in addition to these explanations, were to cling fast also to the general considerations of reality, let him listen to Iamblichus when he says that the memory of children signifies the ever new and flourishing permanent creation of the reason-principles and the 'indelibility of the drawing' or 'the dye' for both readings are extant – the overflowing and neverfailing creation, and the 'enthusiasm' of the teacher the ungrudging supplying of the secondary causes by those superior to them. (trans. Dillon, 1973)

unique cause.[11] Using the imagery of which Dionysius is so fond, Proclus describes emanation as a stream flowing from a cause[12] which fills its effect.[13] Proclus, as with Plotinus, in particular, has a developed concept of reversion, in which he says that the cause perfects the divided multitude of the gods and brings everything back to itself, a view echoed by Dionysius in *CH* 120B.[14] Beyond procession and reversion, Proclus describes the state of remaining, whereby the One remains in itself, undepleted, despite simultaneously emptying itself, creating the universe, and then bringing that creation back into itself.

Dionysian creation, following Plotinus and Proclus, also uses emanation metaphors. Such language has sparked debate concerning whether Dionysius believed in creation as a mechanism, or whether he posited the Christian view of creation through divine will and plan. While some scholars argue that language of 'bubbling forth' does not necessarily lend itself to descriptions of gradual emanation,[15] others argue that gradations necessitate emanation as a mechanism.[16] In *Divine Names* 588C, Dionysius uses such imagery of radiation; however, it is qualified by the description of God's goodness, which might imply an act of will on his part:

> The Good is not absolutely incommunicable to everything. By itself it generously reveals a firm, transcendent beam, granting enlightenments proportionate to each being, and thereby draws sacred minds upwards to its permitted contemplation, to participation and to the state of becoming like it.

Here, divine power processes outward to form creation and bring creation back to God, a double process which is certainly Platonic. Dionysius, however, unlike Proclus, does not speak of this process in strict terms of potency-activity, but rather describes it as a beneficent act, willed by God.[17] Again, Dionysius uses imagery of light bestowal which has parallels with Proclus' descriptions of the effects of creation as irradiations.[18] The purpose of the comparison of language underscores the relationship between the Dionysian creation and Platonist emanation, both of which describe the state of the Good diffusing itself – while Dionysius does speak of God establishing everything out of goodness (*CH* 177C), this description can also be a Dionysian version of the Platonist 'Good diffusing itself' mentioned above. In *DN* 693B, Dionysius describes creation using Platonic imagery of irradiation which points to God's creation as a mechanism:

---

11   Proclus, *In Parm.* 798, 27ff. and *In Tim.* I, 228, 11ff. See *ET*, prop. 11: all that exists proceeds from a single first cause.

12   Proclus, *PT* III, 26, p. 91, 4ff. S–W; see Gersh (1978), 18: Proclus also describes daemons as streaming from Rhea (*In Alc.* 68, 5). This image is at least partly influenced by the *Chaldaean Oracles*.

13   *In Tim.* I, 429, 2–3; *In Tim.* II, 147, 10–11; *In Tim.* III, 164, 2, *PT* IV, 1, p. 8, 10ff. S–W; *PT* IV, 2, p. 13, 3ff. S–W.

14   Proclus, *PT* IV, 15, p. 47, 27ff.

15   Volker (1958), 239–40; Gersh (1978), 21–2.

16   Roques (1954), 101–102; Gersh (1978), 36.

17   See *In Parm.* 868, 9ff. for an example of Proclus' description of the One conferring greatness to creation in terms of potency-activity.

18   *ET* 60, 21–2; for a discussion of this, see Gersh (1978), 23.

Think of how it is with our sun. It exercises no rational process, no act of choice, and yet by the very fact of its existence it gives light to whatever is able to partake of its light, in its own way. So it is with the Good. Existing far above the sun, an archetype far superior to its dull image, it sends the rays of its undivided goodness to everything with the capacity, such as this may be, to receive it.[19]

Both Plotinus and Proclus argue that the Good creates by reason of its goodness, which is to say, an act (or expression) of its essence.[20] Still, in other places, Proclus in particular argues that God's creation is a decision, so that for Proclus he creates according to his will.[21] Dionysius describes the process of procession, reversion, and remaining as a three-part activity involving three types of motion. After clarifying that any motion attributable to God cannot be said to signify a change of place, a movement in space either straight, circular or spiral, he goes on to describe the following motion in procession, reversion and remaining:

> In some mode conforming to what befits both God and reason, one has to predicate movement of the immutable God. One must understand the straight motion of God to mean the unswerving procession of his activities, the coming to be of all things from him. The spiral movement attributed to him must refer to the continuous procession from him together with the fecundity of his stillness. And the circular movement has to do with his sameness, to the grip he has on the middle range as well as on the outer edges of order, so that all things are one and all things that have gone forth from him may return to him once again. (*DN* 916CD)

In his commentary on Euclid's *Elements*, Proclus says that the circle and straight line are based on the principles of Limited and Unlimitedness (*In Eucl.* 103, 1). The circle and circular line correspond to Limit, while the straight line corresponds to Unlimitedness. The spiral is a mixture of Limit and Unlimitedness (*In Eucl.* 104, 27ff.) The behaviour of a line under the influence of Limit and Unlimitedness displays the most elaborate role for lines and circles in the cosmos; Proclus, moreover, links the processive and revertive function to the causal process of remaining, procession, and reversion. Gersh argues that the three geometrical shapes correspond to the three processes, based on Proclus' assertions that the point[22] is most akin to remaining, the line[23] to procession, and the circle[24] to reversion.[25] Proclus describes how these shapes interact with generation in *In Parm.* 1131, 21–8:

---

19 Compare Plotinus, *Enn.* VI, 7 where the One exercises no rational thought.

20 Plotinus describes emanation as the absolute goodness of God and the superabundance of his power. Because of its perfection, the One diffuses itself: *Enn.* IV, 8 (6) 5; V, 4 (7) 1; VI, 9 (9) 6; VI, 6 (34) 10; V, 2 (11) 1; V, 5 (32) 12; II, 9 (33) 3; V, 3 (49) 15. Regarding Proclus and the Good's creation from its own goodness, see *ET*, prop. 25 and 27; *In Tim.* I, 362, 28–63, 7; 366, 20–26; 381, 20; III, 7, 8–17.

21 Proclus, *In Tim.* I, 367, 20–368, 1; 371, 9–372, 19; 372, 19–31; 381, 8–10; see *In Tim.* I, 362, 2–4.

22 Proclus, *In Eucl.* 88, 2ff., 91, 11ff.

23 Iamblichus, *In Tim.* fr. 49 Dillon; Proclus, *In Eucl.* 108, 10–13, 164, 8–11.

24 Proclus, *In Eucl.* 147, 3ff.

25 Gersh (1978), 73.

One may also see on the level of generation these two qualities [line and circle.] One may view in the cycle of existence here (for generation returns to itself cyclically, as is written in *Phaedo* [70Cff.]) the circular; while the straight one may see in the procession of each thing from its birth to its decline, and the middle here, which is in front of the extremes, as its peak of development. (trans Dillon)

Still, this is not to say that line, circle and spiral are limited to the motions of the One and generation. The concept of generation, for Proclus, is particular to soul – souls are constructed out of straight lines and circles, because circles are only one type of line.[26] In his *Commentary on Euclid*, Proclus says:

It is because of the circular revolutions of the heavens that generation returns in a circle upon itself and brings its unstable mutability into a definite cycle. If you divide bodiless things into soul and intellect, you will say that the circle has the character of Intellect, the straight line that of Soul. This is why the Soul, as it reverts to Intellect, is said to move in a circle. (*In Eucl.* 147, 12, trans. Morrow)

That soul moves in a circle because of its revertive tendencies is a common thought in Platonist circles. The soul, however, moves according to different shapes depending on what action it is engaged in:

The demiurgic Intellect has set up these two principles in himself, the straight and circular, and produced out of himself two monads, the one acting in a circular fashion to perfect all intelligible essences, the other moving in a straight line to bring all perceptible things to birth. Since the soul is intermediate between sensibles and intelligibles, she moves in a circular fashion in so far as she is allied to intelligible nature, but in so far as she presides over sensibles, exercises her providence in a straight line. (*In Eucl.* 108, 13ff., trans Morrow)

The soul moves in a straight line when it extends in generation, a circle when it returns during reversion. In this respect, the soul acts as an intermediate, binding together the intelligible and intellectual realms. Dionysius' use of the concept of circular and rectilinear motion can be seen to be firmly grounded in Neoplatonic thought on the subject of the activities of the First Principle and its relation to the hypostases below it.

Articulation of the Hierarchy

In formulating his conception of God's relation to his creation, Dionysius coins the term *hierarchia*[27], which he defines in Chapter 3 of the *Celestial Hierarchy*:

---

26 Proclus, *In Eucl.* 92, 4; Plato, *Tim.* 53C–55C.

27 This term, like a number of Dionysius' other neologisms, has some antecedence in words previously used in much more specialized contexts (*archisynagôgos*, which he uses to describe the activity of God at *DN* 700A and 948D, is a good analogy). The word *hierarchês*, found in a number of inscriptions to describe an official who presides over sacred rites, has a quite restricted meaning. There is also a verb *hierarcheô*, to describe what that official does, but no abstract noun is attested before Dionysius.

In my opinion a hierarchy is a sacred order, a state of understanding and an activity approximating as closely as possible to the divine. And it is uplifted to the imitation of God in proportion (*analogia*) to the enlightenments divinely given to it. The beauty of God – so simple, so good, so much the source of perfection – is completely uncontaminated by dissimilarity. It reaches out to grant every being, according to merit, a share of light and then through a divine sacrament, in harmony and in peace, it bestows on each of those being perfected its own form. (*CH* 164D–165A)

Hierarchy indicates an order set out by God as an expression of divine law and will. God, in creating the universe, does so in the form of a particular arrangement – this harmonious creation is without any disorder as part of God's plan. God is, thus, directly engaged in the arrangement of the universe – not only does he create the hierarchy, but he acts as the *metron*, or measure, of all beings in the hierarchy to maintain the order of the universe (*DN* 648C, 824B).[28] Whereas God is the source of measure in the universe, creation is not said to contain this measure, but rather to be a kind of symmetry as a reduction to the common measure.[29] God assigns to each member of the hierarchy a portion of his own measure, which becomes that member's symmetry (*EH* 373A). The Dionysian hierarchy is thus a highly systematized, highly variegated structure, with each member ordered by God in creation, with the object of the member's return to God.

The Dionysian hierarchy is divided into two universes, the celestial (or intelligible) and ecclesiastical (or sensible). In this way, Dionysius manipulates Plato's dichotomy of intelligible/sensible in the formation of his universe, although the division within the hierarchies is clearly Platonic: each hierarchy is divided into a series of triads with three members arranged vertically, the first member of the triad containing more power than the second. These horizontal ranks are interconnecting, so that the first member of the triad contains the power of the lower two, and so forth. While the two hierarchies are not connected, the ecclesiastical hierarchy mirrors the arrangement of its celestial counterpart. What is at stake in the arrangement of the hierarchies, however, has more to do with reception of divine power, which internal relations also reflect, than mere systematization. The ranks or orders closest to God receive the fullest amount of divine power and hence are better equipped to return to divine contemplation. This concept of a triadic universe has its roots in Plotinus, who gives the three hypostases as the One, Intellect and Soul (*Enn.* V, 1 and II, 9, 1), although it is Iamblichus and, later, Syrianus and Proclus who make this initial triad more intricate with intermediaries, seemingly the basis for Dionysius' hierarchies. In the Iamblichean universe, the Plotinian triad of *on, zôê, nous* is formalized. The Iamblichean triad in the noetic world is, in one version, encompassed by the Demiurge,[30] but Proclus also reports that Iamblichus proposed a much more elaborate system, such was later taken up by Syrianus and Proclus himself, of three levels of the intellective realm, three triads of intelligible gods, followed by three triads of

---

28 In *DN* 824B, God is said to have the shapes and structures of all creation, as well as contain the 'sources, mean terms, and ends of all things'.

29 Roques (1954), 60.

30 Iamblichus, *In Tim*. fr. 7 Dillon.

intelligible-intellectual gods, followed by an intellectual hebdomad (two triads and a seventh entity), and the demiurgic function resided within this third level.

Proclus, in his turn, describes the noetic realm in terms of three triads, attributing the doctrine of three triads in the intelligible orders to the 'theologians in song'; he says that they are exemplified in the second hypothesis of the *Parmenides*.[31] At each level, the three 'moments' of Being, Life, and Mind each contain their own triad of being–life–mind, so that every level of the intellective contains aspects of all three moments. Following on the henadic realm, Proclus sets out a triadic hierarchy of intelligible, intelligible-intellective and intellectual, acknowledging his debt to Syrianus. The hierarchy, as set out by Proclus over the course of the *Platonic Theology*, has been presented above in Chapter 2. Zeus, as the Demiurge, being the third element of the first intellective triad, oversees the demiurgic gods as they exist in the hypercosmic and encosmic realms. Thus, the hypercosmic and encosmic realms mirror the intellective order so that each consists of a triad of which Zeus is a member.

Both hierarchies are divided into ranks or series (*taxeis*). A rank, or level, contains a common element and begins with a monad. In the *Elements of Theology*, prop. 21, Proclus says that each member of a series evolves from or is generated from a unit or monad which is its first member. Because there cannot be a plurality of independent *archai*, each level of reality mirrors the entire cosmos as a whole, so that every level is a unified whole or monad, which engages in procession, reversion and remaining (*ET*, prop. 25). A single series extends vertically downwards to the last order of beings (*ET*, prop. 145), with every member of the series participating in the monad. In Dionysian theology, Dionysius uses the term *taxis*[32] in much the same way as Proclus, describing a vertical order whose members feature a common element, with power diminishing based on a member's distance from the monad at the start of the order. Dionysius, as does Proclus, explains the distribution of power as hierarchical, in so far as superior entities contain all the power of those below, while the subordinates have none of the power of those above them (*CH* 196B). Thus, superior ranks hierarchically govern the inferior (*CH* 260A). A guiding principle that unites all levels of the hierarchy to each other and to God, we may conclude, is a creative application of the Platonic principle 'likeness to God as far as possible' (*homoiôsis theôi kata to dynaton*), used by the Platonic tradition only in relation to man's striving for likeness to God, but applied by Dionysius to the activity of all levels of the hierarchy. At *CH* 165A, he states: 'the goal (*skopos*) of a hierarchy, then, is for each of the beings to be as like as possible to God and to be at one with him'.[33]

---

31 Proclus, *In Parm.* 1090–1091; *PT* II, 24–6.

32 While *seira* and *taxis* appear synonymous, it should be noted that *seira* is used only once, *DN* 680C.

33 This Platonic principle is no doubt easier for Dionysius to assimilate because of parallel with the concept of man as the image of God presented at Gen. 1:26–8.

In the *Celestial Hierarchy*, Dionysius uses nine biblical names to demarcate the triple triad of the hierarchy, a formula which he attributes to Hierotheus.[34] The first group, noted by its perpetual contemplation of God, comprises the Seraphim, Cherubim and Thrones (*CH* 200D). Its status as first rank means that no intermediary exists between God and this group, making it the most divine, since its members receive enlightenment directly from God.[35] In Chapter 7 of the *Celestial Hierarchy*, Dionysius describes the symbolism of the names of those in the first hierarchy as it relates to the capacity of its members to receive divine power without mediation. This rank is the most like God because of its primary participation in the divine light (*CH* 208C). The Seraphim, as the lowest members of the first rank,[36] have the capacity to lift subordinates to the heat in which they participate (*CH* 205C). The second rank, Cherubim, have the power to know and see God (*CH* 205C), while the highest rank, Thrones, have a perfection which allows them to relate directly to God (*CH* 205D). Despite Dionysius' use of scriptural exegesis to manipulate the names of angels to his own categories of beings in the celestial hierarchy, his system is plainly based closely on that of Syrianus and Proclus. The constant motion of the Seraphim, described in the language of fire, has some parallel in Proclus' description of constant intellectual motion in his *Commentary on the Parmenides*. The middle hierarchy consists of the Dominions, Powers and Authorities, all of which achieve purification, illumination and perfection second-hand from the divine enlightenments as they are mediated by the first hierarchical rank (*CH* 240B). The final rank of the hierarchy consists of the Principalities, Archangels and Angels. This group, again, is still further from God and must receive divine power through the mediation of the second hierarchical rank. This last group is said to be in some ways closest to the highest level of the ecclesiastical hierarchy, in so far as this human rank obtains great divine power, albeit proportioned to its lower status.

Still, this is not to say that the celestial and ecclesiastical hierarchies are connected. While the ecclesiastical hierarchy is divided according to the sacraments, rather than its members, the major figures in the hierarchy are divided into a triad: the bishops, priests and monks. The bishop is referred to as the hierarch by Dionysius, whose definition Dionysius gives in *EH* 373C as follows, 'a holy and inspired man, someone who understands all sacred knowledge, someone in whom an entire hierarchy is completely perfected and known'. These hierarchs are the nearest to the angels in terms of place, because they are at the highest rank of the ecclesiastical hierarchy, and as such, Dionysius describes them as 'like gods'. As with the more elevated ranks of the celestial hierarchy, the hierarchs have a 'generous' urge to uplift their subordinates. That the mediation of divine power is described in terms

---

34 This attribution to his master Hierotheus may be seen as a reflection by Dionysius of the fact that Proclus attributes the whole system of intellective triads to his master, Syrianus (e.g. *In Tim*. II, 272, 3–273, 26 = Syrianus, *In Tim*. fr. 16 Wear).

35 *CH* 208A: 'the aim of every hierarchy is to imitate God so as to take on his form, the task of every hierarchy is to receive and pass on undiluted purification, the divine light, and the understanding which brings perfection'. See *ET*, prop. 128.

36 Dionysius actually makes it somewhat difficult to discern the order of entities here, but it emerges below that the Thrones are to be seen as the highest, or the 'remaining' element of the triad.

of generosity speaks to the Christianization of Dionysius' explanation of Platonic relations between members of different ranks.[37] Unlike the higher members of the celestial hierarchy, however, they cannot pass on divine power simply through mediation to subordinates. Instead, they clothe the divine rays in the material form of sacrament, so that they will be more accessible to human minds.[38]

This activity of guiding subordinate members of the hierarchy through the sacraments was commanded, not by the celestial intermediaries, but God himself.[39] Thus, while the ecclesiastical hierarchy is certainly inferior to its celestial counterpart, it is not connected so that the hierarchs are a fourth triad of the angelic realm;[40] rather, the hierarchs are the first triad of their own realm and, as was seen, in connection with the higher *taxis* of the intellective realms, they are the first to behold God, for in the divine order of the hierarchs, 'the whole arrangement of the human hierarchy is fulfilled and completed. And just as we observe that every hierarchy ends in Jesus, so each individual hierarchy reaches its term in its own inspired hierarch' (*EH* 505B). Still, this is not to say that the two hierarchies are wholly divorced: not only did the angels of the celestial hierarchy guide human ancestors towards the divine (*CH* 180B), but they continually lift bishops towards the light of God (*CH* 196C): with this, they have a direct effect on human conversion and spiritual ascension (*CH* 257C, 260B).[41] The clerical functions of the divine hierarchy represent the divine activities so that the three clerical orders are arranged according to beginning, middle and end (*EH* 508D).

Distinctions of Powers

In addition to a breakdown of the universe into two hierarchies, which certainly makes up the bulk of Dionysian cosmos, the universe is also divided into the more general categories of angels, rational souls, irrational souls, plants, and soulless

---

37 Here, Dionysius possibly brings in the missionary aspect of Christianity in terms of the Platonic concept, whereby enlightenment is passed on as a duty.
38 *EH* 376D–377A:

They passed on something united in a variegation and plurality. Of necessity they made human what was divine. They put material on what was immaterial. In their written and unwritten initiations, they brought the transcendent down to our level. As they had been commanded to do they did this for us, not simply because of the profane from whom the symbols were to be kept out of reach, but because, as I have already stated, our own hierarchy is itself symbolical and adapted to what we are.

39 *EH* 377A.
40 The angels are, however, responsible for guiding our ancestors towards the divine reality (*CH* 180B).
41 See Roques (1954), 109, on this phenomenon.

matter.[42] Each of these orders receives divine power according to their ability to receive it, which Dionysius describes in terms of God as absolute Life in Chapter 6 of the *Divine Names*. In this chapter, Dionysius discusses how God bestows power on each level which defines the being of entities; thus, angels and men are granted intelligent life, while animals and plants receive life and warmth (*DN* 868AB). All things, moreover, long for and return to the divine depending on this power: 'the intelligent and rational long for it by way of knowledge, the lower strata by way of perception, the remainder by way of the stirrings of being alive and in whatever fashion befits their condition' (*DN* 593D).[43] This structure is based, generally, on the Plotinian elements of Being, Life and Intellect, but more directly on Proclus' theory of the range of influence of different levels of being, as set forth in his *Elements of Theology* (props. 56–7): the One (or Good), Intellect and Soul have differing ranges of influence. In the third book of the *Platonic Theology*, he describes the levels of existence (*diakosmoi*) and their influence, as follows:

> Prior to the beings themselves, the One substantiates the henads of beings ... Put another way, it is necessary that those which exist as primary beings participate in the first-most Cause through these unities which lie immediately next to them. For each of the second is attached to those prior to them through those that are similar to them, bodies through their own particular souls to the universal soul, souls through their intellectual monads to the universal intellect, and real-existents, which are primary, through their unified existence to the One...but the henads of beings are substantiated by the imparticipable and totally

---

42 *DN* 696CD:

Next to these sacred and holy intelligent beings are the souls, together with all the good peculiar to these souls. These too derive their being from the transcendent Good. So therefore they have intelligence, immortality, existence. They can strive towards life. By means of the angels as good leaders, they can be uplifted to the generous Source of all good things and, each according to his measure, they are able to have a share in the illuminations streaming out from that Source. They too, in their own fashion, possess the gifts of exemplifying the Good and they have all those other qualities which I described in my book *On the Soul*.

And, if we must speak of the matter, all this applies to the irrational souls, to the living creatures which fly through the air or walk the earth, those that live in the waters, the amphibians as well as those which are burrowed into the ground, in short, every sentient and living being. They all have soul and life because of the existence of the Good. And the plants too have nourishment and life and motion from this same Good. So also with soulless and lifeless matter. It is there because of the Good; through it they received their state of existence.

43 See also *DN* 700B:

All things are returned to it as their own goal. All things desire it: Everything with mind and reason seeks to know it, everything sentient yearns to perceive it, everything lacking perception has a living and instinctive longing for it, and everything lifeless and merely existent turns, in its own fashion, for a share of it.

transcendent Unity, and so are capable of linking the beings to the One and of making them return to themselves. (*PT* III, 3, p. 13, 4–17 S–W)

A noteworthy parallel to Proclus' scheme, however, occurs in Dionysius' description of the three functions of the respective classes: purification, illumination (or contemplation) and perfection (*katharsis, ellampsis/phôtismos, teleiôsis*) (*CH* 208Aff.) are said to be both the activity of God, with respect to the angelic and human minds, and the activity of the angels and clerical orders.[44] The purpose of purification is to free the intelligence of everything other than God – in the celestial hierarchy, this takes place at the intelligible level only, while in the ecclesiastical hierarchy, purification is sensible and intelligible.[45] Illumination is a more exalted activity than purification, although it cannot take place without purification. When the intelligence is free from all elements other than God, illumination reveals God (*CH* 165D), transmitting the science of God and divine things; at the hierarchic level, illumination is thus the progressive transmission of divine light. The third activity of hierarchy is the perfection of the union with God. This is characterized by the ability of the intelligence to contemplate the sacred mysteries. In terms of divine knowledge, then, Dionysius summarizes the three activities of the hierarchy in *CH* 209C:

Purification, illumination, and perfection are all three the reception of an understanding of the Godhead, namely, being completely purified of ignorance by the proportionately granted knowledge of the more perfect initiations, being illuminated by this same divine knowledge (through which it also purifies whatever was not previously beheld but is now revealed through the more lofty enlightenment), and being also perfected by this light in the understanding of the most lustrous initiations.

Purification, illumination and perfection refer to degrees of spiritual knowledge, with the more advanced orders operating perfection, the middle orders, illumination, and the lower orders, purification. The diversity of the functions of the hierarchy speaks to the diversity of the hierarchy itself, a diversity summarized in the thearchy, which engages in all three activities with respect to the hierarchy.[46] In the celestial hierarchy, the three functions appear at each level to one degree or another (see *CH*, Ch. 3), although in the ecclesiastical hierarchy, the distribution of power and function of each member tends to be more strictly defined.[47] In the ecclesiastical hierarchy,

---

44 EH 508D: 'The divinity first purifies those minds which it reaches and then illuminates them. Following on their illumination it perfects them in a perfect conformity to God'.

45 Roques (1954), 94.

46 Roques (1954) 96; see *CH* 168A:

And so it comes about that every order in the hierarchical rank is uplifted as best as it can toward co-operation with God. By grace and God-given power, it does things which belong naturally and supernaturally to God, things performed by him transcendently and revealed in the hierarchy for the permitted imitation of God-loving minds.

47 Still, the higher orders contain the power of the lower ones. For instance, the bishop consecrates and perfects, while the priests, who illuminate, also purify (*EH* 508C). See Roques

the powers are demarcated according to groups of individuals, and primarily according to the power of sacraments: the *synaxis* and the sacrament of anointing are perfecting (*EH* 424Cff., 484Bff.); baptism is purifying and illuminating, while the final anointing at death (extreme unction) makes it also perfecting (*EH* 404C, 484C). Hence, the three powers exist in each of the three sacraments.[48] This division of function is also reflected in the clerical orders, although, again, the functions and duties overlap: the hierarchs consecrate and perfect, the priests illuminate, and the deacons purify and discern the imperfect (*EH* 508C). The division of divine light and divinizing activity is thus further divided in the ecclesiastical hierarchy than in the celestial hierarchy.[49]

The three-fold activity of purification, illumination, and perfection, or their equivalents, appears in the later Platonist doctrine of prayer, especially prayer accompanied by religious rites. In Book V of the *De Mysteriis* (26, 237–40), Iamblichus describes three levels of prayer: an introductory level, which leads to acquaintance with the divine; a conjunctive, which produces a sympathy with the gods; and a stage of unification, which establishes human souls in the divine. Following this, Iamblichus sets forth three advantages of these levels of prayer which connect the one praying with the divine:

> According to the distinction of these three levels, then, which measure out the whole range of interaction with the divine, prayer establishes links of friendship between us and the gods, and secures for us the triple advantage which we gain from the gods through theurgy, the first leading to illumination (*epilampsis*), the second to the common achievement of projects, and the third to the perfect fulfillment (*teleia apoplêrôsis*) of the soul through fire. (trans. Clarke)

Iamblichus goes on to note that prayer is required for all connections with the divine, whether the prayer be preceded or completed by rites. He says that prayer is effective in that it 'enlarges very greatly our soul's receptivity to the gods, reveals to men the life of the gods, accustoms their eyes to the brightness of divine light, and gradually brings to perfection the capacity of our faculties for contact with the gods'. The three stages of prayer, thus, prepare one for divine power, and are often connected to theurgic ritual.

The stages as laid out by Iamblichus are taken up by Proclus in his *Timaeus Commentary*[50] where Proclus expands the stages of prayer to five. In the first stage, the one praying acquires knowledge of the divine orders; in the second stage, one is linked to the divine through a series of three stages: assimilation – likeness with the divine; linkage – the subjection of human soul to divine control; and approach – increasing the closeness of the linkage.[51] At the final level, Proclus describes a level of *henôsis*, whereby the soul is united with the divine, a state of 'establishing

---

(1954), 99.

48 Rorem (1993), 236, note 150.

49 Roques (1954), 101.

50 *In Tim.* I, 209, 1–212, 28; See Dillon (2002), 288.

51 See Dillon (2002), 289.

the One of the soul in the actual One of the gods, and making our activity one with that of the gods'.[52]

For Dionysius, each member of the celestial hierarchy operates its power in a double capacity in so far as each is participated in by a lower rank. Not only must each rank receive light, but it must, in turn, pass the divine power on to the rank below it. This conception of participation, indeed, mirrors the participation of the thearchy, in so far as the thearchy itself is unparticipated, despite being participated in by others (*DN* 644AB).

Iamblichus describes this phenomenon in *In Tim.* fr. 60: where intelligence is prior to soul, but not directly connected, 'For the transition from the transcendent to the participating should not be immediate, but there should be as median those essences which are combined with things that participate' (trans. Dillon).[53] Iamblichus describes how the intellectual order presides over soul and is participated by it, but only through intermediaries, whereas Proclus describes the same phenomenon in *ET* 21,[54] 99[55] and 101.[56] In his *Commentary on the Parmenides*, Proclus describes the relationship between the One and the triad of being, life and intellect as a series of levels of participation which begin with the One, which is wholly unparticipated (1069). He adds that those which follow, however, are participated:

> For in every ruling order the participated multiplicity should be presided over by the unparticipated and primal form, or even a causal principle superior to form; in this way, after all, prior to the forms-in-matter there are the immaterial Forms, and prior to that life which comes to be in something else we have that which is separate and on its own and unmixed, and everywhere those things which come to be in something else are presided over by those which subsist on their own. For instance, the multiplicity of souls which have taken charge each of its own body are presided over essentially by the unparticipated Soul, which goes about 'in the place of the heaven'; and the multiplicity of intellects are presided over by the single unparticipated Intellect, that one which is separate and eternally established in itself and gives coherence from above to all intellectual essence; and the multiplicity of intelligibles are dominated by the primal intelligible object, which is unmixed and established singly on its own, for that object of intellect in the individual intellect is distinct from that which is established prior to this on its own, and this latter is the intelligible object pure and simple, while the former is an intelligible object in relation to intellectual entities. Even so, beyond the multiplicity of participated henads there is an unparticipated One, transcendent, as has been said, over all the divine realms. (*In Parm.* 1069–70, trans. Dillon)

---

52 *In Tim.* I, 211, 25–6; see Dillon (2002), 290.

53 See Dillon's discussion at (2002), 342.

54 *ET*, prop. 21: 'Every order has its beginning in a monad and proceeds to a manifold co-ordinate therewith; and the manifold in any order may be carried back to a single monad'.

55 *ET*, prop. 99: 'Every participated term arises *qua* unparticipated from no cause other than itself, but is itself the first principle and cause of all the participated terms; thus the first principle of each series is always without origin'.

56 *ET*, prop. 101: 'All things which participate intelligence are preceded by the unparticipated Intelligence, those which participate life by Life, and those which participate being by Being; and of these three unparticipated principles Being is prior to Life and Life to Intelligence'.

While Proclus attributes the level of the unparticipated to each of Being, Life and Intellect, in addition to the One, the Procline triads constitute themselves in three terms: imparticipable, participable, participated. Each term is attached to the One through the henad which presides over it; the henads manifest the One as imparticipable and attach themselves to the One.[57] This theory appears to have originated with Iamblichus, whom Proclus credits in *In Tim.* II, 240.6–7 (fr. 54 Dillon)[58] with the doctrine that every order is headed by an unparticipated monad.[59] The singularity of the unparticipated monad, at every level of existence, further serves to unite the cosmos in so far as every entity participates in that member and bears some aspect of that member, as Proclus argues in *ET*, prop. 21.[60]

In *CH* 257C, Dionysius says that every hierarchy has a first, middle and last power, with the middle power containing aspects of the ranks before and after it as a mean between extremes. This concept is certainly Platonist, appearing both in Iamblichus (e.g., *DM* V, 8, 225, 5–8) and Proclus (e.g. *PT* IV, 19, p. 54, 21–55, 4 S–W).

Analogy

Hierarchy is both an object, as the organization of the universe, a psychological rendering of the organization of the universe, and a process. The activity of the

---

57 Roques (1954), 75; *ET*, prop. 116: Every god is participable, except the One. Only the One is imparticipable, a characteristic which helps to preserve its uniqueness. The gods or henads, on the other hand, are participable:

> What is self-complete will then be this unity whereby it is linked to the One itself, so that once more, the god, qua god, will be this component, while that which came into existence as not-one exists as one by participation in the unity. Therefore every henad posterior to the One is participable; and every god is thus participable.

58 Dodds makes the point that the triadic formulation of this doctrine is probably Procline. See *ET* (1992), 236.

59 Iamblichus speaks of the Soul in particular, which is an unparticipated monad: 'for at the head of every order is the unparticipated monad before the participated, and it is the number which is distinctive of and naturally related to the unparticipated, and from the One is the Dyad, as in the case of the gods themselves' (fr. 54 Dillon).

60 *ET*, prop. 21:

> Since, then, in every order there is some common element, a continuity and identity in virtue of which some things are said to be co-ordinate and others not, it is apparent that the identical element is derived by the whole order from a single originative principle. Thus in each order or causal chain there exists a single monad prior to the manifold, which determines for the members of the order their unique relation to one another and to the whole. It is true that among members of the same series one is cause of another; but that which is cause of the series as a unity must be prior to them all, and qua co-ordinate they must all be generated from it, not in their several peculiarities, but as members of a particular series.

verb *hierarcheô* relates to the noun *hierarchia* as depicting its aim – the activity of the hierarchy is the act of God's creation, and the desire of that creation to return to God using hierarchy as the means of doing so. One of the keys to understanding the passage mentioned above is the term *analogia*, Dionysius' designation for the relation of God and creature. 'Analogy' or some variation of the term, occurs 66 times in the corpus and is integral to the double nature of God's activity in creation (God's creation and the necessary reciprocity of that creation).[61] Analogy, thus, refers to the proportion between God and created things which allows the created things to have some form of contact with God. Not all members of the hierarchy, however, have the same proportion – rather, Dionysius uses *analogia* to refer to the faculty by which entities can conform themselves to the power of God.[62] The faculty or aptitude of the created being to receive the divine varies depending on where that entity resides in the universe – entities located closer to the divine are better able to receive divine power and hence, are better assimilated to God. Analogy thus reflects the fitness or suitability to receiving divine power, which is received in a lesser degree by those further away from its source.[63]

Analogy in Iamblichus denotes a certain psychic state, a suitability for receiving gods,[64] while Proclus elaborates this notion to indicate how some are fit for participation in a particular Form, so that some receive more or less power depending on their status.[65]

In *ET*, prop. 32, reversion occurs through likeness to God. Dionysius, as in other instances, seems to use this term slightly differently from the Platonists, in so far as he uses *analogia* as an active principle inciting entities to return to their source, while for Proclus, the universe holds together because of *analogia*.

In *Celestial Hierarchy* 165A, Dionysius shows how members of the hierarchy connect by imitating the divine activity. Once higher members have received the divine light, they pass on the light to lower members:

> Hierarchy causes its members to be images of God in all respects, to be clear and spotless mirrors reflecting the glow of primordial light and indeed of God himself. It ensures that when its members have received this full and divine splendour they can then pass on this light generously and in accordance with God's will to beings further down the scale.

Unlike the mechanical symmetry between ranks in the Platonic world, the distribution of divine light by members of higher orders to lower is described in terms of beneficence in the Dionysian world. Just as God creates out of goodness, so do intelligences enlighten subordinates. Thus the hierarch, as the 'angel of God', guides those lower to him out of 'kindly love' and 'models himself on the divine goodness by seeking, as though on his own behalf, the gifts meant for others' (*EH* 564A). A member of the hierarchy mimics the activity of God by passing on the (now-diluted) divine rays to the those lower to it – again, while the power is diluted, it is

---

61 Lossky (1930), 289.
62 Lossky (1930), 290.
63 *In Parm.* 842, 38–843, 2.
64 *DM* 105, 1, 233, 1–2; See Gersh (1978), 37–8.
65 *In Parm.* 843, 13; 903, 36; 859, 11; 874, 14; *ET*, prop. 132; *In Eucl.* 146, 13–15.

diluted according to the inferior member's ability to receive it.[66] Still, the ultimate power resides in God who is the source of the power which orders and arranges the cosmos.[67] The concept of analogy or proportion is thus also connected to power and participation, in so far as the higher entities are higher because they contain more power and are participated in by those which follow it. The hierarchy itself is the entity through which divine light transmits itself to its members, and the hierarchy portions out God's power analogously.[68]

Entities receive divine light depending on their ability to gaze upon it. Although Dionysius does not describe the process using the language of free will, there seems to be a degree of freedom in an entity's ability to take in divine power, depending on whether the entity chooses to look upon it – a phenomenon developed in Dionysius' discussion of evil.[69] Nonetheless, regardless of whether an entity decides to look upon the divine, it is still limited by its nature, as given by God. Beings who participate in divine power are conformed to that power proportionately to the power of each of their own minds (*CH* 165B). Later in this same passage, Dionysius shows how higher entities mimic the activity of the divine by passing on the divine power to lower entities, who have the capacity only to receive a lessened degree of that power:

> When the hierarchic order lays it on some to be purified and on others to do the purifying, on some to receive illumination and on others to cause illumination, on some to be perfected and on others to bring about the perfection, each will actually imitate God in the way suitable to whatever role it has. (*CH* 165B)

While this passage does not use the term *analogia*, implicit in it is the concept of proportion, in so far as each member of the hierarchy imitates God in the way it is

---

66 In *DN* 696C, Dionysius describes how the souls, a rank below the angels, receive divine power mediated through the angels:

Next to these sacred and holy intelligent beings are the souls, together with all the good peculiar to these souls. These too derive their being from the transcendent Good. So therefore they have intelligence, immortality, existence. They can strive towards angelic life. By means of the angels as good leaders, they can be uplifted to the generous source of all good things and, each according to his measure, they are able to have a share in the illuminations streaming out from that Source.' The angels guide and transmit the souls connected below them so that the souls receive power as is appropriate to their ability to receive it.

67 *EH* 257C.
68 *EH* 504D:

Therefore the founding source of all invisible and visible order quite properly arranges for the rays of divine activity to be granted first to the more godlike beings, since theirs are the more discerning minds, minds with the native ability to receive and to pass on light, and it is through their mediation that this source transmits enlightenment and reveals itself to inferior beings in proportion to capacity.

69 To be presented in detail in Chapter 5.

able, according to the power God has given to it.[70] In the *Ecclesiastical Hierarchy*, the hierarchs not only pass on divine power to lower members, but they portion divine power appropriately, as men are fit to receive it:

> They understood quite well that those empowered by God to lay down sacred norms went about organizing the hierarchy into fixed and unconfused orders, giving each, as was due, its appropriate allotment. (*EH* 377A)

Just as God and the angels distribute divine power using the principle of *analogia*, so do the hierarchs, under God's instruction. Each of the sacred orders is arranged so as to pass on divine light through instruction of the faithful: bishops, monks, priests: illuminated, ministers, purified. Thus, while, in the celestial hierarchy, the sacrament means the knowledge of every aspect of God's immateriality, in the ecclesiastical hierarchy the sacrament carries with it a material nature, so that the hierarchy can be expressed through a division of sacrament, initiator and initiated.[71]

Attached to this concept of *analogia* is the term *axia*, or the merit proper to the intelligence, which designates the approach of the will to God and the initiative of the entity engaging in contemplation. Roques explains the relationship between *axia* as 'that which bridges the divide which separates our actual *analogia* from the ideal *analogia*, assigned to each of the orders of being'.[72] Dionysius describes the function of *axia* as follows:

> The beauty of God – so simple, so good, so much the source of perfection – is completely uncontaminated by dissimilarity. It reaches out to grant every being, according to merit (*axia*) a share of light and then, through a divine sacrament, in harmony and in peace, it bestows on each of those being perfected in its own form. (*CH* 164D)

The principle of *axia* speaks to the free will of the member of the hierarchy in so far as divinization, and the contemplation required for such divinization, is not the result of an intelligence's rank as determined by God (as every member can return to God according to its ability), but is the result of its own desire to seek God. In the ecclesiastical hierarchy, the hierarch has a being, proportion and order which is perfected by God, and the hierarch has the role of imparting perfection and deification to those below, according to their merit (*axia*) (*EH* 372D).[73] Thus, the amount of

---

70 *CH* 168A:

And so it comes about that every order in the hierarchical rank is uplifted as best it can toward cooperation with God. By grace and a God-given power, it does things which belong naturally and supernaturally to God, things performed by him transcendently and revealed in the hierarchy for the permitted imitation of God-loving minds.

71 Roques (1954), 69.
72 Roques (1954), 63.
73 This is expressed on a number of occasions: See *EH* 373B: 'Actually, it is the same one whom one-like beings desire, but they do not participate in the same way in this one and the same being. Rather, the share of the divine is apportioned to each in accordance with merit'.

divine power received by an intelligence depends not merely on its hierarchical rank, but its willingness to receive the power. Dionysius explains this using the example of a seal, which, although unchanging, will leave differing impressions on surfaces depending on the pliability of the wax involved:

> Maybe some will say that the seal is not totally identical in all the reproductions of it. My answer is that this is not because of the seal itself, which gives itself completely and identically to each. The substances which receive a share of the seal are different. Hence, the impressions of the one entire identical archetype are different. If the substances are soft, easily shaped, and smooth, if no impressions have been made on them already, if they are not hard and resistant, if they are not excessively soft and melting, the imprint on them will be clear, plain and long-lasting. But if the material is lacking in this receptivity (*epitêdeiotês*),[74] this would be the cause of its mistaken or unclear imprint or of whatever else results from the unreceptivity of its participation. (*DN* 644B)

This has its parallel in Proclus' discussion of the permanence of Form in *In Parm.* 884, which is not attributable to some common element in individual phenomena, Proclus argues, but rather to lack of change in the Form. Change is thus attributed to differences within those receiving the Form.[75]

The principle of the higher entities being better able to receive divine power than those below it is likewise found in Proclus' *ET*, prop. 62, according to which those nearer to the One are greater in power, and hence, more like the One.

A hierarchy, moreover, as an object, is an instrument used by God for salvation:

---

74 We may note the use here of this characteristic Neoplatonic term for the receptivity of influences from above, which Dionysius employs quite frequently, e.g: *DN* 593D, 680B; *EH* 392A, 429D, 508A.

75 Proclus says that if form is exemplified in particulars, form is always the same but is imprinted on substrata of varying receptivity. *In Parm.* 883, 37–884, 26:

> Others again have attributed the permanence of the Forms to the common element in individual phenomena (for man begets man, and like in general springs from like), but these people must first address themselves to the problem as to whence the common element in individuals takes its origin. For this could not be the genus, being immanent in Matter and divisible and not absolutely eternal, nor, if it comes from another causal principle, could this be one that is subject to motion and change; for in that case it itself would be totally changeable. But in fact inasmuch as it is a Form, it remains always the same, like one identical seal impressed upon many pieces of wax. They may change, but it remains uninterruptedly the same in all the instances of wax. What, then, is the immediate cause of the imposition of the seal? Matter is in the place of the wax, and the individual man is to be identified with the imprint, so what are we to identify with the signet-ring that descends upon its objects, if not Nature that permeates matter and thus moulds the sense realm with its reason-principles? With the hand wielding the signet-ring we may identify the Soul, which directs Nature, Soul as a whole directing Nature as a whole, and individual souls directing individual natures; and with that which does the impressing of the seal by means of the hand and the signet-ring may we not identify the Intellect, which through Soul and Nature fills the sense-realm with Forms, that which we may truly characterize as Resource, the begetter of those reason-principles which flow forth as far as Matter? (trans. Dillon)

The goal of a hierarchy, then, is to enable beings to be as like as possible to God and to be at one with him. A hierarchy has God as its leader of all understanding and action. It is forever looking directly at the comeliness of God. A hierarchy bears in itself the mark of God (*DN* 165A).

Another use of the term analogy is, thus, both subjective and objective divine love: the love of God for creation and creation's love of God.[76] In Dionysius' Christianized Platonism, the basis for an entity's power is its place in the hierarchy, but this power, moreover, is best described as its love for God. Members of the hierarchy play an active role in conforming themselves to God.[77] This love of God, moreover, creates a symmetry or unity of purpose which holds the entire hierarchy together as a whole, despite its numerous parts:

> This – the One, the Good, the Beautiful – is in its uniqueness the Cause of the multitudes of the good and beautiful. From it derives the existence of everything as beings, what they have in common and what differentiates them, their identicalness and differences, their similarities and dissimilarities, their sharing of opposites, the way in which their ingredients maintain identity, the providence of the higher ranks of beings, the interrelationship of those of the same rank, the return upward by those of lower status, the protecting and unchanged remaining and foundations of all things amid themselves. Hence, the interrelationship of all things in accordance with capacity. Hence, the harmony and the love which are formed between them but which do not obliterate identity. Hence, the innate togetherness of everything. (DN 704BC).

Not only do the members of the hierarchy share a love of God, but this shared love turns into a love between ranks. Love orders the participation so that the degree of participation in the hierarchy depends upon the free choice – the decision to love God or the member of the cosmos above or below – of members of the hierarchy.[78] Here, elements of Christian charity appear in Neoplatonic concepts of *analogia* and *homoiôsis*.

The term *analogia* also signifies the divine love or plan which God has for all of creation, in so far as this love is manifested as theophanies, the divine Ideas which are suited to each creature depending on that creature's ability and potential responsiveness to God. Through these theophanies, God makes himself known to his creation:

> The exemplars of everything preexist as a transcendent unity with it [sc. the Good]. It brings forth being as a going-forth of being. We give the name of 'exemplar' (*paradeigma*) to those principles which preexist as a unity in God and which produce the essences of things. Theology calls them predefining, divine and good acts of will which determine and create things and in accordance with which the Transcendent One predefined and brought into being everything that is. (*DN* 824C)

---

76 Lossky (1930), 294.

77 *DN* 701A.

78 Lossky (1930), 296.

Analogy, as it refers to the divine Ideas, is the measure of God's love for his creation.[79] The divine Ideas pre-exist in God and proceed in the form of divine light, the material through which God can be known by his creation.[80] Causality, as the manifestation of the invisible causes or divine Ideas, makes possible a connection between the causes and the effects of the causes, through the participation of effects in causes or imitation of the divine. The effects possess images of their causes, albeit in an imperfect way (*DN* 645D). Thus, the divine Ideas are the creative principles and the final ends of creation, by which, according to the analogy of those things, he is the cause of all things (*DN* 821B–824B).

The act of creation, by way of the concept of *analogia* described above, connects the creator with his creation. In *DN* 869D, God creates the hierarchy from his preexistent Ideas, and the hierarchy forms a kind of analogy by which creation can know God: 'But we know him from the arrangement of everything, because everything is, in a sense, projected out from him, and this order possesses certain images and semblances of his divine paradigms'. Each creature was assigned, by being placed in a particular rank at the time of creation, an analogy by which he can come to participate in the divine ideas.[81] There is, thus, a connection between love of creator and creation, expressed through analogy, because creation contains images of the divine ideas – in defining the analogies of individual creatures, God determines out of love to produce things which desire to return to him, by using the analogy, out of their love of God.[82] Analogy for Dionysius represents the union between the will of God in creation and the will of creatures, who must select whether to seek God (*DN* 913C).

The major difference between Dionysius' interpretation of God's creation and the subsequent ordering of that creation and the Neoplatonic one resides in the motivation of the creator. While both use *analogia* and *axia* to describe a cohesive universe, only Dionysius describes God as processing out of himself for love of creation, with the decision whether or not to turn to divine love left up to the created being. Still, there appears a doctrine of divine 'warmth' for creation, although the emphasis lies on the reception of that warmth by creation. Plotinus, in his treatise *How the Multitude of the Forms came into Being, and on the Good* (VI, 7 [38], 22), describes the One's activity as follows:

When anyone, therefore, sees this light (sc. from the Good), then truly he is also moved to the Forms, and longs for the light which plays upon them and delights in it, just as with bodies here below our desire is not for the underlying material things but for the beauty imaged upon them. For each is what it is by itself; but it becomes desirable when the Good colours it, giving a kind of grace (*hôsper charitas*) to them and passionate love to the desirers. Then the soul, receiving into itself an 'outflow' (*aporrhoê, Phdr.* 251b2) from thence, is moved and dances like a bacchant and is all stung with longing and becomes love. Before this it is not moved even towards Intellect, for all its beauty; the beauty of Intellect is inactive till it catches a light from the Good, and the soul by itself 'falls flat

---

79 Lossky (1930), 304–306.
80 Lossky (1930), 285.
81 Lossky (1930), 300.
82 Lossky (1930), 305.

on its back' (*Phdr.* 254b8) and is completely inactive and, though Intellect is present, is unenthusiastic about it. But when a kind of 'warmth' (*thermasia*, cf. *Phdr.* 251b2) from thence comes upon it, it gains strength and wakes and is truly 'winged'; and though it is moved with passion for that which lies close by it, yet all the same it rises higher, to something higher, to something greater which it seems to remember. And as long as there is anything higher than that which is present to it, it naturally goes on upwards, lifted by the giver of its love. (trans. Armstrong)[83]

Here, the warmth from the One is received by the Intellect when the Intellect seeks it. The One, in turn, is described by Plotinus as benign, 'the Good is gentle and kindly and gracious, present to anyone when he wishes' (V, 5 [32],33f.), which is still not to say that the One cares, per se, about us, although it is presented as generally benign.[84]

There is, then, much that is Platonic in Dionysius' concept of hierarchy and of the process of *analogia*. Only the active love of God for his creation may be claimed as distinctively Christian, and even of that, as we have seen, certain adumbrations may be discerned, at least in the thought of Plotinus.

A Note on Angels as Henads

From a Neoplatonic perspective, the triads of intelligible (angelic) entities set out in the *Celestial Hierarchy* should not properly be classed as henads. For Syrianus and Proclus (and likely for Iamblichus before them),[85] the class of beings known as henads or 'unities' (*henades*) are inhabitants of the realm of the One, not properly that of Intellect. They were postulated in order to contribute a sort of bridge between the absolute unity and transcendence of the One and the (relative) multiplicity of what proceeds from it at the level of Intellect. These entities, products of the archetypal Limit and Unlimitedness, together constitute what is termed 'the Unified' (*hênômenon*), which is the element of the henadic realm which connects most immediately with the intelligible realm, appearing there as One-Being (*hen on*), the ruling monad of the realm of Intellect. However, the *hênômenon* can also be viewed as an assemblage of 'henads', also denominated 'gods', which serve as the unitary archetypes of the Forms in the realm of Intellect.

---

83 For a lengthy discussion of this passage, see Dillon (1997), 327ff.

84 In a discussion on this topic, Dillon (1997), 329, points to the following passage which illustrates that the One does not care for its creation:

> The Good, then, is master also of this derived power (sc. of Beauty), although he does not need the things that have come into being from him, but leaves what has come into being altogether alone, because he needs nothing of it, but is the same as he was before he brought it into being. He would not have cared if it had not come into being; and if anything else could have derived from him he would have grudged it existence; but as it is, it is not possible for anything else to come into being; all things have come into being, and there is nothing left. (*Enn.* V, 5 [32], 21ff.)

85 On this debate, see Dillon (1972, 1993).

It is against this background that certain significant turns of phrase employed by Dionysius may be viewed.[86] First of all, cf. *DN* 588B, he refers to God, among a string of other epithets, as a 'henad unifying every henad' (*henas henopoios hapasês henados*). With this one phrase he seems to betray a knowledge of the whole later Neoplatonic system, according to which the One contains within itself, and gives unity to, a multiplicity of entities which have not yet properly proceeded forth from it. What Dionysius has in mind here is not clear, since he has no use for a system of henads as such. However, later in the work, at *DN* 892D, we find the most interesting phrase 'the immortal lives of the angelic henads', which the power of God preserves 'unharmed'.

How can it be that Dionysius refers to the angels as 'henads', since by definition they have proceeded forth from God? The answer may lie in the fact advanced earlier (Chapter 3, pp. 45–8), that Dionysius has adopted Porphyry's view of the relation between the subjects of the first two hypotheses of the *Parmenides*, which makes the subject of the second hypothesis also God in his creative and procreative aspect, enabling Dionysius to introduce the Trinity within the realm of the One.[87] The divine classes of entity depicted there will therefore still count as 'henads', as being intimately connected with God, despite their various degrees of plurality.

On the other hand, however, the three triads of angelic beings in the celestial hierarchy can be assimilated also to the three levels of beings distinguished within the realm of Intellect, first by Iamblichus, and then after him, more elaborately, by Syrianus and Proclus. Dionysius is not, of course, concerned to reproduce as such the distinction between the intelligible, intelligible-intellective and intellective levels of being, but he does make it clear that his three levels of angelic being differ in degrees of purity and illumination, thus differentiating them in an analogous manner to the Neoplatonic entities. So we may conclude, after all, that these inhabitants of the Dionysian universe are enjoying the best of both levels of being.

---

86 J.P. Sheldon-Williams (1972) has postulated a relationship between Pseudo-Dionysius' use of variations of the term 'henad' and the Neoplatonic concept of henad, drawing a relationship between henad and Form for Pseudo-Dionysius.

87 Cf. the fine turn of phrase at *CH* 212C *henas trisupostatos*, 'henad triply hypostatized'.

Chapter 5

The Problem of Evil

Dionysius' discussion on the place of evil in the universe – that it does not exist – and its relation to matter has long been one of the key documents which linked him to Proclus.[1] The treatise, a lengthy excursus in Chapter 4 of the *Divine Names*, seems to be directly dependent on Proclus' monograph *On the Existence of Evils*. While the task of discerning precisely to what extent Dionysius is borrowing Proclus' exact terminology is made somewhat more complicated by the circumstance that the work survives chiefly in the mediaeval Latin translation by William of Moerbeke,[2] one can still construe the Greek text with some accuracy, thanks to William's methods of translation, which are determinedly literal.[3] More importantly, Dionysius formulates the same argument as Proclus, using the same examples and technical vocabulary, in arriving at the same conclusions.[4]

Nevertheless, Dionysius' account of evil does exhibit differences, in so far as he Christianizes his response and does away with the structural argument as it appears in Proclus. While Proclus structures his argument in the scholastic manner, with two positions stated and refuted before his own opinion is given, Dionysius states his views without discussion as to how the conclusion was derived. While Dionysius adopts much of Proclus' argument on evil, he not only re-arranges the argument, but he also simplifies things, ontologically changing Proclus' conclusion regarding the mode of existence of evil.[5] Proclus' argument focuses on the question as to what mode of being evil belongs to and is primarily addressed to two groups of philosophers: the first group, including, in Proclus' view, Plotinus, argues for a positive existence for evil among beings, while the second denies the existence of evil. To this former group, Proclus responds that because the Good is the cause of everything, evil cannot belong to beings, for whatever participates in the Good participates through being. In addition, Proclus argues that if the Good is beyond being, then evil would have to be beyond non-being – a status which would make non-being ontologically prior to being, something no Platonist would admit. Finally, Proclus argues that a good demiurge could not have created evil.[6]

---

1   Stiglmayr (1895), 253–73, 721–48; Koch (1895), 438–54.

2   We also have three treatises on evil and providence by the Byzantine prince Isaak Sebastokrator, in which he shamelessly pillaged Proclus, indicating that Proclus' Greek text was still extant in Byzantium in the thirteenth and fourteenth centuries. See Opsomer and Steel (2002), 7.

3   See the Greek retroversion of Boese (1960).

4   Steel (1997), 88.

5   Steel (1997), 96.

6   See also Proclus, *In Tim.* 374, 28–9.

Against the second group of philosophers, Proclus argues that evil cannot be the lowest form of the Good, because, if it were on the same scale as the Good, its strengthened state would only make it more removed from the Good, whereas good and evil are clearly opposites. Next in his argument, Proclus shows that evil is really opposed to the Good, but it does not have its own character, as a Form – hence, it is either a failure or a deviation. With this, Proclus offers the alternatives that absolute evil as absolute privation is impossible. Instead, Proclus adopts Iamblichus' solution that evil is a perversion which cannot survive on its own, but instead acts as a parasite upon the Good – a *parhypostasis*.[7] Thus, the focus of Proclus' discussion is not on whether evil exists, but on its mode of being. Using the Platonic structure of the universe, Proclus argues that absolute evil cannot exist ontologically, but enters reality when mixed with being.[8]

Dionysius makes use of the arguments against the two positions set out by Proclus, but does not deal with them systematically or identify them as the philosophical stances of others. Instead, Dionysius seems to adopt what Proclus offers as the first position, while taking up the second in the form of objections. The bulk of Dionysius' discussion on evil, then, concerns the question of whether evil has existence – a position Dionysius opposes using arguments similar to the ones maintained by Proclus, although somewhat simplified. Because Dionysius sides with the first position Proclus states, that evil does not exist, it may be helpful to show where he borrows from *On the Existence of Evils*, Chapters 2 and 3, which address this topic.

The most notable examples of Dionysius adopting Proclus occur in the first few chapters of Dionysius' account of evil. In Chapter 2 of *On the Existence of Evils*, Proclus argues that, because the Good is the cause of everything, the Good would not create evil. Section 2.2–23, cited below, has numerous parallels to *DN* 716BC:

> Indeed, how is it possible that something exists which utterly lacks a share in the principle of beings? For just as darkness cannot participate in light nor vice in virtue, so is it

---

7   Simplicius credits Iamblichus with this theory at *In Cat.* 418, 15. Proclus, also, says that there can be no absolute deficiency of the Good, so that evil only exists when it is mixed with matter:

> Thus, all things are good to the father of the all, and there is evil in those things that are not capable of remaining established in complete accordance with the Good; for this reason evil is 'necessary', as we have said earlier. In what sense evil exists and in what sense it does not is clear from our argument. For both those who assert that all things are good, and those who deny this, are right in one respect and wrong in another. Indeed, it is true that all beings are, but non-being, too is interwoven with being. Therefore all things are good, since there is no evil that is unadorned and unmixed. And also evil exists, namely for the things for which indeed there is evil: it exists for the things that do not have a nature that is disposed to remain in the Good in an unmixed way. (*DMS* 10, 11–21 trans. Opsomer–Steel)

In this passage, Proclus shows how evil is limited to the particular, because there can be no absolute deficiency of the Good.

8   Steel (1997), 96.

impossible that evil should participate in the Good. Suppose light were the first cause; then there would be no darkness in the secondary beings – unless it had its origin in chance and came from somewhere other than the principle. Likewise, since the good is the cause of everything, evil can have no place among beings. [For there are two alternatives.] Either evil, too, comes from the Good – but then the question arises: how can that which has produced the nature of evil still be the cause of all good and fine things? Or evil does not come from the Good – but then the Good will not be the good of all things nor the principle of all beings, since the evil established in beings escapes the procession from the Good.

In general, if anything, in whatever way it exists, derives its existence from being, and before it is being it is one – and if it neither was nor will be permitted to secondary beings to do what they do without the beings above them – for Intellect must act with Life, Life with Being, and everything with the One – then evil again is subject to one of the following alternatives: either it will absolutely not participate in being, or it is somehow generated from being and must participate at the same time in the cause beyond being. And a direct consequence of this argument is the following: either there is no principle, or evil does not exist and has not been generated. For that which has no share in being is not being, and that which [proceeds] from the first cause is not evil.

And again in Chapter 41, Proclus says:

Hence, one of two things must follow: either evil must not be said to be evil, if it is of divine origin, or evil exists and has no divine origin. But we have shown above that it exists. Therefore, "there must be other causes of evil, not god" – as Plato himself somewhere teaches, establishing that for all good things the procession is from one cause, and referring the generation of evil things to other causes, not to the divine cause. (41, 8–12)

Dionysius, likewise, argues that the Good cannot produce what is not good (*DN* 716BC):

Evil does not come from the Good. If it were to come from there it would not be evil.[9] Fire cannot cool us, and likewise the Good cannot produce what is not good.[10] If everything comes from the Good – and the Good naturally gives being and maintains, just as evil naturally tries to corrupt and to destroy – then no being comes from evil.[11] Nor will evil itself exist if it acts as evil upon itself, and unless it does this then evil is not entirely evil but has something of the Good within it which enables it to exist at all.[12]

---

9   Proclus, *DMS* 2, 8–9; 41, 9–10 (trans. Opsomer–Steel).

10   *DMS* 2, 41, 7–8: 'But, as they say, it does not pertain to fire to refrigerate, nor to good to produce evil from itself'; 2, 9–13:

How can that which has produced the nature of evil still be the cause of all good and fine things? Or evil does not come from the Good – but then the Good will not be the good of all things nor the principle of all beings, since the evil established in beings escapes the procession from the Good'. (trans. Opsomer–Steel)

11   *DMS* 5, 4–6: 'For all things have their being from the Good and are preserved by the Good, just as, conversely, non-being and corruption occur on account of the nature of evil'.

12   *DMS* 42, 6–8: 'Evil is not unmixed evil, as we have said repeatedly, but it is evil in one respect and good in another'.

Proclus' argument against the second group appears in 2, 23–32:

> If, then, the Good is, as we say, beyond being and is the source of beings – since everything, in whatever way it exists and is generated, strives for the Good according to its nature – how then could evil be any one thing among beings, if it is actually excluded from such a desire? Thus, it is far from true to say that evil exists because 'there must be something that is completely contrary to the Good.' For how could that which is completely contrary [to something] desire the nature that is contrary to it? Now, it is impossible that there is any being which does not strive for the Good, since all beings have been generated and exist because of that desire and are preserved through it.

DN 716C seems to be an interpretation of the above passage from Proclus:

> Now if it is the case that things which have being also have a desire for the Beautiful and the Good, if all their actions are done for what seems to be a good, and if all their intentions have the Good as their source and goal[13] (for nothing does what it does by looking at the nature of evil),[14] what place is left for evil among the things that have being and how can it exist at all if it is bereft of good purpose?"

He continues (716D) by arguing that evil cannot have existence because of its metaphysical relation to being:

> Evil is not a being; for if it were, it would not be totally evil. Nor is it a non-being; for nothing is completely a non-being, unless it is said to be in the Good in the sense of beyond being. For the Good is established far beyond and before simple being and non-being. Evil, by contrast, is not among the things that have being nor is it among what is not in being. It has a greater non-existence and otherness from the Good than non-being has.

Dionysius excludes evil from beings and non-beings based on the absolute transcendence of the Good. In *On the Existence of Evils* 3, 1–11, Proclus states that if the Good is beyond being, evil must be a non-being:

> For if the One and what we call the nature of the Good is beyond being, then evil is beyond non-being itself – I mean absolute non-being, for the Good is better than absolute being. Thus, one of these two implications follows. Non-being is either absolutely-not-being or what is beyond being. But it is impossible that evil is beyond superessential non-being, which is the Good. If, on the other hand, non-being is absolutely-not-being, then evil even more is not; for evil is even more wraith-like, as the saying goes, than that which absolutely does not exist, since evil is further removed from the Good than non-being. This is what is shown by those who give priority to non-being over being evil. However, that which is further removed from the Good is more insubstantial than that which is

---

13 *DMS* 2, 23–8: 'If, then, the Good is, as we say, beyond being and is the source of beings – since everything, in whatever way it exists and is generated, strives for the Good according to its nature – how then could evil be any one thing among beings, if it is actually excluded from such a desire?'

14 *DMS* 49, 3–5: 'But since souls pursue what is in every way good and do everything, including evil things, for its sake, someone might perhaps think that for evils, too, the Good is the final cause'.

closer; thus, that which is absolutely not has more being than the so-called evil; therefore evil is much more deprived of being than that which is absolutely not.

Proclus' argument here rests on the point that the Good, as the source of being, is itself beyond being, so that evil, if it was postulated as its opposite, would have to be regarded as 'beyond non-being', which is absurd.

Next, Dionysius reformulates Proclus' question on the mode of being of evil in the direction of the origin of evil, with a view to discovering the ontological status of evil. In *DN* 716D–717A, he argues that evil is not just a lesser good, but in opposition to the Good, and he uses language and examples cited by Proclus in 4, 1–37. Dionysius says:

If evil does not have being, then virtue and vice must be exactly the same, both totally and in particular details. And whatever conflicts with virtue cannot be evil. Yet the opposite of moderation is excess and the opposite of justice is injustice. Nor am I talking here of the just or unjust man, of the temperate or intemperate man, for long preceding the visible evidence for the virtuous man or his opposite is the distinction made within the soul between virtue and evils, and the inner conflict between passion and reason. Hence one must concede that there is something contrary to goodness and that this is evil. Goodness is not contrary to itself. It comes, rather, from a single cause so that it rejoices in communion, unity and concord. A lesser good is not the opposite of the greater good. What is less hot or cold is not the opposite to what is more so.

This passage parallels *DMS* 4, 1–37:

The argument that banishes evil from being could go like this, and along these lines it may sound probable. The argument that gives voice to the opposite viewpoint, however, will require that we first look at the reality of things and declare, with that reality in mind, whether or not evil exists; so we must look at licentiousness itself and injustice and all the other things that we usually call vices of the soul and ask ourselves whether we will accept calling each of them good or evil. *For if we admit that each of these [vices] is good, we must necessarily affirm one of the two following: either virtue is not contrary to vice – that is, virtue on the whole is not contrary to vice on the whole, and particular virtues are not contrary to the corresponding vices – or that which opposes the Good is not in every respect evil.* But what could be more implausible than each one of these positions, or what could be less in accordance with the nature of things?

For the vices oppose the virtues; how they oppose one another becomes clear if one takes a look at human life, in which the unjust are opposed to the righteous, and the licentious to the temperate, and also if one looks at what one might call the discord within souls themselves – for instance, when people lacking continence are drawn by reason in one direction; and in the fight between the two the better is overcome by the worse, but sometimes the worse by the better. For what else is happening in these people than that their souls' temperance is in discord with their licentious manners? What is happening in those who are fighting with anger? Is it not something similar? And what about the other cases of evil in which we perceive our souls to be in discord? Indeed, in general the manifest oppositions between good and evil men exist long before in a hidden way within the souls themselves. And the stupidity and disease of the soul are then extreme when the better part in us and the good rational principles that exist in it are overcome by worldly, vile passions. But to adduce many more examples would be foolish, would it not?

Now, if vices are contrary to virtues, as we have said, and evil is in every respect contrary to good – for the nature of the Good itself is not so constituted as to be in discord with itself, but being an offspring of one cause and one henad, it maintains a relation of likeness, unity, and friendship with itself, and the greater goods preserve the lesser goods, and the lesser goods are beautifully ordered by the more perfect – then it is absolutely necessary that the vices be not merely vices 'by way of speaking', but each of them must also really be evil and not just something less good. *For the lesser good is not contrary to the greater good, just as the less hot is not contrary to the more hot nor the less cold to the more cold.* Now if it is agreed that the vices of the soul belong to the nature of evil, it will have been demonstrated that evil pertains to beings.

In the third part of his treatise, Proclus reaches his discussion on the mode of existence and nature of evil in Chapters 50–54, where he determines that evil is a parasitic entity (*parhypostasis*) which can only survive when mixed with being; as such, it is part of a class of things which have their being accidentally, it is without efficient cause and indefinite.[15] The agent is, thus, at fault, for evil *qua* evil arises when a person aims at what seems good to him, but is indeed not good. With this explanation, Proclus sets out to counter any relationship between evil and the Good as first cause – because the Good causes everything in the universe, evil must then have no cause.[16]

Dionysius simplifies this description, giving evil an ontological place in the universe, as is pointed out by Carlos Steel.[17] As with Proclus, he sets out to eliminate the first principle as the source of evil, while still maintaining that God is the source of everything. Evil, for Dionysius, exists as an accident,[18] as was seen in Proclus' treatise, and is a deficiency. Although Dionysius describes evil as being mixed with the Good (*DN* 732D and 733B: 'evil has no share of being except in an admixture with the Good'), he uses the term *parhupostasis* only three times (*DN* 732C, 720D, 728D). In *DN* 732C, Dionysius describes evil as 'existing by means of something else', while he uses the verb (*parhyphistamenê*) in *DN* 720D in reference to the mode of existence of a disease, and in *DN* 728D, where evil has a contingent existence, being parasitic even without a body. In other passages, however, evil is not presented as a parasitic entity relying on being for existence, but rather as a deficiency in a subject's ability to participate in the Good.[19] By making evil a level of deficiency in the participants' ability to partake of the Good, Steel argues, Dionysius gives evil

---

15 'Therefore it is appropriate to call such generation a parasitic existence (*parhypostasis*), in that it is without end and unintended, uncaused in a way and indefinite'. (*DMS* 50, 29–31, trans. Opsomer–Steel).

16 'For there is no way of existing for that which neither is produced, in any way whatsoever, from a principal cause, nor has a relation to a definite goal and a final cause, nor has received in its own right an entry into being, since anything whatever that exists properly must come from a cause in accordance with nature – indeed, without a cause it is impossible for anything to come about – and must relate the order of its coming about to some goal.' (*DMS* 50, 3–9)

17 Steel (1997), 100.

18 *DN* 732C.

19 The lack of participation in God can be intentional or unintentional, as Dionysius argues. *DN* 736AB.

its own level of reality.[20] Still, Proclus and Dionysius both ultimately attribute evil to a deficiency on the part of the agent: for Proclus, the agent, mistaking the Good, acts in such a way that evil becomes intermixed with being; evil uses a mistaken understanding of the Good as an opportunity to attach itself to being as a parasite. Dionysius, on the other hand, attributes evil to an agent's inability to participate in the Good – hence, evil is an insufficient level of Good.

As regards the category of souls, Proclus attributes evil to all classes of being after heroes, because they descend or move to generation, transitions which allow for the occurrence of evil (*DMS* 20). Proclus divides souls into three categories: (1) immaculate souls, which remain in contact with the divine even during descent, and hence contain no evil; (2) fallen human souls, which fall from their state of contemplating the gods;[21] (3) irrational souls (souls of animals) (chs. 25–6). In this last case, Proclus says that evil arises when animals lack the appropriate virtue and, hence, do not act according to their nature.

Dionysius divides the last two categories into human souls and irrational animals, both of which fall into evil through a lack of participation in the Good (*DN* 728A, 728B). Again, the explanation of evil he offers relates to the concept of nature, and this provides a particularly close parallel to Proclus' theory of evil. Proclus says that there is no evil in the nature of the universe as a whole, although for particular beings, who are not in accordance with their nature, evil arises (Chs. 27–9). Similarly, Dionysius argues that evil in the realm of nature only exists in particulars (*DN* 728C), in so far as things are unable to reach their natural state of perfection. Again, both thinkers coincide in so far as they attribute evil to an agent who does not act appropriately to its natural or anticipated behaviour. Ontologically speaking, evil for the levels of existence discussed from gods (or angels) down to nature arises when entities do not behave in a way fitting to their appropriate level in the cosmic hierarchy, which, for both thinkers, (although emphasized to a greater extent by Dionysius) seems to be a level of participation in the Good.

As regards matter, the lowest level of the universe, both Proclus and Dionysius argue that matter is not evil because evil does not exist in itself, as a state of being (i.e. as matter), but it is in other things contrary to the Good. Proclus first presents the view of Plotinus in *Enn.* I, 8 (51), 3, which says that absolute evil, as unmeasured

---

20 'Certes, celui-ci admettra volontiers qu'il y a plusieurs degrés du bien, et différents modes de participation (c.f. 6, 3–6), mais le degré le moins parfait dans la participation au bien n'est jamais, en tant que tel, le mal. Le mal arrive quand il y a un être qui a la possibilité d'être privé du bien et que cette possibilité est effectivement réalisée: c'est le cas de l'âme particulière et de tous les êtres sublunaires. Mais ce mal, nous l'avons vu, ne peut jamais être considéré comme un forme amoindrie du bien dans l'échelle de gradation. Le moindre bien reste toujours le bien: il n'est pas encore une forme de mal (c.f. 170, 23–24....) et le moindre mal reste toujours mal. Même si le mal ne peut exister qu'en parasitant le bien et en empruntant l'être et la puissance de ce dernier, ce qui définit formellement le mal, c'est son opposition au bien. En concluant que le mal est "un bien imparfait", Denys a donc imprudemment simplifié la doctrine de Proclus et enlevé au mal sa réalité.' (Steel (1997), 100)

21 Again, when Dionysius offers a parallel explanation for evil in devils, he greatly simplifies Proclus' lengthy discussion of the fall and the subsequent alteration of internal activity.

and formless, can be identified with matter, as something without form (Ch. 30). To this, Proclus replies that matter is neither good nor evil, but a cosmic necessity. Steel shows how Dionysius uses three passages in Chapters 31–2, 36 and 37 of Proclus' treatise to make his argument on evil and matter, although he first introduces the combined passages with a citation from Matthew 7:18.[22] Regarding matter, Dionysius says that matter cannot be evil because it has a place in the cosmos, having derived its existence from the Good, Proclus' argument in *DMS* 31. Dionysius proposes, as a second argument, that matter is necessary for the fulfilment of the cosmos, because matter produces and sustains the nature of the Good, whereas evil is ineffectual and unproductive (*DN* 729B).[23] This argument seems to be a condensed version of *DMS* Chapters 32, 36 and 37, in which Proclus argues (in Ch. 32) that matter is necessary for the universe and any degree of unmeasure in matter is seen as matter's need or desire for measure, in which case it cannot be evil. Both Proclus and Dionysius ultimately reject the concept that matter is evil, based on the belief that all created beings in some way partake of the Good – because the Good was their creator and because, by their mode of creation, all things exist through participation (to some degree) in the Good.

The concept that absolute evil cannot exist because the Good creates everything gives rise to the question of how a providential god could permit any degree of evil in the universe (*DN* 733A). To this, Dionysius (again, condensing an argument made by Proclus in *DMS* 58–61) responds that (1) evil has no being and nothing with being is overlooked by providence (*DMS* 58, 1–4); (2) evil has no existence unless mixed with the Good (*DMS* 61, 1); (3) if no being is without some share in the Good, Providence must be in all things (*DMS* 61, 5; 58, 24–5). The last major point Dionysius makes on evil and providence does not occur in *DMS*, but is taken from Origen's *De Principiis*, III, 1, 18–24.[24] In *DN* 733BC, Dionysius says:

---

22 Steel (1997), 101.

23 Dionysius, however, merely states that matter is necessary for the universe without building any kind of proof or argument. In Chapter 34 of *DMS*, Proclus explains that matter contributes to the fabrication of the world, which makes it good. He next connects this concept with the argument that God as the creator of matter would not create anything evil. In *DN* 729, Dionysius borrows this connection without Proclus' explanation, stating that matter is necessary for the fulfilment of the cosmos and that the Good would not have created anything evil. Proclus reiterates the point that matter is generated by God in Chapter 35. Again, it is the concept that the Good created the universe and all entities partake in the Good (and hence, no absolute evil can exist) which shapes the arguments of both Proclus and Dionysius on the topic.

24 In these sections, Origen discusses the relationship between free will and providence using a series of examples, e.g.:

But it must certainly not be understood from this that if the hand moves, for instance, to strike someone unjustly or to steal, this is from God; for only the power of movement is from God, and it is our part to direct those movements, the power of exercising which we have from God, either to good or to evil purposes. Thus what the apostle says is, that we receive from God the power of willing, but it is we who use the will either for good or for evil desires. (trans. Butterworth)

Therefore, we should ignore the popular notion that Providence will lead us to virtue even against our will. Providence does not destroy nature. Indeed its character as Providence is shown by the fact that it saves the nature of each individual, so that the free may freely act as individuals or as groups, in so far as the nature of those provided for receives the benefactions of this providing power appropriate to each one.

The second section of Proclus' treatise addresses the question of where evil exists (Chs. 11–39). Here, Proclus goes through the various ontological levels of the universe and explains how evil exists at the levels of the gods, angels, daemons, heroes, souls (immaculate souls, fallen human souls, irrational souls), nature and matter. Again, Dionysius simplifies this account somewhat, as would be expected from a Christian adopting a non-Christian hierarchy of beings. He thus limits his discussion to the lower levels of being, angels, daemons (for Dionysius, of course, fallen angels, or devils), souls, irrational animals, nature, and matter. Regarding the existence of evil, Proclus says that evil does not exist in the gods because they are eternally identical to the Good (Chs. 11–13), just as it does not exist in angels, who are contiguous with the gods (Ch. 14).

Dionysius, as a Christian, does not mention the gods, and furthermore, he reformulates the question, answering it with the blanket statement that evil cannot reside at any level of beings because all proceed from the Good, in which no evil can exist.[25] Still, his discussion of evil in angels comes closest to Proclus' treatment of evil in gods, as Dionysius argues that no evil exists in angels because they are an image of God (and hence, one would assume, eternally self-identical, as Proclus had described gods).[26] Proclus, likewise, excludes evil at the daemonic level, arguing that *daimones* are evil neither to themselves nor to others: they are not evil to themselves because they derive their existence from the gods, and they are not evil to others because, by punishing wrongs, they do good deeds (Chs. 16 and 17). This last argument is used by Dionysius to show how angels are not evil, in so far as the punishments they mete out are for sinners only (*DN* 724B). Rather than addressing Platonic *daimones*, Dionysius discusses Christian demons, from whom he also excludes evil, much in the manner of the Neoplatonists, who say that evil does not exist at the intelligible levels. In *DN* 725A, he reiterates his earlier claim that things which owe their origin to God, as do devils, cannot be essentially evil. Devils are, thus, not evil with respect to their being, but in their failed activity or lack of participation in God. Using (and adjusting) Proclus' argument in favour of the permanence of daemons in Chapter 17, Dionysius argues further that devils cannot be wholly evil, because evil is a state of impermanence, and devils are always in the same condition.[27] Simultaneously, however, he attributes their evil to a state of

---

25 *DN* 721C–724A.

26 *DN* 724B.

27 Proclus, *DMS* 17:

For if they [demons] were evil in themselves, a dilemma would arise: either they remain in evil perpetually, or they are susceptible to change. And if they are always evil, [we will ask]: how can that which receives its existence from the gods be always evil? For not to be at all is better than always to be evil. On the other hand, if they change, they do not belong

'moving away' or 'lapse', by which is meant a permanent state of rejecting God (*DN* 725BC). With this explanation, Dionysius' description of evil in devils is essentially parallel to Proclus' description of evil in fallen human souls, as discussed below, in so far as both groups neglect their expected duty of contemplation of the Good (*DMS* 23–4).

Despite some aspects of Dionysius' arguments, then, which may owe more to Origen, or to his Christian background in general, than to Proclus, we can see from this detailed comparison of the two how deeply he is indebted to Proclus, apart from the intrinsic tenets of the argument, which stretch Christian orthodoxy to the limit in the direction of a monistic system. Dionysius' excursus on evil thus helps to constitute a definitive link between the two thinkers.

---

to the beings that are daemons in essence, but to beings that are such by relation: for the latter may be both better or worse, and [that is] another kind of life. Daemons, however, without exception, always fulfill the function of daemons, and every single one of them always [remains] in its own rank.

Chapter 6

Scriptural Interpretation [*Theoria*] as Onomastic Theurgy

Introduction

The following passage summarizes the mode of Dionysian contemplation [*theoria*]:[1]

> We use appropriate symbols [*symbola*] for the things of God. With these analogies [*analogiai*] we are raised upward towards the truth of the mind's vision, a truth which is simple and one. We leave behind us all our own notions of the divine. We call a halt to the activities of our minds and to the extent that is proper, we approach the ray which transcends being. Here, in a manner no words can describe, pre-existed the goals of all knowledge and it is of a kind that neither intelligence nor speech can lay hold of, nor can it at all be contemplated, since it surpasses everything and is wholly beyond our capacity to know it. Transcendently, it contains within itself the boundaries of every natural knowledge and energy. At the same time, it is established by an unlimited power beyond all celestial minds. And if all knowledge is that which is limited to the realm of the existent, then whatever transcends being must also transcend knowledge. (*DN* 592D)

This passage outlines the appropriate track for *theoria* to pursue. Contemplation begins with the material *symbola* – primarily that of scriptural interpretation, especially the divine names found in scripture (as will be argued in the next chapter, sacraments are not to be interpreted but enacted).[2] These symbols are a necessary means of conveying the transcendent divine, which cannot be known in its nature. Symbols serve as analogies not in the sense that they bear a similarity to the thing, but rather because they bear images of the divine paradigms, which may in themselves be dissimilar.[3] However, because these symbols carry divine light intertwined with

---

1   The descriptions of *theoria* here derive from passages where the word *theoria* or its cognates is explicitly mentioned (as opposed to descriptions of theoretic activity). The noun *theoria* occurs 42 times in the corpus, predominantly in the *Ecclesiastical Hierarchy*. The verb *theoreo* occurs 13 times in the corpus, predominantly in the *Divine Names*. Daele (1941).

2   Peter Struck notes that Dionysius' use of Procline symbols in his interpretation of scripture makes him 'one of the most important authorities in the medieval period on figurative language'. See Struck (2004), 255.

3   The concept of 'unlike likeness' (*anomoios homoiotês*), of which Dionysius makes much use (*DN* 916A; *CH* 137D, 141C; 144C, 145A, 337B), he borrows from the later Platonist tradition; cf. e.g. Syrianus, *In Met.* 153, 5–6 (where Syrianus refers to it as 'well-known' (*thrylêtheisa*), and Proclus, *In Remp.* II, 232, 20; *In Alc.* 189, 16; *In Parm.* 741, 13; 751, 19; 760, 7.

sensibility, they must be systematically unfolded to isolate divinity according to the ability of the participant. In this way, Dionysian *theoria* is schematized into spatio-temporal and moral distinctions:[4] – spatio-temporal in that each hierarchic rank represents a different degree of *theoria*, and moral in so far as members of each rank contemplate according to their spiritual ability. Using negative theology, the soul gradually sheds its discursive reasoning – the soul must eventually break away from being into a state of mystical contemplation. Discursive theology, however, is limited in so far as the human intellect cannot enter the hyper-noetic realm, except by a rare attainment of mystical *theoria*. This higher *theoria*, only occasionally experienced by man though continually experienced by the first hierarchy of angels, is marked by an initiation into the divine work (*theourgia*). It seems that *theoria* when used to refer to the divine names is simply another one of Dionysius' terms for onomastic theurgy. Possibly, our author uses a patristic commonplace so as not to be accused of over-Platonizing. This chapter will discuss Dionysian scriptural interpretation as a mode of theurgy comparable to Proclus' inspired reading of the Homeric poems – both see their respective texts as containing divine power which can be unlocked through a ritualized reading.

Power of Names: Names as *Symbola*

For Dionysius, scriptural interpretation, particularly of the divine names in scripture, fulfils the Hellenic definition of theurgy, with the divine names acting as symbols *par excellence*. Dionysius' scriptural interpretation is not merely anagogical and allegorical, although it certainly has these elements. Primarily, Dionysius refers to passages and even to particular words in scripture as symbols that signify a higher reality. Names refer to the *ousia* of what they signify. These symbols have been placed by God during the creation of the universe and thus contain creative *dynamis*. The divine names in scripture are efficacious in this way because they contain the power of the gods. The word itself performs a generative function unleashed at the divine level, but still potent when it functions as human language.

Dionysius explains that scripture functions as a theurgic *symbolon* because it directs us to a higher power that we could not access on our own:

> [The divine] revealed all this to us in the sacred pictures of the scriptures so that he might lift us in spirit up through the perceptible to the intelligible, from sacred shapes and symbols to the simple peaks of the hierarchies of heaven. (*CH* 124A)

Scriptural symbols are adapted to limited human understanding. At the beginning of Letter 9, Dionysius says that we contemplate the divine mysteries in scripture through perceptible symbols – one must strip these in order to see the mysteries in themselves.[5] Proclus explains that Homer sometimes depicts the gods using base images because these base images sit in the same chain of being as the gods. The

---

4   Roques labels this division 'quantitative and qualitative' – quantitative as proximity to the divine, qualitative as contemplative ability; see Roques (1952), col. 1890.

5   *Ep.* 9, 1104B.

lower images, thus, are symbols of these higher principles.[6] Proclus describes this phenomenon in his *Republic Commentary:*

> Moreover, when we consider each chain of the gods descending from above down to the lowest creatures and passing through all the ranks of beings encountered in reality, we can see that the ends of these chains manifest properties like those the myths assign to the gods themselves and that they produce and maintain aberrations comparable to those by which the myths have hidden the secret doctrine of first causes. (*In Remp.* I, 77, 29–78, 6, trans. Struck)

Dionysius, likewise, argues that descriptions of God, which are divided and multiple by their nature, are symbols of God:

> And what could anyone say about sacred compositions [*synthemata*] that attempt to render the form of God by putting forward and multiplying the visible shapes of things hidden, the divisions of things one and undivided, and shapes and many forms of things shapeless and formless? With regard to these, if anyone is able fittingly to see and distinguish their inner meaning, he will discover that they are all mystic things, of a divine form, and filled with much theological light. (*Ep.* 9, 1105C, trans. Hathaway)[7]

Symbols are composite in that they render the form of God in visible shapes.[8] God uses poetic imagery to represent the formless as a concession to the human mind.[9] The composite language, thus, reflects the diversity of our expressions in a non-unified structure of reality. Proclus has a similar understanding of language as symbol, placing language as a mediator between the world of sense experience and the higher realities. Language is human because it exists uniquely on the psychic level. Still, the ability of the gods to create by naming underlies the human use of language as in the relationship of archetype to copy.[10] Even though he explains that language is a fragmented image of reality, Proclus prohibits the direct procession from the phenomena of language to a nature of the understanding of reality: the soul must proceed through beings that are 'more partial' down to 'diversity' of existence in this world.[11] As Dionysius specifies, this mode of dual-transference is necessary because we are composite:

---

6   See Struck (2004), 245.

7   For a parallel passage, see Proclus, *In Tim.* III, 243, 8–13.

8   'The whole of philosophy is divisible into the study of intelligible things and the study of parts of the physical world and rightly so, since the ordered whole (*kosmos*) is itself double, on the one hand intelligible, and on the other hand, perceptible' (Proclus, *In Tim.* I, 13, trans. Hathaway).

9   *CH* 137B.

10   'The gods name and create by their act of thought. In us, however, the ability to impose names is measured by our participation in divine knowledge. In so far as we yield to the passivity of impressions, we introduce into language an arbitrariness', Trouillard (1974), 242.

11   See Proclus, *In Remp.* I, 111, 16–27 and *In Tim.* I, 352, 11–19. In this way, language accommodates itself to each level of reality. While the highest level of reality contains language synonymous with power and essence, the lower levels have disjunctive speech. In

Divine knowledge should illuminate human life as such, which is both undivided and divided, in a way suitable to itself; in such a way that the impassible [*apathes*] part of the soul should define the simple, more inward meaning of godlike images, while the passionate element, as befits its nature, should honor and elevate itself to the most divine realities through the construction of expressed (*typôtika*) symbols which have already been combined, since these veils (*parapetasmata*) are akin by nature to it, a thing which is proved by the fact that those who have heard clear theological teachings without such covering shape in themselves a certain form which leads them to the idea of such a theological doctrine. (*Ep.* 9, 1108AB,[12] trans. Hathaway, emended)

The two parts of the soul respond differently to the double nature of the cosmos. The impassive nature is the divine, true self[13] that is able to comprehend the intelligible truth in reality, whereas the passive nature is the part attached to images and discursive expressions.[14]

Proclus has a similar notion. In the *Eclogae de Philosophia Chaldaica* he explains that every soul is composed of intellectual *logoi* and divine *symbola*. The former come from intellectual forms, while the latter arise from divine henads and make union with the divine possible.[15] This distinction also occurs in Dionysius, especially in a reading of the Platonic parts of the soul as seen in Letter 8:[16] 'So define for yourself what is proper for your passion, anger, and reason and for you let the divine ministers [define what is fitting]'.[17] Later in the Letter, Dionysius rebukes Demophilus about his behaviour towards his parishioners, warning him to correct his 'untamed passions'.[18] Hathaway notes that mythic language is used throughout the text because Demophilus does not yet have his *nous apathês*.[19] As with Demophilus, the perceptible aspect of symbols is geared for our untrained intellects.

In Tim. II, 255, 1–25, Proclus explains how each divine order has a power of naming identified with its own efficacy.

12 See Proclus, *In Tim.* II, 352, 15–19: 'but we must appreciate that the mode of knowing varies according to the diversity of the knowing subject. For the same object is known by God in the mode of unity, by intellect in the mode of totality, by reason in the mode of universality, by soul under the aspect of figure, and by sense-perception as a received impression. So it is not true that, because the object known is the same, the knowledge of it is also the same'.

13 Proclus, *ET*, prop. 80: 'The proper nature of all bodies is to be acted upon, and of all incorporeals to be agents, the former being in themselves inactive and the latter impassible; but through association with the body the incorporeal too is acted upon, even as bodies too can act through partnership with incorporeals' (trans. Dodds).

14 Hathaway (1969), 120.

15 Fragment 5 *Eclogae de philosophia Chaldaica* in Des Places (1971), 206–212. See Sheppard (1980), 152.

16 Hathaway (1969), 77.

17 *Ep.* 8, 1093C.

18 *Ep.* 8, 1097A.

19 Hathaway (1969), 149.

Power of Names: Names Signify *Ousia*, Act as *Dynamis*

These symbols are not allegories – they directly signify a higher reality:

> For the *logos* lying before [the theologians] [in the form of scriptural symbols] taken both as a whole and in its parts, is not a sterile narrative but rather a vivifying perfection. In opposition to vulgar misconceptions, we must therefore enter into the holy symbols [which are] becoming to God and not dishonour them, being as they are offspring and copies of divine characters and visible images of inexpressible, marvellous visions.
> (*Ep.* 9, 1105C–1108D, trans. Hathaway)

Because God emanated names at the time of creation and as the source of creation,[20] names refer to particular *ousiai;* the name is an illumination of the divine.[21] Proclus says that names issued from gods are more intellectually powerful, perfectly adhering to the nature of the underlying realities.[22] In his *Commentary on the Parmenides*, Proclus praises those who think that the Forms have given their names to the sensible realm so that names are images in words of the objects they indicate:

> It is clear from all this that names refer primarily to intelligible Ideas, and that sense-objects get their names, together with their being, from that source. But we must recognise that what has been said is about the names that our mind is able to consider. There are many grades of names, as of knowledge. Some are called divine, the names by which the inferior gods designate the beings above them; some angelic, the names by which the angels designate themselves and the gods; some are demonic, and some human.
> (*In Parm.* 852, 38–853, 7, trans. Dillon–Morrow)

Not only do the names in this realm correspond to the higher realm, but various intelligible and psychic levels have their own names, corresponding to their own essences and powers. Dionysius makes a similar statement in Letter 9:

> For not only are transcendent light and intelligible things and in a word things divine depicted in numberless symbols, as for example, God is said to be fire, and intelligible oracles of God are said to be consumed in fire, but even the godlike orders of intelligible and intelligent angels are depicted in varied shapes and forms and fiery configurations. The image of fire itself is understood in one way when attributed to the God beyond knowing; in another [when attributed] to his providential activities or reason-principles, in yet another [when attributed] to angels; the first [being understood] as causal; the next as substantial, the last as participative,[23] each in its own way as contemplative and scientific ordering [chose to] define them. (*Ep.* 9, 1108C–1109A, trans. Hathaway, emended)

---

20 Trouillard (1974), 242.

21 *PT* I, 29, p. 124, 22 S–W; *In Parm.* 81, 8; *In Crat.* 51, p. 19, 16.

22 Proclus, *In Tim.* I, 273, 25–7; *In Tim.* III, 243, 8–13; *In Remp.* I, 198, 13–24.

23 Dionysius is here, interestingly, making use of a standard Neoplatonic distinction (originating, it would seem, with Iamblichus), between three modes of subsistence of intelligible entities: *kat' aitian, kath' hyparxin* and *kata methexin*, cf. Proclus, *ET*, prop. 65; *In Tim.* I, 8, 17ff.; 234, 23ff.

As with Proclus, each level of being has its own essence correlated to a nane, so that even the same name (e.g. 'fire') reveals a different essence depending on which level of reality it reveals. Proclus elaborates further on the relationship between name, *ousia* and *dynamis* in his *Commentary on the Cratylus*. Here he says that the name functions as an instrument which has two sorts of powers, one communicating thoughts, the other producing sameness and otherness as manifesting essence.[24]

Dionysius reflects the power of names as noted by Proclus. He says that the scriptural symbol contains 'natural knowledge and energy and unlimited power (*dynamis*)',[25] such that names are not to be interchanged.[26] The following passage shows how names express activity in Dionysian thought:

> Why is it, however, that theologians sometimes refer to God as Yearning and Love and sometimes as the Yearned-for and the Beloved? On the one hand he causes, produces, and generates what is being referred to, and on the other hand, he is the thing itself.
> (*DN* 712C)

Here, name refers to activity, in this case yearning as the power of generation.

The relationship between symbol and thing signified is a rather complicated one, especially because the modern understanding of words such as 'symbol' or 'likeness' differs so drastically from the late Platonist usage. In the Platonist tradition of exegesis, symbols in the form of words or stories are identified with the nature of reality in the same way that copies relate to archetypes.[27] The relationship is not an allegorical approach, but rather a hieratic relationship of one-to-one correspondence. Depending on the notion of sympathy, the word acts as a symbol of the intelligible reality so that the theurgic practice of animating statues with *symbola* can be equated with the giving of names to things so that the name is like the thing named.[28] Proclus has a similar understanding of symbol in his *Commentary on the Republic:*

> Symbols are not representations of those things of which they are symbols. For that which is the contrary of something else cannot be a representation of that thing, such as the ugly of the beautiful or that which is contrary to nature of that which is natural. For symbolic wisdom hints at the nature of reality through the medium of elements totally contrary in their nature. (*In Remp.* I, 198, 15–19, trans. Coulter)

It is necessary to understand here what is at stake for Dionysius and Proclus. Unlike the Alexandrian interpretation of scripture,[29] this late Platonic interpretation reads texts in light of a hierarchical metaphysics.

---

24 Proclus, *In Crat.* 51, p. 20, 18–21.
25 *DN* 593A.
26 *DN* 640C.
27 Lamberton (1986), 201.
28 Sheppard (1980), 155. See Proclus, *In Crat.* 19, 12; cf. 25, 1–7.
29 The Alexandrian interpretation of scripture is embodied by the Christian Origen and the Jewish thinker Philo, although its modes of examining texts is certainly not limited to a Judeo-Christian approach; rather it has its roots in Stoic or Stoicizing allegorical exegesis of the Homeric poems. This method of reading is characterized by a multi-level, anagogic approach to texts. As with the Dionysian and Procline method, it appreciates that the reader

In a series of passages in the *Celestial Hierarchy*, Dionysius addresses the question of how divine and heavenly things are revealed. He explains that God 'proceeds naturally though sacred images in which like represents like';[30] these shapes lift us from multiplicity to simplicity. The meaning of the term 'likeness' (*homoiotês*) sheds light on the term 'image' (*eikon*). The notion is that of likeness or analogy, the Platonic relationship between cause and effect as seen in Proposition 28 of the *Elements of Theology*. As part of a great, interlocking chain of being, symbols embodied in the lower levels of reality contain the same intelligibility that exists at the higher levels.[31] The substance of this intelligibility is able to remain the same at various levels because as God emanates, he emanates the same light in varying degrees of power. Thus, the reality of God's existence at the highest level of reality is the same in the material words of scripture – for those receptive to the intelligibility existing in scripture will be simultaneously receptive to the complex order of reality.[32]

Following in the Procline tradition of divine names as symbols, Dionysius holds that the divine names in scripture refer to the processions of God.[33] The divine names function as theurgic light:

> This is the kind of theurgic enlightenment into which we have been initiated by the hidden tradition of our inspired teachers, a tradition at one with scripture. We now grasp these things in the best way we can, and as they come to us, wrapped in the sacred veils of that love towards humanity with which scripture and hierarchical traditions cover the truths of the mind with things derived from the realm of the senses. (*DN* 592B)

The names have the same double power as other scriptural *symbola*: we mentioned that they are intelligible, as 'theurgic light', and they are perceptible, cloaked in material images. Proclus gives names the same significance that he gives other *symbola*: each name carries a likeness of the object to which it is applied – 'which

---

can approach the text at different levels depending on his own moral disposition, which can be raised with proper training. For Origen, the structure of scripture relates to the order of reality. The sensible world of scripture holds the meaning of the intelligible realm, so that when read correctly, the allegorically-bent Christian can see the connection between spiritual events and mystical intelligibilities. The reader begins at the literal level and progresses through the guidance of Jesus in the form of faith. Cf. Origen (*De Princ*. IV, 3, 5). A correct reading sees the connection between the sensible reality and the higher intelligible world. The two realms are connected in scripture in that scriptural stories speak allegorically – the words point to something higher, but they do not contain the higher reality themselves. This is the fundamental difference between the Alexandrian method of interpretation and the later Neoplatonic. For more discussion on allegorical interpretation in Origen, see Dawson (1998) and Torjeson (1985).

30   *CH* 140C, 136D.

31   Lamberton (1986), 190.

32   Coulter (1976), 53.

33   In *DN* 589D; Proclus seems to make the divine names into Platonic Forms that descend as processions: 'The divine word exists as a unity in the gods but as a plurality in the daemons and the further they are removed from the gods, the greater is their extension and the lower their descent into plurality' (*In Parm*. 673, 5–8, trans. Morrow–Dillon).

means that they refer primarily to immaterial Forms, and derivatively to sensible things, so that things in this world derive both their being and their designation from that world'.[34] Dionysius adapts this Procline description of names for his explanation of biblical names. These crass signs [*synthemata*] function as a goad for the materially inclined to look for the intelligibility existing in the name. Proclus explains the same phenomena but stresses the 'place-holder' aspect of the name. In the *Parmenides Commentary* he proposes a homonymous use of names. Giving the example of the name 'man', he says that man can mean two separate things depending on its application. Primarily, 'man' is a likeness of the intelligible reality – in this case a likeness of a paradigm; secondarily, it is a sensible thing – a likeness of a likeness.[35] For both Dionysius and Proclus names act as *symbola* that refer to the essence of a being. When names act in their primary capacity they engage the powers of similarity (*homoiôsis*) to become a fragmented image of their paradigm.

Onomastic Activity: Enactment of Names

Acting as symbola, names carry a performative capability. Just as we saw the powers of other textual symbols unleashed through proper reading, the power of names is unearthed through ritual chanting:

> In my opinion, it would be unreasonable and silly to look at words rather than at the power of their meanings. Anyone seeking to understand the divine things should never do this, for this is the procedure followed by those who do not allow empty sounds to pass beyond their ears ... People like this are concerned with meaningless letters and lines, with syllables and phrases which they do not understand, which do not get as far as the thinking part of their souls, and which make empty sounds on their lips and in their hearing. (*DN* 708BC)

This relation between words and the essences the words convey is certainly Procline, rather than Chaldaean or Iamblichean. Whereas Iamblichus and the *Chaldaean Oracles* insist that the chanter not change the barbarian names because he should chant the meaningless sounds of the barbarian names, Proclus and Dionysius insist that the power of the name resides in its relation to the essence it reveals.[36] Thus, Proclus and Dionysius, it would seem, both see no problem with the translation of

---

34 Proclus, *In Parm.* 851, 8–10, trans. Morrow–Dillon.

35 Proclus, *In Parm.* 852, 11.

36 See Proclus, *In Tim.* I, 99, 3–7; *In Crat.* 71, p. 32, 5–12, unlike Iamblichus, *DM* VII, 5 on the chanting of names, where Iamblichus warns against changing the barbarian words. Also, *EH* 428AB:

The variegated and sacred material construction of the symbols is not taken for granted by them, although it presents only the external properties of the symbols. For, on the one hand, the most holy chanting of scripture and the uplifting knowledge leads the way to a virtuous life, and above all it teaches the complete purification from destructive evil.

magical terminology. Still, Dionysius does not describe the names as having the same sacramental powers as do the eucharist or baptism, for instance.[37]

Moreover, names function as powers that correspond with hierarchic ranks, as we see with Proclus in the *Platonic Theology*:

> In short, therefore, it must be admitted that the first, most principal and truly divine names are established in the gods themselves. But it must be said that the secondary names, which are imitations of the first and which subsist intellectually, are of a daemonic allotment. And again, we may say that those names which are third from the truth, which are logically devised and which receive the ultimate resemblance of divine natures, are revealed by skilled practitioners, acting now under divine inspiration, now intellectually, and generating moving images of their inward visions.[38] (*PT* I, 29, p. 124, 3ff. S–W)

This passage is of interest because it expounds the various degrees of divine names that exist in the hierarchy. The last degree is of the most interest to us. This degree refers to the ritual unfolding of divine names that takes place on our level – at this

---

37 A number of Christian writers and liturgies, however, do discuss the power of names as performative. In the *Contra Celsum*, Origen heartily agrees with Celsus that, indeed, Christians do hold the name of Jesus itself as having magical powers. He explains that when the name is pronounced, daemons are driven out of men. In fact, he adds, the name of Jesus is so powerful against daemons that sometimes it is effective even when pronounced by bad men. In *C. Cels*. 1, 6, Origen says:

> For they do not get the power which they seem to possess by any incantations, but by the name of Jesus, with the recital of the histories about him. For when these are pronounced they have often made daemons to be driven out of men, and especially when those who do utter them speak with real sincerity and genuine belief. In fact the name of Jesus is so powerful against the daemons that sometimes it is effective even when pronounced by bad men. Jesus taught this when he said: 'many shall say to me in that day, in thy name we have cast out daemons and performed miracles' [Mt 7:22)]. (trans. Chadwick)

On Origen and divine names see Dillon (1990), 206. This corresponds to the fourth-century Church debate as to whether or not the personal attitude of the priest determines the effect of the ritual words he speaks. Chanting the name of Christ or the name of the Trinity as protection against evil spirits becomes widely popular in the Middle Ages; for example the incantations attributed to St Patrick in which he invokes the Trinity to aid him against the enchantments of women. See Thorndike (1943), 640.

38 Cf. Proclus, *In Parm*. 851,7–853, 11, where Proclus summarizes his theory of language, including how hierarchic names correspond to our knowledge of both names and gods.

level both Dionysius and Proclus[39] draw a connection between names and statues.[40] Proclus identifies the divine names with the ritual use of statues as harbourers of the gods.[41] In drawing this analogy, he emphasizes their role as theurgic symbols.[42] Dionysius continues this tradition: the 'sacred symbols' [*symbola*] are actually the perceptible images (*agalmata*) of intelligible realities'[43] and 'we must examine all that is manifested to us from these *agalmata* that are the divine names'.[44] For Dionysius, they are the images that must be transcended by those wishing to see the true types, and the hierarchy causes its members to be divine images.

Moreover, there is a connection between these degrees because the higher orders necessarily contain the power of the lower,[45] described in terms of interlocking triadic ranks. Dionysian scriptural interpretation can be understood in light of

---

39 Proclus, *In Crat.* 18, 27–19, 17: through language the soul makes verbal representations of the gods, as the sculptor carves his statues. John of Scythopolis has an extremely interesting comment upon Dionysius and the relation between divine names and statues in the following scholion: 'In what consists the art whereby names are made?' And he replies:

It is that there exists in the soul a certain power which has the capacity to make copies ... and by virtue of that power, the soul can assimilate itself to superior beings, gods, angels, and demons; ... that is why it makes statues of god and demons; and when it wants to bring into being likeness in a certain way immaterial and engendered by reason alone, of the First Beings, it produces out of itself, and with the help of verbal representation, the substance of the names; and just as the art of mysteries by means of certain ineffable symbols makes the statues here below like the gods and ready to receive the divine illuminations, in the same way the art of the regular formation of words ... brings into existence names like statues of the realities. (*PG* 4, 264 BC. Quoted by Saffrey (1990), 8)

40 *Agalma* occurs six times in the Dionysian corpus: *CH* 145A, 165A; *EH* 428D, 473 B, 476A; *MT* 1025B. Daele (1941).

41 Plutarch speaks a good deal about statues as symbols in ritual. 'Thus men make use of consecrated symbols, some employing symbols that are obscure, but others those that are clear in guiding the intelligence toward things divine ...' *De Is.*, 378A. Plutarch dispels the rumours that statues contain the gods: 'Some Greeks don't speak of statues as statues but as gods themselves, claiming that although we should regard them as 'devices of the god who orders all things ... the divine is not engendered in forms or in polished surfaces', 379CD, 382A. Plutarch holds a much different view from the later Platonists on symbols because, in his metaphysics, God does not descend to the level of the material.

42 'For it generates every name as if it were a statue of the god. And as the theurgic art through certain symbols calls forth the ungrudging goodness of the gods into the illumination of artificial statues, thus also the intellectual science of divine matters, by the compositions and divisions of sounds unfolds the occult essence of gods ... For it is necessary to venerate even the ultimate echoes of the god and venerating these to become established in the first paradigms of them.' (Proclus, *PT* I, 19, 8, 124, 22–125, 8, trans. Taylor, adapted)

43 *EH* 397C.

44 *DN* 909B.

45 Cf., Proclus, *ET*, prop. 145: 'The distinctive character of any divine order travels through all the derivative existents and bestows itself upon all the inferior kinds' (trans. Dodds).

Proclus' theory of participation;[46] that is, each rank is ordered so that the highest member is 'not partaken of' (*amethekton*) – it is the unaffected cause of ranks below. The middle member is 'partaken of' (*metechomenon*) – it participates in the higher rank while being unaffectedly participated in by the rank below. The third member 'partakes' (*metechon*). Thus, each hierarchic rank unfolds the symbol according to its own spiritual receptivity – but nonetheless these levels all participate in one another. When the reader approaches the symbol, he does so by corresponding himself to the suitable hierarchic rank. The importance of divine receptivity or aptitude is discussed in Letter 8:

> Each class of beings around God is more divine than that which stands farther away. And those nearer the true light are more full of light and able to shed light by virtue of being nearer to the True Light. Do not take this nearness, however, in a spatial sense, but according to the sense of aptitude [of each class] for receiving the gift of God (*kata tên theodokhon epitêdeiotêta*). (*Ep.* 8, 1092B, trans. Hathaway)

Hathaway explains that 'aptitude' came to refer to the receptivity of a medium to divine inspiration through symbols. Proclus links magic ritual and symbols in myth in the following passage:

> The art, therefore, governing sacred matters distributes, in a fitting way, the whole of ritual among the gods and the attendants of the gods (i.e. daemons) in order that none of those who attend the gods eternally should be left without a share in the religious service due them. This art calls on the gods with the holiest rites and mystic symbols, and invokes the gifts of the daemons through the medium of a secret sympathy by means of visible passions. In the same way, the fathers of such myths as we have been discussing, having gazed on virtually the entire procession of divine reality, and being eager to connect the myths with the whole chain which proceeds from each god, made the surface images of their myths analogous to the lowest races of being which preside over the lowest, material experiences. However, what was hidden and unknown to the many they handed down to those whose passion it is to look upon being, in a form which revealed the transcendent being of the gods concealed in inaccessible places. As a consequence, although every myth is daemonic on its surface, it is divine with respect to its secret doctrine. (*In Remp.* I, 78, 18–79, 4, trans. Coulter)[47]

Textual interpretation is not merely the mode of commentary, rather it is a hieratic process: *theoria* is *theourgia*.

Onomastic Activity: Progression of Initiates

Symbols are unfolded with reference to their level of meaning which also corresponds to the progression of the listener. The reading of scripture is not a haphazard affair: 'One should not confuse holy symbols by some chance criterion but rather interpret

---

46 This may in fact have been first propounded by Iamblichus, cf. *In Tim.* fr. 60 Dillon, and Dillon's commentary (1973), 342.

47 Struck, in addition to Coulter, also offers a commentary on this passage, to show how the theurgist uses *sympatheia* as it can be found in poetry. Cf. Struck (2004), 246–7.

them with reference to the causes or substances or powers or orders or values of which they are composite significations'.[48] The method of reading corresponds to the theurgic progression of the listener:[49]

> Let us not believe that the visible appearances of composite things were modeled for their own sake, but rather that they protect inexpressible and invisible knowledge from the many, since things in all respects holy are not easily accessible to the unholy, but are revealed only to the genuine lovers of holiness, as those who lay aside their childish fancies about the sacred symbols and are ready to pass in simplicity of mind and with an aptitude for the faculty of contemplation to the simple, supernatural, and more elevated truth behind symbols. (*Ep.* 9, 1105CD, trans. Hathaway)

In the second chapter of the *Celestial Hierarchy*, Dionysius explains that modes of symbolic images, especially anthropomorphic or animal images,[50] are a concession to the nature of our human minds.[51] Thus, scriptural imagery aids every soul unable to be raised directly to conceptual contemplations by its nature as soul and it aids those unable to see past the material aspect of symbols – whom Dionysius refers to as *hoi polloi*.[52] Using the language of mystery ritual, Dionysius explains that images as stumbling blocks separate the initiated from the uninitiated, so that only those who are ready can approach the deeper mysteries.[53] This is not to say that one rank of initiation is more sacred than another. When Dionysius compares loftier images of God as 'mind' in the *Divine Names* with the baser images of God he notes that 'these sacred shapes are actually no less defective than this latter, for the deity is far beyond every manifestation of being and life'.[54] As a *symbolon*, the base image contains the divine just as the lofty image might. Proclus makes similar remarks in his *Commentary on the Republic* when he speaks of the allegorical interpretation of indecent myths:

---

48 *Ep.* 9, 1109A.

49 Proclus warns that only those with proper training can understand myths. He uses the image of a veil in I, 74, 19 to speak of allegorical meaning as protecting the uninitiated from approaching the text. See Sheppard (1980), 146, on a comparison between Proclus' language here and mystery language.

50 Dionysius and Proclus explain these images in a similar way: see Dionysius, *Ep.* 9 where he discuss the drunkenness of God and Proclus, *In Remp.* I, 74–6, where Proclus says blasphemies in stories act as screens for those who cannot go beyond the superficial meaning of the text. They explain this unlikely image as a symbol to deter the uninitiated. Proclus is quite fond of picking apart unseemly behaviour of the gods as depicted by Homer.

51 *CH* 137B.

52 *CH* 140B.

53 Proclus, *In Remp.* I, 76, 24ff. where Proclus distinguishes not just levels within a single myth, but two types of myths: the first aims at the education of the young and are free of words contrary to the gods. The second type are myths which are addressed to the inspired state of the soul and these myths use universal sympathy to connect the soul with its cause. This passage corresponds to what we see in Dionysius, *EH* 432A: '[The uninitiated] are not permitted to join in following sacred acts and in contemplation reserved for the perfect sight of the perfected'.

54 *CH* 140B.

Because [myths] lend themselves to being favorable both to the vulgar and to those who are awakened to understanding – that is to say, a small number –, they reveal the affinity with the reality of things to furnish the assurance, founded on the same operations of the hieratic art, of their connaturality with the divine. And in effect, the gods lend themselves to attend to the sorts of symbolic formulas, they obey the wishes of those who invoke them, they manifest their singular property in the midst of those invoking them. (*In Remp.* I, 83, 10–15)

Furthermore, the initiate would be able to approach the divine should he be able to read the loftier imagery in the text.[55] The necessity of spiritual/sacramental preparation before ritual is commonplace enough.[56] The next chapter will explore Iamblichus, and Dionysius' levels of preparation[57] and methods to restrain the uninitiated from the higher mysteries, for which they are unprepared.

---

55 Struck (2005) explores the use of *ainigma* to show the relationship between allegorical reading and the reading of oracles.

56 Proclus, *In Parm.* 670, 4–16 on the importance of knowledge before approach and union:

Souls being led must be linked with the objects of their desire through knowledge and attention, of which the learning of the name is an image (for names are the product of the cognitive part of the soul) and it sometimes happens that souls which still are imperfect do not lay hold on the thing that they know but see it partially and incompletely and at other times they see it as a whole, when they grasp it perfectly and through it know also other names that are higher than it. The name, then, when the Clazomenean asks to know is a symbol of the thing's being …. (trans. Morrow–Dillon)

This passage links spiritual preparation with names as symbols. With proper knowledge of the name, the soul grasps the symbol within itself.

57 Dionysius distinguishes different levels of spiritual and sacramental preparation but he does not create the same levels in the text as do the Alexandrian commentators. That is, he does not specify a literal, allegorical, ethical, and spiritual level of text. For him, there are only the intelligible and sensible parts of symbols.

Chapter 7

Hierourgia and *Theourgia* in Sacramental Activity

Introduction: Cosmic Sacrament

For Dionysius, the closest parallel to the Hellenic term *theourgia* is the term *hierourgia*,[1] the ritual enactment of divine works. Dionysian sacraments, given by God, are enacted to recreate the divine work – the incarnation of Christ. Dionysius uses the Hellenic vocabulary for theurgic tokens (*synthema, symbolon, sphragis, typos*) to describe the Christian sacraments, the efficacy of which divinize the soul, just as in Hellenic theurgy. The sacraments and Hellenic *symbola* are salvific in that they are the material cosmogonic causes embedded both in the universe and in the soul. When the soul is re-awakened to the causes, it remembers its own divine source.[2] As in Hellenic usage, the symbols come from the divine, humans serve merely to enact them. Also, symbols are efficacious without our thinking, although we need to be spiritually prepared to be receptive to them. There are a number of differences, certainly, between Dionysius' use of *theourgia* and the Hellenic usage. He distinguishes between human enactment of divine works and the divine work itself, and he works within an ecclesiastical framework, rather than a Timaean cosmos.[3] These differences, however, do not profoundly disguise Dionysian *hierourgia* from its roots in theurgy.

Recent debate concerning Dionysian theurgy has centred on the author's use of the term *theourgia*. Paul Rorem, both in his doctoral dissertation and in his notes to the recent translation by C. Lubhéid, says that our author, unlike Iamblichus or Proclus, used the term 'theurgy' to mean 'work of God', not as an objective genitive indicating a work addressed to God but as a subjective genitive meaning God's own work.[4] Andrew Louth, in his follow-up article, 'Pagan Theurgy and Christian Sacramentalism in Denys the Areopagite', agrees. He claims that in the Dionysian

---

1 *Hierourgia*, the verb *hierourgeo*, and the adjective *hierourgikos* appear a total of 59 times in the corpus. Daele (1941), 82.

2 *EH* 484D; Proclus, *In Tim.* I, 213, 16–18.

3 Shaw (1995), 599.

4 P. Rorem, 'Our author used the term "theurgy" to mean "work of God" , not as an objective genitive indicating a work addressed to God (as in Iamblichus, e.g. *DM* I, 2, 7, 2–6) but as a subjective genitive meaning God's own work' (*EH* 3 436C, 41; 440B, 27; 440C, 29; 441D, 46; 445B–C, 22 and 28), especially in the incarnation (*EH* 3 429C, 38f.; 432B, 18 and 22f.; 441C, 34 and 39). See Rorem (1987), 52, n.10. Rorem also argues that anagogical movement takes place not through rites and symbols themselves, as with Iamblichus, but rather in their interpretation. See Rorem (1984), 116, and (1979), 453–5. Louth (1986) agrees

corpus, the word *theourgia* seems never to be used of religious rituals. Neither of these authors points to the use of the term *hierourgia* as a replacement for *theourgia* in this context. Rather, both discount the notion entirely, based on their assessment of Dionysius' use of the term *theourgia*. Gregory Shaw, in his recent article 'Neoplatonic Theurgy and Dionysius the Areopagite', contends that the term is a subjective, rather than objective genitive. He explains that implicit in the meaning of *theourgia* is man's enacting of the divine work. This, however, also does not seem entirely accurate. When Dionysius speaks of *theourgia*, he specifically means the work of God, the incarnation of Christ. However, when we enact this work, through *hierourgia*, we become *theourgikoi:* participants of the work, co-workers of the work. Thus, Rorem and Louth correctly assert that *theourgia* pertains only to divine works, while Shaw rightly points out that the principle of theurgy does, as propounded by Iamblichus and Proclus, indeed exist in Dionysian thought. Peter Struck gives a convincing examination of Dionysian theurgy, particularly in the acts of Jesus as theurgy.[5] Struck argues that Dionysius describes Jesus' performance of actions in terms of theurgy in order to ritualize them.[6] More recently, Dylan Burns also lays out similarities between Hellenic and Dionysian treatment of theurgy in his article, 'Proclus and the Theurgic Liturgy of Dionysius'.[7]

Theourgia – Hierourgia

For Dionysius, the closest parallel to the Iamblichean/Procline term *theourgia*[8] is, then, the term *hierourgia*, the ritual enactment of divine works. Dionysian sacraments, given by God, are enacted to recreate the divine work of the incarnation of Christ. With respect to terminology, the only real distinction between Dionysius'

---

with Rorem. See also Rist (1985), 150, who notes that liturgical acts are God's working as an 'enlightened theurgy'.

   5   Struck (2001).

   6   Struck (2001), 32.

   7   Burns (2004).

   8   The term *philosophia* rarely appears in the corpus. It occurs five times, referring to a secular Hellenic knowledge, that is, interestingly enough, not disparaged by our author. In Letter 7, however, Dionysius chastises the Greeks for 'using the wisdom God gave them' to banish reverence, *Ep. 7*, 1008B. Moreover, in the same letter, Dionysius says that the knowledge of beings, rightly called *philosophia*, was described by Paul as wisdom of gods. These two ideas together seem to suggest that Hellenic *philosophia* is equatable to Pauline *philosophia*, in that both are given by god. In *DM*, Iamblichus makes a three-fold division regarding his method of inquiry: 'But in all things we shall give to each that which is appropriate. And such questions, indeed, as are theological, we shall answer theologically; such as are theurgy, theurgically; but such as are philosophical, we shall explore philosophically', I, 7, 3ff. Andrew Smith deals at length with this passage in (1993), 74–86. Smith concludes that for Iamblichus, philosophy includes the highest levels of reality in its scope that Iamblichus regarded the traditional gods and divinities as the subject of theology and Platonic hypostases as the domain of philosophy at its highest level (77). Smith explains that philosophical ideas are compared with the theurgical equivalent in order to better explain theurgy (84). See also Smith (1974), 84.

usage and that of the later Platonists is that Dionysius distinguishes between human enactment of divine works and the divine work itself. Both Iamblichus and Proclus use one word, *theourgia*, to denote these two actions. In some ways, Iamblichus, in particular, would have been better off distinguishing between the two words when he argues against Porphyry that *theourgia* is not human work that compels the gods, but rather divine work enacted by humans. The Dionysian innovation in this way better explains the concept of *theourgia*. It seems, however, that Dionysius' use of the two terms could have been his way of separating himself from his Hellenic counterparts, so as not to be accused of heresy, or even to protect his assumed apostolic identity.

It seems, then, that Dionysian theurgy distinguishes between the divine works and those who enact the works, and in this way it differs from Hellenic theurgy. Moreover, the major distinction occurs when Dionysius places the metaphysical concept of theurgy and the mechanics of its enactment in an ecclesiastical situation. While the Iamblichean classes refer to the different spiritual capacities for three types of souls, the Dionysian classes reflect church history as embodied in the Old and New Testaments. The Old Testament, forecasting the divine works of Jesus (*theourgia*), wrote by way of images. On the other hand, the New Testament described how Jesus actually achieved his works: thus, the divine works are the consummation of the divine words (*theologia*)[9] – the theurgy of the New Testament is the fulfilment of the prophets. Dionysius explains that the ecclesiastical hierarchy sits smack in the middle between the extremes of the legal hierarchy of the Old Testament and the celestial hierarchy of the New Testament. With the former, it shares the use of varied symbols derived from the realm of sense-perception; with the latter, it shares the contemplation of understanding.[10] All worship, then, must begin in the ecclesiastical hierarchy and it must employ both material symbols and contemplation.

While the last chapter showed how Dionysian *theoria* functions theurgically, this one will demonstrate how *hierourgia* and *theourgia* are all descriptions of theurgy as set out by Iamblichus. In short, Iamblichus explains theurgy as worship given by the gods, enacted by humans.[11] It is a worship that always begins with the symbols

---

9   *EH* 432B.

10   *EH* 501D.

11   See *DM* IV, 1–4, where Iamblichus is concerned to explain that, despite appearances, the theurgist does not compel the gods, but is in effect authorized by them to act on their behalf. Cf. esp. 2, 184:

The whole of theurgy presents a double aspect. On the one hand, it is performed by men, and as such observes our natural rank in the universe; but on the other, it controls divine symbols (*synthêmata*), and in virtue of them it is raised up to union with the higher powers, and directs itself harmoniously in accordance with their dispensation, which enables it quite properly to assume the mantle of the gods. It is in virtue of this distinction, then, that the art both naturally invokes the power from the universe as superiors, inasmuch as their invoker is a man, and yet on the other hand gives them orders, since it invests itself, by virtue of the ineffable symbols (*aporrhêta symbola*), with the hieratic role of the gods. (trans. Clarke–Dillon–Hershbell)

cloaked in different degrees of matter,[12] divinely placed in the cosmos for human ascent, and a worship divided into different modes so as to suit the ability of the performer. At every stage, both higher and lower, theurgy is a ritual enactment, not simply a spiritual understanding of symbols. For Dionysius, *theourgia* is first and foremost the sacred acts of Christ, particularly the incarnation, which is enacted by men through sacramental *hierourgia*. In addition to meaning the salvific works of Jesus, *theourgia* refers also to human co-operation in this salvific work (as *theourgikos*), a state very rarely achieved through *henôsis* and *theôsis*.

The following passage shows the relation between *theourgia* and *hierourgia* for Dionysius:

> [The theologians] teach that God himself thus gives substance and arrangement to everything that exists, including the legal hierarchy and society ... they praise the divine works of Jesus the man (*hai andrikai Iesous theourgiai*) ... and [they engage in] sacred writing about the divine songs, which have as an aim to praise all the divine words [*theologiai*] and divine works [*theourgiai*] and to celebrate the sacred words [*hierologiai*] and operations [*hierourgiai*] of sacred men, forms a universal song and exposition of divine things, granting to those chanting the sacred words sacredly the ability to receive and distribute the entire rite of the hierarchy. (*EH* 429CD)

This passage shows the difference between *theourgia* as the works of Jesus and *hierourgia* as the operations of sacred men, as well as the connection between the two: *hierourg*ia is the ritual engagement and reproduction of *theourgia*. Iamblichus, in the *De Mysteriis*, on the other hand, presents *theourgia* as the work of men, albeit possible only through the power of the gods, so that 'the theurgic priest, through the power of ineffable emblems, commands the cosmic spirits, not as a human being'[13] nor as one employing a human soul but existing above them in the order of the gods: but nonetheless, theurgic acts, according to Iamblichus, are performed by man, not God. Dionysian (and Eastern Church, for that matter) sacramental theology is thus fundamentally similar to Hellenic *theourgia* in that both use material *symbola* to harness divine *energeia*, but there is a subtle shift in terminology as between Dionysius and his Neoplatonic predecessors.

---

12 Cf. *CH* 121C: 'For it is quite impossible that we humans should, in any immaterial way, rise up to contemplate the heavenly hierarchies without the aid of those material means capable of guiding us as our nature requires'.

13 *DM* 247. See also Iamblichus, *DM* 48, 5–11:

> And if one were to consider also how the hieratic prayer-formulae have been sent down to mortals by the gods themselves, and that they are the symbols of the gods themselves and not known to anyone but them, and that in a way they possess the same power as the gods themselves, how could one any longer justly believe that such supplication is derived from the sense-world and is not divine and intellectual? (trans. Clarke–Dillon–Hershbell)

Symbolon – Synthema

While in the last chapter we examined *symbolon* as the written word of sacred text, in this chapter we will examine material *synthemata* that are impressed upon the physical self to effect a moral and hierarchical change. The sacrament re-orders the soul disordered by embodiment and makes man a Christ. Modern sacramental theology points out the unity in the sacramental act – although there are a multiplicity of sacraments, each of which progress the Christian to a different stage of divinization, there is an essential unity in the meaning incarnate in ritual material elements.[14] These rites, when applied to the morally prepared individual, cannot help but divinize the participant. As we saw in the previous section on *theoria*, this divinization is salvific for every prepared man (i.e. Christian), but each man partakes in the divine only so far as he is able – again, only the fully initiated hierarch fully participates in God.

As with the Hellenes, Dionysius explains how the theurgist (for him, the hierarch) mimics the divine activity of differentiation and unity, and full reversion. Dionysius, however, inserts a third major player into this cosmic mimesis: that of the sacrament itself, both as rite and as Christ. The following passage is worth quoting in full:

> For the blessed godhead above all, although he proceeds in divine goodness with a view towards the communion (*koinônia*) of those sacred men participating him, still he does not come outside of his own unmoved stability and steadiness according to his essential being, he enlightens all those in proportion (*analogia*) to their likeness to God, he truly remains in himself, of his very own being.
>
> Similarly, the divine rite of the synaxis, although holding on to its unique, simple and indivisible cause, still becomes pluralized in a sacred multitude of symbols (*symbola*) because of love for man, and it travels to the whole range of hierarchic images (*eikonographia*), but it draws back together all these images unitedly into its own unity and it makes united with those being led sacredly towards it.
>
> In the same godlike way, the divine hierarch, although he sacredly hands down his unique knowledge of the hierarchy to the subordinates, travelling in a multitude of sacred enigmas (*ainigmata*), but again as free and not held back by those below him, restores himself to his own cause without loss and he makes an intellectual journey to the One of himself (*to hen heautou*)[15] by seeing purely the unified *logoi* of the rites, making the divine return (*epistrophe*) to primary things the goal of his philanthropic going out (*proodos*) to secondary things. (*EH* 429AB)

This passage reveals a cosmic relationship between all three movements (Godhead, sacraments and hierarch) in that they all process and return. The three, however, are also different in so far as their processions vary – a difference in this activity signifying a difference in their essential being.

---

14 Powers (1967), 85.

15 This reference to 'the One of himself' is of great interest, in view of the Iamblichean and Procline concept of 'the One of the soul', cf. Iamblichus, *In Phaedr.* fr. 6.

Teletê

Because the previous chapter examined the divine motion in creation, this section will start with the *teletê* as the activity of differentiation and unity. Here, Dionysius combines the New Testament theology of Jesus as sacrament[16] with a Hellenic understanding of soul as an intermediary. According to sacramental theology, Christ exists as *teletê*[17] because he mirrors the sacramental order of divine power from above and the 'cultus of love' below.[18] As with the *symbolon* of scriptural interpretation, he contains an intelligible and sensible component. The intelligible component consists of the *logoi* that comprise the cosmos. This notion appears in the Hellenic passages examined so far, but it also exists in the tradition of the Eastern Church. The Eastern Church Fathers speak of the cosmos as the universal sacrament, so that individual sacraments are a manifestation of what the world and human history already is.[19] Moreover, Christ as sacrament seems to bear a certain analogy to the activity of the Iamblichean soul as mean between the intelligible and sensible. In contrast to Plotinus' view that the highest part of the human soul remained 'above' in permanent contact with the intelligible world, Iamblichus (and the Platonists after him) maintained that the soul descends as a whole, and that its essence, as well as its activity, is thoroughly mixed. The activity of the soul in Iamblichus is encapsulated by the later Platonist Priscianus thus:

> But if, as Iamblichus thinks, a distorted and imperfect activity cannot proceed from an impassible and perfect substance, the soul would be affected somehow even in its essence. Thus also in this way it is a mean not only between the divisible and the indivisible, or what remains and what proceeds ... but also between the ungenerated and the generated ...The generated aspect of it, however, also never proceeds without the stable and ungenerated, while the ungenerated aspect of it is sometimes removed from all association with generation from body. (*In De An.* 89, 33–90, 2, 5)[20]

This passage throws some light, I think, on the activity of the *teletê*, most pronounced in Christ's ability to mediate between the intelligible and sensible universes. Just as the Iamblichean soul is a mean between the world of the immortal and mortal,

---

16 Vorgrimler (1992), 27, explains that Jesus as the sacrament of God is deeply rooted in the New Testament. Augustine, in particular, saw the humanity of Jesus Christ as the primordial sacrament. Note that for convenience, the Greek term *teletê* will be generally translated 'sacrament'. It should be born in mind, however, that the term is the same as the traditional Greek term for a religious rite or initiation, whereas the Latin term *sacramentum* has the connotation of a military oath.

17 Church Fathers commonly speak of the 'remaining' aspect of the sacrament:

When this bread is taken, each individual has no less than all together; one receives the whole, two receive the whole, a greater number receive the whole without any diminution; because the blessing of this sacrament knows how to be distributed, but knows not how to be destroyed in the distribution. (Jerome, *Homily on the Body and Blood of Christ*; PL 30, 280–4, translation in Stone (1909), 129).

18 Vorgrimler (1992), 34.

19 Vorgrimler (1992), 40.

20 Trans. Finamore–Dillon (2002), 235.

differentiation and remaining, so does Christ mediate between God the Father and the angelic and ecclesiastical cosmos. In the Eastern Church (prior to the liturgical changes imposed by the Western Church), the entire liturgy functioned as cosmos, with the eucharistic events as actual recreations of the divine incarnation. The Dionysian sacrament, in particular, has a cosmogonic role – Christ descends not because of human sin, but rather as a cosmic mechanism. With his necessary descent, he unfolds cosmic unity into differentiation. Sacrament, in this regard, bears some similarity to the Hellenic concept of number[21] or time. With a dual divine-human aspect, Christ is the ultimate *symbolon* – Karl Rahner developed the concept of real symbol, which describes the 'expression' of a particular, present reality in a symbol as distinct from an arbitrarily chosen sign. It is important to bear in mind, throughout this discussion of sacrament, that *teletê* in Dionysius refers to the element of sacrament and to Christ. This is because the material sacrament contains the divine as the true incarnation of Christ.

The hierarch, likewise, mirrors the activity of the divine. His activity is expressed in the lines of Priscianus' *De Anima* commentary that follow the ones just quoted: 'But our soul is differentiated in itself. It is pure, on the one hand, insofar as is appropriate for it, receiving immortality, permanence, and indivisibility from the separated and intellectual life'.[22] For Iamblichus, the human soul engages in a procession and return different from that of the world soul. When the human soul progresses, however, its immortality becomes filled with mortality and its indivisibility is divided.[23] Dionysius seems to agree with this in so far as he suggests that the human soul becomes disunited when it is in the material world. But the hierarch is a different kind of soul. Dionysius (like Iamblichus, cf. *De An.* §§28–30) uses a hierarchic schema in which souls at different levels partake in different activities, which in turn affect their being. The soul of the hierarch behaves to some extent like that of the theurgic priest – on the one hand, we have no reason to doubt

---

21 Proclus in *PT* V, 34, p. 101, 1ff. S–W explains that the divine monadic numbers, more simple than Forms, exist ontologically prior to intelligible entities. As with sacrament, these numbers are both one and many. Theurgy, when it employs these numbers, takes part in monadic sympathy to effect ineffable rites. Metaphysically, numbers exhibit a creative ability – the monadic numbers create the universe when they emanate into infinity. Later in the same passage, Proclus shows that monadic numbers also have an anagogic power. Because the monadic number is beyond all intelligible number, it collects numbers into itself – it elevates souls from things 'apparent', i.e. intelligible number. Cf. *In Remp.* II, 16, 3–22, 19. Time, moreover, is connected to number in that it proceeds according to number and measures the celestial periods, comprehending in itself the first causes of the perfection of the periods. It exists as a monad and that proceeds into differentiation: 'Time by its essence and through the activity resting in itself is thus eternal and a monad and a centre, and simultaneously, it is continuous and number and circle, in respect of that which is proceeding and participating', Simplicius, *In. Phys*, p. 795, 4–26. trans. Sambursky–Pines. Cf. Sambursky (1968), 153–67 for more discussion. These examples point to the active, generative function of number and time. In this way, sacrament bears a similarity to number and time – these analogies also shed light on the possible generative function of Christ as sacrament.

22 Priscianus, *In de An.* 89, 3–90, 25.

23 Cf. Plotinus, *Enn.* IV, 2.

its mortality, on the other hand, it is extraordinary, and in this case, angelic.[24] This angelic quality is due to its proximity to God, in relation to the rest of the human hierarchy.[25] Still, as will be specified below, the hierarchs seem to have a divine origin, in addition to divine activity.

Contemplation as Hierarchic Activity

Fully initiated, the hierarch reverts in contemplation while he administers the sacred rites: he reverts both to the thearchic One and to the One inside himself (*to hen en heautôi*). Unlike the situation in Hellenic Platonism, where the One is the only entity that reverts fully because it alone embarks on no other activity, the Dionysian hierarch reverts completely because he engages in a special task. Dionysius says that the hierarch 'rises to the contemplation of primary things after having proceeded to the secondary' in order that he may 'never cease to travel from one divine reality to another and that he may remain ever under the guidance of the divine spirit'.[26] With this, Dionysius either paints the highly unlikely portrait of a man who engages exclusively in contemplation of primary things or he describes the ecclesiastical duty of disseminating the eucharist. The hierarch remains undistracted while he engages in his ecclesiastical duties thanks to a purificatory rite. After he transforms the bread and wine, Dionysius explains that the bishop washes his hands in water:

> With his extremities thus purified he preserves the utter purity of his conformity to God and he will then be able to turn benevolently to secondary tasks while yet remaining free and unsullied. For being completely at one, he can immediately turn back to the One to whom he remains so bound by a pure and untarnished return that the fullness and the constancy of his conformity to God is maintained. (*EH* 440Aff.)

Dionysius distinguishes between 'primary contemplation' and 'secondary activities' based on monadic activity and pluralization: the sacrament is single while it sits on the altar, many when it moves out to those receiving the sacrament.

This complete reversion divinizes the hierarch so that he partakes in cosmogony (the entire hierarchy is perfected in him)[27] and so that, through sympathy, he can perfect those below him. Hierarchs, as men, have a thearchic origin but behave as

---

24 Dionysius says: 'Hence, I see nothing wrong in the fact that the Word of God calls even our hierarch an 'angel', for it is characteristic of him that like the angels he is, to the extent that he is capable, a messenger and that he is raised up to imitate, so far as a man may, the angelic power to bring revelation'. (*CH* 293A)

25 *DN* 817C.

26 *EH* 397A.

27 *EH* 373C:

Our hierarchy is, and is called, the function embracing all the sacred rites in itself, in accordance with which the divine bishop, once he is perfected, will have a participation in all the most sacred rites which pertain to him ... Nevertheless, the one who speaks of 'hierarch' indicates a man divinely inspired and god-like, one knowing all sacred knowledge and in whom the whole hierarchy is purely perfected and known.

divine beings [*hôs theoi*] after being sent down from the divine goodness itself.[28] Dionysius says that the first leaders of our hierarchy received their sacred gift from God and then 'like divine beings, they had a generous urge to secure uplifting and divinization for their subordinates'.[29] The hierarchs clearly take on the role of the divine, not just in their ability for full reversion, but because they behave with the same beneficent desire to divinize, just as the angels desire to divinize them. The hierarch is defined as one who 'desires all men to be saved by taking on a likeness to God'.[30] In this way, he bears a similarity to the Iamblichean theurgic priest. In the following passages, Iamblichus first argues that the theurgist is invested with divine powers because of his ritual duties:

> The whole of theurgy presents a double aspect. On the one hand, it is performed by men, and as such observes our natural rank in the universe; but on the other, it controls divine symbols, and in virtue of them is raised up to union with the higher powers, and directs itself harmoniously in accordance with their dispensation, which enables it quite properly to assume the mantle of the gods. (*DM* 184)

The invocations to the gods depend on a connection between caller and called, for the operations to be divine rather than human work. The same energy is imparted by the divine and received by the invoker.[31] In this way, the description of the theurgist bears a resemblance to the description of one type of soul in Iamblichus' *De Anima*. Here, Iamblichus argues that embodiments differ based on the purpose of descent.[32] Iamblichus believes in a class of pure souls who descend willingly for the salvation of the human race. These souls are not weighed down by generation in the material realm because they are closely connected to the intelligible realm – although this connection allows them to ascend with greater ease, they still require theurgy.[33] It is possible that Dionysius sees his hierarch as a similar character. On the one hand, the hierarch is human, but he has a higher rank than the other members of the ecclesiastical hierarchy. The hierarch has a semi-divine *ousia*, and hence an angelic status.

---

28 *EH* 376D:

The first leaders of our hierarchy received their fill of the sacred gift from the transcendent Deity. Then divine goodness sent them to lead others to this same gift. Like gods, they had a burning and generous urge to secure uplifting and divinization for their subordinates. And so, using images derived from the senses they spoke of the transcendent. They passed on something united in a variegation and plurality. Of necessity they made human what was divine. They put material on what was immaterial. In their written and unwritten initiations, they brought the transcendent down to our level.

29 *EH* 376D.
30 *EH* 393A.
31 *DM* 185.
32 §28, Finamore–Dillon.
33 Iamblichus, *De An.* 397, 22–4.

The Trinity, the sacrament (both as material rite and as Christ) and the hierarch create a special situation that allows for a theurgic *mimesis* of the divine work. The sacrament, as a material element that proceeds into differentiation and remains in its unity, projects a divine *ousia* with its divine activity. When the intelligible sacrament adopts a material covering, it repeats the activity of the incarnation: it contains the divine, and yet it is accessible to man through its sensible aspect. The hierarch, moreover, can tap into the power of the sacrament (and the divine) because there is no separation between his energy and the divine energy.

The next section of this chapter will present the Dionysian sacrament as compared with its Hellenic cousin. Specifically, the mode and efficacy of the sacrament will be discussed through an examination of the technical terms *sphragis* (seal) and *eikon/ typos* (image/imprint). The second half will examine the sacraments of baptism and the eucharist as intended for the initiates and those ready to be perfected.

Efficacy of Sacrament: *Sphragis*

For Dionysius, the sacrament as a *symbolon* imitates the creation of the cosmos, when God impressed (*apotypoô*) the world with living images (*eikones*). Dionysius borrows from the Platonic concept of the intelligible Forms imprinted as from a seal (*sphragis*) at the time of creation: this *sphragis* is embedded into the psychology of the soul.[34] This demiurgic imprinting takes on a hieratic significance for the later Platonists – the *sphragis* is one description of *synthemata* which were implanted in the soul in creation and are awakened through theurgy.[35] The Hellenic Platonists describe the Demiurge as imprinting Platonic Forms that reveal the divine order.[36]

Using the term *sphragis*, Dionysius explains that the sacrament impresses [*apotupôutai*] its mark on all souls who ritually partake in it – the divine hierarch receives the divine light as a *sphragis* in accordance with his status as fully-initiated:

> The divine Light, out of generosity, never ceases to offer itself to the eyes of the mind, eyes which should seize upon it as always there, always divinely ready with the gift of itself. And it is on this that the divine hierarch models himself when he generously pours out on everyone the shining beams of his inspired teaching, when in imitation of God he remains ever ready to give light to whoever approaches, and when he displays neither a grudge nor profane anger over previous apostasy and transgressions. In godlike and hierarchical fashion he gives to all who approach his guiding light and does so in harmonious and orderly fashion and in proportion to the disposition of each one toward the sacred. (*EH* 400AB)

---

34 This is seen both in *Timaeus* 39E where the demiurge moulds [*apotupoumenos*] this world after the nature of the model, and in *Theaetetus* 191D, with the description of memory. Plato says that whatever we wish to remember, we think of it in our own minds and hold this as wax under the perceptions and imprint them upon it, just as impressions are made from seal rings. It should also be noted, however, that the metaphor of the seal is given Christian authorization by such passages as 2 Cor. 1:22 and Heb. 1:3.

35 Proclus, *In Tim.* I, 4, 32–3. See Shaw (1995), 165.

36 Shaw (1995), 164.

and later in the passage, the divine blessedness

> grants a share of itself to someone uplifted thus, marks him with its light as a certain sign (*symbolon*), receives him into the company of those who have earned divinization and who form a sacred assembly. (*EH* 400CD)

and again in 476A:

> They are the truly divine images (*agalmata*) of the infinitely divine fragrances. Because this is the truly fragrant, they have no time to return to the counterfeits which beguile the mob, and it truly impresses (*entypousa*) only those souls which are true images (*eikones*) of itself.

The divine light stamps its own power and essence upon the hierarch, divinizing him so that he can engage in the divine work. As the hierarchy also bears the marks of God,[37] so does it actively mark the hierarch, making him a *sphragis*, while the hierarch simultaneously subsumes the entire hierarchy within himself.

The key passage for the sacrament as *sphragis* occurs in the *Divine Names* 644AB:[38]

> Or take the example of a seal. There are numerous impressions (*sphragides*) of the seal and these all have a share in the original prototype. It is the same whole seal in each of the impressions and none participate in only a part. However, the non-participation of the all-creative Godhead rises far beyond comparisons of this kind, since it is out of the reach of perception and is not on the same plane as whatever participates in it. Maybe someone will say that the seal is not totally identical in all the reproductions of it. My answer is that this is not because of the seal itself, which gives itself completely and identically to each. The substances that receive a share of the seal are different. Hence the impressions of the one entire identical archetype are different. If the substances are soft, easily shaped, and smooth, if no impressions have been made on them already, if they are not hard and resistant, if they are not excessively soft and melting, the imprint on them will be clear, plain and long lasting. But if the material were lacking in this receptivity, this would be the

---

37 *CH* 165A.

38 This passage seems to be a condensed version of *In Parm.* IV, 839–44. In these passages, Proclus explains participation in the divine as a seal upon wax: 'Participation is like an impression made by a seal [*sphragis*] upon wax; for the seal, I mean the Idea, leaves a trace and an impression of itself' (col. 839, 27–9); and: 'For the creative action of the Forms is not alone sufficient to bring about participation; at all events, though these Forms are everywhere to the same degree, not all things participate alike in them; nor is the appetency of the beings that participate adequate without their creative activity...' (843, 23–6); and again: 'But inasmuch as it is a Form, it remains always the same, like an identical seal impressed upon many pieces of wax. They may change, but it remains uninterruptedly the same in all the instances of wax' (884, 8–10).

Athanasius, Cyril of Jerusalem and Basil all speak of the Holy Ghost as the *sphragis* by which the character of Christ is impressed upon creation. Cf: Athanasius, *Ep. Serapion* 1, 23, 385A; Cyril, *Comm in Joh.* 3.5, 564B; Basil, De *Spir.* 64, 185C. Gregory of Nazianzus argues that the personal worth of the minister does not affect the sacrament, since the seal, whether made of iron or gold, impresses itself equally upon the wax, *Or.* 40, *PG* 36, 396.

cause of its mistaken or unclear imprint or of whatever else results from the unreceptivity of its participation.

The sacrament leaves different impressions not because it gives itself differently, but rather because the substances that receive a share of the *sphragis* are capable of varying degrees of participation.[39] This is understandable when viewed in light of a hierarchical universe. Again, we see the theurgic principle of receptivity at work in the nature of the sacraments. As *eikones*, these souls can recognize the models for their own impression.[40] In the fourth century, the indelibility of the seal is strongly asserted by Cyril of Jerusalem and Basil, who claim that the seal remains even in the sinner.[41] This is possible because of the difference between the seal and grace – while grace can be lost, the seal is permanent as an everlasting commitment to Christ. More discussion on this issue will follow later in the chapter.

Christian Liturgy and Hieratic Ritual

With the sacramental system of Dionysius, we see a liturgy composed of the basic elements of the Eastern Church, described according to the phenomenology of theurgy. In the *Ecclesiastical Hierarchy*, Dionysius describes the progress from initiation to perfection most profoundly brought forth in the sacraments (*teletai*) of baptism and the eucharist. These particular sacraments each bring about a different level of participation, both of which are salvific, but only the perfecting sacrament of the eucharist completes man to make him a christ, or *theourgos*. As with theurgy according to Iamblichus and Proclus, Dionysian sacraments are efficacious only when they contain divine power – this power is harnessed by invoking the divine (in this case, the Holy Spirit), which comes down upon the matter of its own accord. The sacrament, moreover, works upon man once its materiality is re-ordered by divine power. This re-elementation, in turn, transfigures man when he has physically partaken of the material sacrament. This section will investigate the parallels between Dionysius' descriptions of the Christian liturgy and the Iamblichean liturgy, and it will include other Christian parallels from the Eastern Church Fathers on just how the sacrament works.

In the *Ecclesiastical Hierarchy*, the power of the sacrament corresponds to a particular person's ability to receive it, which, in turn, depends on that person's particular rank in the hierarchy. This is based on the structure of the universe: i.e. the ecclesiastical hierarchy mirrors its triadic celestial counterpart; its three levels are divided on the basis of the three functions of purification, illumination and perfection (500D–509A). For a start, the initiates are purified by priests through a proper reading of scripture; this is the lowest level, and yet it contains, in the best later Neoplatonic manner, three levels of its own (again, of purification, illumination and perfection). The catechumens make up the middle level – they are illuminated by deacons through baptism (but they are also purified, 508AB). The fully initiated constitute the third

---

39 *DN* 644B.
40 *EH* 397C.
41 Leeming (1960), 169.

and highest level. The sacraments of the *synaxis* (eucharist) and confirmation, which bring about perfection, are administered by the hierarch (bishop). The differences of the clerical functions represent the different divine activities (508D). Dionysius elaborates primarily on the sacraments of baptism and the *synaxis*. The sacrament of baptism is a necessary step to full participation in the divine.

Although faith and contemplation are necessary steps for salvation, they are ineffective without the sacred rites. Dionysius explains that before the sacred rites (*hierourgia*), the participant's soul must be shaped for reception of the holy words and operations. Only when the soul loves God, and the mind makes an anagogic movement towards him will the soul be able to engage in the rites.[42] For, as Gregory says, 'without the laver of regeneration it is impossible for the man to be in the resurrection'.[43] Iamblichus certainly says the same thing, and like Dionysius, he adds that mere thought (*ennoia*) does not join theurgists with the gods;

> since if this were the case, what would hinder those who philosophize theoretically from having a theurgic union with the gods? No, truly it is the accomplishment of ineffable acts, acts beyond comprehension, and the power of the unutterable symbols, understood solely by the gods, which establishes theurgic union.[44]

The issue remains, for both Dionysius and Iamblichus, that the source of all unification and salvation is the divine. Iamblichus has a most interesting section on prayer as a purificatory rite, midway between contemplation and material ritual (*DM* V 26, 237–40).

Invocation: Rites Begin and End with the Divine

The concept of invocation reveals two important aspects of the sacrament – because the invocation must follow a particular formula and must take place at a particular time, it reveals the importance of precise ritual. Also, when Dionysius or the Greek Fathers speak of the invocation, they go to great lengths to explain that Christ (or the Father or the Holy Spirit) is the ultimate source of the invocation and the power of the rites. These two aspects of invocation, particularly the latter, are the keystones of Hellenic theurgy as well: they show how theurgy is an essentially hieratic ritual in technique, and yet it is not magic because it does not involve a commanding of the divine.

As explained in the introduction to this chapter, Dionysius innovates with regard to his language, using the term *theourgia* to refer to the incarnation as the work of Jesus and *hierourgia* to refer to man's enactment of the divine work. This explanation stresses that Jesus is the source of every theurgic act:

> Jesus who is the most divinely transcendent and super-essential mind, the source and essence of the entire hierarchy, all holiness, every theurgic act, who is the most transcendent

---

42 *EH* 392B.
43 Gregory of Nyssa, *Catechetical Lectures* XXXV, trans. Moore–Wilson (1972).
44 *DM* 96.

power, enlightens our most sacred superiors in a manner more sacred and more intellectual and it makes them as similar as possible to its own light. (*EH* 372AB)

Jesus is the source of the power that the hierarch wields. The rites themselves come from him, as, in Iamblichean theory, they do from the gods in general, and when the rites are in a liturgical setting, the hierarch, like the theurgist, can tap into the divine power to enact the *theourgia*:

The most sacred performers of the sacred operations [*hierourgia*] ... sing with a universal hymn the cause that is the worker of good and bestower of good from whom the salvific rites are revealed to us, to enact [*theourgousai*] the sacred divinisation of those being perfected. (*EH* 436C)

Once the hierarch has sung the 'universal hymn', he is attuned to the power of Christ and obtains his power for sanctification. Nonetheless, Dionysius makes it clear that the holy works which the divine hierarch performs are, indeed, very much beyond him and would not be possible, were they not handed down by God. Likewise, when Iamblichus answers Porphyry's claim that theurgic rites command the gods, he explains that 'everything is accomplished solely by a divine cause'.[45] Rather, the things which truly summon the gods are the divine *synthemata*, which were sown into this realm by the divine.[46]

In his commentary on the passage above, Struck notes that the theurgies mentioned are not merely the acts of Jesus, but the whole of God's providential care for men. Struck examines the passage more fully; We quote his translation of this section in full below, with some minor modifications:[47]

Some call this hymn a confession, others a symbol of worship, but others, more divinely I believe, call it a hierarchical thanksgiving, since it embraces all the blessed gifts that come to us from God. For it seems to me to be the validation (*pragmateia*)[48] of all the theurgies praised among us, a validation which benevolently establishes our being and life, and shapes our divine form by means of beautiful archetypes, and brings us into participation of a more divine unity and uplifting, and observes the bereftness that arose in us from a lack of attention to the divine gifts; it seems to recall us to our original condition through restored goodness, and to benefit us with a most perfect imparting of his particular nature by his complete taking on of our own, and in this way to give us a communion with God and with divine things. (*EH* 436C)

Struck's suggestion here, that 'theurgies' refers to the providential acts of God through Jesus, seems a reasonable one. The ritual aspect implicit in theurgy, moreover, can be maintained by arguing that the eucharist contains all these providential acts.

In the Eastern Church, emphasis is placed on the epiclesis and the coming of the Holy Spirit as the efficacious seal of the sacrament (whereas the West focuses on

---

45 *DM* 65.

46 *DM* 98.

47 Struck (2001), 33.

48 This term, which Dionysius does not appear to use elsewhere, seems to have more or less this force here.

Christ's act of offering).[49] From the middle of the fourth century, as seen in Cyril's *Catechetical Lectures*, the epiclesis becomes directed to the Holy Spirit, that it may descend on the gifts for the fulfilling of the offering.[50] Gregory declares that 'it is prayer and the invocation of heavenly grace, and water, and faith, by which the mystery of regeneration is accomplished'.[51] The invocation itself transforms the elements from bread and wine to the body and blood of Christ.[52] Athanasius declares that 'as long as the prayers and invocations have not been said, this bread and wine are simply bread and wine. But when the great prayers and the holy invocations have been uttered, the Word descends upon the bread and wine and the body of the Word is present'.[53] Athanasius marks a turning point in the eucharistic formula. After Athanasius (AD 373), the invocation must be directed towards the Holy Spirit.[54]

Dionysius explains that the rites are not efficacious unless presided over by the proper men and performed with the proper elements:

> But it is to this [hierarchic] order especially, rather than to the other orders, that divine law has bestowed the more divine workings of the sacred ministry. Their rites are images of the power of the divinity, by which the hierarchs perfect the holiest of symbols and all the sacred ranks. Even if the priests can preside over some of the reverend symbols, a priest could not perform the sacred divine birth without the divine ointment. For it is the ordinance of God that only the sacramental powers of the God-possessed hierarchs can accomplish the sanctification of the clerical orders, the consecration of the ointment, and the rite consecrating the holy altar. (*EH* 505BC)

The hierarchs are specially chosen by God to perform the sanctifying task. The elements lack power unless empowered by the hierarchs – they have a unique relationship with the divine. Iamblichus, likewise argues that the perfecting rites must follow ritual procedure:

> So, therefore, certain invisible spirits, each having by allotment a different function, are constituted to perform that office only as it has been arranged. If, then, anyone shall undertake to celebrate the perfective rites in proper order, and shall change them in another direction and do something contrary to prescribed custom, there will be a particular degree of injury resulting for making use of the sacred rites in an unlawful manner. (*DM* IV, 1, 182)

---

49 Dalamais (1960), 76.

50 Dalamais (1960), 91.

51 Gregory of Nyssa, *Catechetical Lectures* XXXIII, trans. Moore–Wilson.

52 Tertullian warns us that not only will matter remain matter without the invocation, but that evil spirits could descend upon it: 'Are there not other cases, too, in which, without any sacrament, unclean spirits brood on waters, in spurious imitation of that brooding of the Divine Spirit in the very beginning? Witness all shady founts, and all unfrequented brooks' (*On Baptism* 5, 4, trans. Coxe (1973)).

53 Athanasius, *Ep. Serapion*, *PG* 86, 240, 1, trans. Robertson (1953).

54 Labauche (1922), 260.

Efficacy of Sacraments

Sacraments work their power by re-arranging the soul's disorder and divinizing the human entity. This occurs because when the sacrament, which is truly God, is ingested or makes physical contact with man it intermingles with him. Dionysius explains that when the eucharist is consumed the disorder is ordered and the formless is enformed. With this, the soul is purified and able to purify others, it is 'formed of light' (*phôtoeidês*), 'an initiate in God's works' (*theourgikos*). The divinized, perfect soul is a co-worker with God; it is a god itself. In 372AB, Jesus uses theurgy to help unify us with the divine:

> Jesus enlightens our blessed superiors (sc. the angelic orders), Jesus who is transcendent mind, utterly divine mind, who is the source and the being underlying all hierarchy, all sanctification, all the workings of God, who is the ultimate in divine power. He assimilates them, as much as they are able, to his own divine light. As for us, with that yearning for beauty which raises us upward (and which is raised up) to him, he pulls together all our many differences. He makes our life, disposition, and activity something one and divine, and he bestows on us the power appropriate to a sacred priesthood.
>
> Approaching therefore the holy activity of the sacred office we become closer to those beings who are superior to us. We imitate as much as we can their abiding, unwavering, and sacred constancy, and we thereby come to look up to the blessed and ultimately divine ray of Jesus himself. Then, having sacredly beheld whatever can be seen, enlightened by the knowledge of what we have seen, we shall be able to be consecrated and consecrators of this mysterious understanding. Formed of light, initiates in God's work, we shall be perfected and bring about perfection.

Theurgy, in the Dionysian sense as well as in the Neoplatonic, works by helping to assimilate those contemplating the divine with the divine. Here, the theurgy in question is Jesus' work as divinity, particularly his work in bestowing power appropriately so that we mimic the activity of the angels.

Conclusion

As seen in this chapter, there are many elements common to Dionysian and Hellenic theurgy. For both, the rites are the necessary route for reaching divinization. The rites themselves are controlled by the gods (or the Trinity, and in particular Christ) and individuals can only participate in the rites after they are mentally prepared through a series of initiations that permit receptivity. For both it is also extremely important that the rites take place in a liturgical context: they are performed in a holy setting and in a particular order. Dionysian theurgy, however, differs from its Hellenic counterpart in that while every item contains divinity, only particular items can be liturgically enacted to reach the divine. It is unclear as to how the three levels of participation in the ecclesiastical hierarchy correspond with Hellenic theurgy. That is, it seems that church laymen correspond with varying stages of initiation: the baptized can only participate through those who partake of the eucharist, and thus, fully partake of the divine. As for the hierarchy of church leaders, however, the relationship is less clear. Specifically, is the priest less of a theurgist than the bishop?

It would seem that the priest would have to possess greater divinatory powers than, say, the catechumen and yet he occupies the same hierarchic rank as the baptized.

These problems, of course, are distinctively Christian. One salient distinction between Dionysian and Iamblichean ritual is that, for Dionysius, the hierarchs are conduits of divine theurgy to their congregations. The Neoplatonic theurgist, on the other hand, appears as more of a lone figure, concerned only, or primarily, with his own personal unification. The 'congregation', if any, remains very much in the shadows.

Chapter 8

Union and Return to God:
The Mystical Theology and the
First Hypothesis of the *Parmenides*

Introduction

The objective of both the celestial and ecclesiastical hierarchies, for Dionysius, is a union to the divine which mirrors the union of the Godhead with Trinity. Although descriptions of this union exist throughout the corpus, Dionysius dedicates his *Mystical Theology* to this topic, whereby union takes place beyond intellect, for the purpose of divinization – becoming as much as possible like and in union with God (*EH* 373D).[1] Because Dionysius stresses the ecstatic, direct ascent of the soul to the unknowable God, he describes union using negative theology. This negative approach to divine union, particularly of the union beyond intellect, appears thoughout Proclus' writings on the subject, as well as Damascius' treatment of the topic.

Union with God

Before a discussion on what is meant by the term 'union', it is necessary to discuss what, in particular, Dionysius is suggesting a union to or with, in order to understand the nature of the union itself. Dionysius seems to posit a series of items as the object of union: God (*EH* 376A, 392A, 393A, 400C);[2] the One (*EH* 401AB[3], 425A, 437A,

---

1   See *EH* 373D: God divinizes men for their own salvation.
2   On participation in God: *EH* 376A:

> The common goal of every hierarchy consists of the continuous love of God and of things divine, a love which is sacredly worked out in an inspired and unique way, and before this, the complete and unswerving avoidance of everything contrary to it ... It consists of an inspired participation in the one-like perfection and in the one itself, as far as possible.

EH 376A: 'I have said in solemn fashion that our greatest likeness to and union with God is the goal of our hierarchy'; *CH* 165A: 'The goal of every hierarchy, then, is to enable beings to be as like as possible to God and to be at one with him ... Hierarchy causes its members to be images of God'.

3   On participation in the One: *EH* 425A: 'Each of the hierarchic sacraments is incomplete to the extent that it does not perfect our communion and "gathering" to the One'. *EH* 437A: 'For it is not possible to be gathered together toward the One and to partake of peaceful union with the One while divided among ourselves'. *EH* 440A (regarding the hierarch who

440A, 533D, 424D); the divine monad (*EH* 429A,[4] 533A); the divine life (*EH* 444C);[5] and the divine perfection (*EH* 400C). To take the first term, God as the object of union calls for a union and assimilation to God; the divine thearchy itself allows us to achieve this union (*EH* 441BC).[6] When Dionysius speaks of union to the One, or as Lubhéid often translates it, 'communion with' or 'assimilation to', the text reads *pros to hen* or *pros theon*, 'likeness' and 'union' being *aphomoiosis* and *henosis*. Dionysius speaks of unification of itself (*EH* 437A, 533D) towards the One (*EH* 401B, 404C) and to the One (*EH* 440A) and elevation to the One (*EH* 402D).[7] Unity also takes place with respect to the other members of the Trinity which results in divinization – neither union to the Spirit nor to Christ results in divinization, but both serve to help prepare the soul for union in God. Union to Christ is a union to the Christian life in so far as one participates in the life and death of Christ (*EH* 293B, 401D, 404A, 437C, 440B, 444C; 553B, 556D, 560A). Jesus, as the light of the Father, can be called upon to gain access to the Father (*CH* 121B). His concern for humans, moreover, helps lift the soul to the divine. Dionysius also describes union to the spirit to conduct Christians to contemplation on the mystery of God (*EH* 424C), inspiring Christians to prayer and contemplation of the divine realities.

Dionysian union is a union of defined intellects, separated from all superessentiality; the technical term for the union is *henosis hyper noun*, or 'union beyond intellect'.[8] Dionysius describes such a union in *Mystical Theology* where, through an inactivity of knowledge, one knows 'beyond the mind' and is united with the divine – thus, the union beyond intellect places the soul in connection with the ineffable God (*DN* 872CD, 585B). For Dionysius, this is necessary because the superessential essence exceeds any union, which is to say that intellect is not affected by union, but only

---

has already reached some communion with the One): 'For being completely at one, he can immediately turn back to the One to whom he remains so bound by a pure and untarnished return that the fullness and the constancy of his conformity to God is maintained'.

4   Especially with respect to God as *monê*, conferring unity upon entities as it brings them into union with it: see *EH* 429A:

> Enlightening anyone conforming as much as possible to God, the Deity nevertheless maintains utterly and unshakably its inherent identity. Similarly, the divine sacrament of the synaxis remains what it is, unique, simple and indivisible and yet, out of love for humanity, it is pluralized ... It extends itself so as to include all the hierarchical imagery. Then it draws all these varied symbols together into one unity, returns to its own inherent oneness, and confers unity on all those sacredly uplifted to it.

5   With respect to Jesus, by his kindly activities he 'called the human race to enter participation with himself and to have a share in his own goodness, if we would make ourselves one with his divine life and imitate it as far as we can, so that we may achieve perfection and truly enter into communion with God and with the divine things' (*EH* 444CD).

6   De Andia (1996), 292; she says that thearchy elevates to God and allows one to live in God. See section on cataphatic theology.

7   De Andia (1996), 293.

8   Dionysius uses three biblical citations to illustrate this (*DN* 592C): 1 Cor. 15:54; 1 Th. 4:17 and Lk 20:36. See De Andia (1996), 223.

the ranks of processions (*DN* 816B).[9] Thus, because God is superior to every kind of knowledge, union can only exist beyond intellect (*DN* 593B; *MT* 1001A). In Chapter 5 of the *Divine Names*, Dionysius expresses this phenomenon through a series of analogies, including that of union of lines in the centre of a circle. Here, rays unite without confusion in the centre of a circle; just as union is a union of paradigms of things with the One (*DN* 821A). What is meant by Dionysius' extensive discussion of union without confusion of *logoi* (*DN* 821B) or union superior to paradigms, is an emphasis on the unity which takes place without confusion particular to the intelligible realm.

This concept of *henosis hyper noun*, moreover, appears in Procline thought, especially in *Platonic Theology* I, 3, p. 14, 8–9, where Proclus discusses how Plato argues that the soul is not suspended from intellect but from superior monads which allow for unions above intellect. Here, union of soul takes place beyond intellect, which is superior to soul. In addition to the phrase *henosis hyper noun*, this concept appears in Platonist writings, as writers distinguish between the 'flower of the intellect' and the union beyond intellect. In *PT* I, 3, Proclus describes how the flower of the intellect, or the summit of the intellect, unites the henads to everything in existence. Proclus describes three parts of the soul, each of which corresponds to a different mode of knowledge: the senses, the discursive faculty and the flower of the intellect, whereby the soul engages in an action superior to intellection.[10] In *In Tim.* II, 203, 30–204, 13, Proclus distinguishes five stages of the return of the soul, with the third being the flower of the intellect, whereby the summit of the soul touches – without making union with – the divine essence. At the fifth and final stage, the one of the soul is established in a union with the *monê* of the One. In *In Tim.* I, 211, 9–212, 24, Proclus describes how the intelligible union has a place by the lower intellect through which the henads come to a union with the One.

Despite God's existence beyond the realm of intellect, the journey to the divine, for Dionysius, begins at the level of discourse, including the divine names, scripture and liturgy; here, one can find God in his accessible, perceptible form. The soul, thus, obtains union with the divine through a series of stages which can be distinguished into two groups: the cataphatic, or stage of mystical union centring on God's existence in the perceptible universe, and the apophatic, mystical stage in which, after obtaining a limited degree of knowledge of the divine through perceptible things, the soul undergoes a process of 'unknowing', in which the knowledge of God as obtained through the perceptible images of God proves insufficient, so the soul must strip its understanding of God of everything gained through perceptible things.

As an example of union beyond intellect, Dionysius turns to the figure of Moses as the model for mystical ascension. In the *Mystical Theology* (1000C–1001A), Moses unites to that which is beyond the 'shadow of the unknowable' through a union beyond intellect – here, an elevation of intellect in the form of Moses' climbing of Mt Sinai. In this way, Moses is the model of the intellect elevated to God in a state of unknowing. The structure of Moses' union (*MT* 1000D–1001A) follows the structure Dionysius sets out in chapter 7 of the *Divine Names*, where Moses is first separated

---

9   De Andia (1996), 254.
10   De Andia (1996), 216.

from all things and then united to the divine rays of wisdom, which illuminate him. Dionysius sets out four stages of ascension, beginning with separation from the universe, and followed by purification, illumination, and ascension to the summit. Dionysius, moreover, discusses Moses' entrance into darkness as the elevation of intellect through purification from the limits of knowledge. The figure of Moses was also of interest to both Philo and Gregory of Nyssa, the former having discussed Moses in terms of an ascension from darkness. Dionysius follows this example as he turns to advice for others on how to connect with the One: as with Moses, one avoids darkness in order to look towards the divine, in the form of light:

> But since God is the source of this sacred arrangement in accordance with which the intelligence of sacred beings acquires self-awareness, anyone proceeding to examine his own nature will at the start discover his own identity and he will acquire this first sacred gift as a consequence of his looking up toward the light. Having duly examined with unbiased gaze what he himself is he will avoid the dark pits of ignorance. He will not yet be sufficiently initiated into complete union with and participation in God nor will his longing for this come from within himself. Only gradually will he [the catechumen] be uplifted to a higher state and this because of the mediation of people more advanced than he. Helped on by those at a higher level, helped on as far as the very first ranks, followed by the sacred rules of order he will be uplifted to the summit where the Deity is.
> (*EH* 400CD)

Here, the process of union towards God is outlined fairly clearly: one examines God as he appears in the hierarchy, the contents of which are his own essence; such an examination results in a certain self-awareness which prepares the candidate for gradual uplifting through progressive denial of self-longing and desire, by those in higher spiritual ranks than he; when he is helped as far as possible by those humans above him, he has reached the outer boundary of where God exists. The central point of the passage above is, thus, to remind the catechumen that the aim of his life in the ecclesiastical hierarchy is to learn how to focus all of his attention on God as the first step to union.[11] This style of contemplation, moreover, is exemplified in the life of the monk who renounces all things in his daily life which conflict with his single-mindedness towards God. Of the monks, Dionysius says that they alone have 'a duty to be at one only with the One, to be united with the sacred unity' (*EH* 533D). In addition to centring one's life around God in order to reach God, the sacrament brings one (presumably, received by a person in full contemplation of God) 'towards the One', as well.[12] While all of the above provides one with a method of achieving an approach to God, while stopping at the point of actually reaching God – *The Mystical Theology*, in turn, treats the question of how union and divinization are reached.

---

11 *EH* 401A: 'One cannot participate in contradictory realities at one and the same time, and whoever enters into communion with the One cannot proceed to live a divided life, especially if he hopes for a real participation in the One'.

12 *EH* 424D: 'For scarcely any of the hierarchic sacraments can be performed without the divine Eucharist as the high point of each rite, divinely bringing about a spiritual gathering to the One for him who receives the sacrament, granting him as a gift from God its mysterious perfecting capacities, perfecting in fact his communion with God'.

The Unknowing of God

Because cataphatic theology limits the soul to God as he appears in the world below intellect, apophatic theology is required to transcend intellect and forms of knowing in order to reach the supra-noetic God:

> But the real truth of these matters is in fact far beyond us. That is why their preference is for the way up through negations, since this stands the soul outside everything which is correlative with its own finite nature. Such a way guides the soul through all concepts of the divine, concepts which are themselves transcended by that which is far beyond every name, all reason and all knowledge. (*DN* 981B)

Dionysius' mention here of the negation of divine concepts which are in turn negated, divides the process of unknowing into two stages. In the first, one strips the intellect of all perceptible or tangible ways of thinking about God, as acquired through scripture, liturgy and the divine names of God. In the second stage, the soul then negates even the negative names which result from the first stage – at this stage, the soul transcends every position, including that of negation.

The argument that even the negative propositions about God must be transcended has its root in Platonic discussions of the negative propositions on the One, as outlined in Proclus' commentary on *Parmenides* 142 A (*In Parm.* VII, 64, 25–70, 18). Iamblichus protects the absolute unknowability of the One by suggesting that there are two Ones, the first a totally transcendent entity, 'the ineffable' (*arrhêton*), the second presiding over the henads. For, as Iamblichus argues, whenever something is said of the One, this attribute is added to it, putting the One in danger of being 'particular to something' rather than simply One – any terms attributed to the One, including negative ones, would diminish the One. Iamblichus argues that in order to protect the transcendent unity of the One, the One as cause must be separate from its effect. Syrianus, on the other hand, says that the negative propositions are tied to the positive, in so far as identifying what the One is not is another way of attributing something to the One – that is, negative statements specifically say that the One is other than all these things. At the intelligible level, Syrianus notes that we speak in a specificatory way with our negative statements (on the level of the intelligible); rather than being just negative; this approach looks back to the *megista gene* of the *Sophist*,[13] where one type of being 'is not to be'.[14] Syrianus argues that negative propositions in both the intelligible and sensible spheres say something about the thing which they are negating; at the intelligible level; each Form has its own identity, so that we can say 'is not' when speaking of rest, because it is not movement, or identity or difference. Each Form is different and specific, but still communicates with other Forms.[15] Terms trying to characterize the One, then, are

---

13 Plato, *Soph.* 255E: 'And we shall say that (the character of difference) pervades all (the forms) ...' and 257E: 'The character of difference seems to me to have been parceled out'.

14 On the sensible level, a negative proposition implies a reference to some reality for which we are denying the attributes. Steel (1999), 356.

15 Steel (1999), 356.

specifics that do not affect the integrity of the One. Proclus and Syrianus explain that negation at the sensible level is privative, not specificatory, as it is on the intelligible level.

In contrast to the intelligible and sensible levels, however, at the level of the One, both positive and negative propositions say something about the One. The propositions about the One do not express anything about it, rather, they express our conceptions of it, i.e. negations of the One are the negations of our concepts about it:

> Negative propositions about the One do not really express anything about the One. For nothing at all applies to it, either specifically or privatively, but, as we have said, the name 'one' names our conceptions of it, not the One itself, and so we say that the negation also is about our conception, and none of the negative conclusions that have been stated is about the One, but because of its simplicity, it is exalted above all contrast and all negation. So he rightly added at the end that these negative propositions do not express anything about the One. (*In Parm.* VII, 70, 11–18 K)

Thus, Syrianus credits negative statements with the same metaphysical weight as positive statements – both are limited manners of expressing the One.

The first stage of negation is outlined in Chapter 5 of the *Mystical Theology* (*MT* 1045D–1048B), in which the following are denied:[16]

1.   the spiritual realities, including the divisions of the three hypostases, intellect, and faculty of soul
2.   the categories of the *Parmenides*: number, more or less, motion or rest
3.   the names of God.

Lastly, Dionysius affirms the unknowability of God (*MT* 1048A): 'We make assertions and denials of what is next to it, but never of it, for it is beyond every assertion, being the perfect and unique cause of all things'. God is known through the unknowing typified by darkness and silence. In addition to the union begun through contemplation and abandonment, union takes place through love, although Dionysius does not seem to have a theology of metaphysical ecstasy like many of the Platonists. Unlike Plotinus, who speaks explicitly of the love of the One which drives the soul towards divinisation, Dionysius only uses the term 'ecstasy' when referring to the role of love in the return process, both for the soul returning and God enacting the soul's return: 'This divine yearning brings ecstasy so that the lover belongs not to self but to the beloved … it is shown by the subordinates in their divine return toward what is higher' (*DN* 712A)[17] and 'The very cause of the universe in the beautiful, good superabundance of his benign yearning for all is also carried outside of himself … he does so by virtue of his supernatural and ecstatic capacity to remain, nevertheless, within himself' (*DN* 712B). The crucial difference between Dionysius

---

16 De Andia (1996), 391.

17 Dionysius uses the example of Paul in 2 Cor. 5:13: 'This is why the great Paul, swept along by his yearning for God and seized of its ecstatic power, had this inspired word to say: "It is no longer I who live, but Christ who lives in me"'.

and Plotinus in the process of the soul's return to God lies in this discussion of love; namely, and unlike Plotinus, for instance, the love is not one-sided – rather, not only does the soul love God and wish to return to him, but God, in turn, loves the soul and urges its return. This may reasonably be regarded as a distinctively Christian feature of his thought, since the most that can be attributed to the Neoplatonic One is a general, impersonal benevolence towards all creation.

Dionysius outlines how the soul may go about obtaining a unity with the divine through an abandonment of, or disattachment from, creation, including the created names of God. Prior to complete disattachment, the soul undergoes the process of purification, illumination and contemplation which prepares it for abandonment and entry into the divine. After a hymn invoking the Trinity, Dionysius advises Timothy to leave behind everything perceptible in order to arrive at a union with the ineffable, imperceptible Godhead: 'by an undivided and absolute abandonment of yourself and everything, shedding all and freed from all, you will be uplifted to the ray of the divine shadow which is above everything that is' (*MT* 1000A).[18] That is, once one has become informed in the nature of the divine, initiation takes place into the divine by use of negative theology, since the Godhead is beyond assertions, and even denials (*MT* 1000B). Dionysius here denies not only the names posited in the *Divine Names*, but the categories of being which he attributed to God in the other treatises:

It is not soul or mind, nor does it possess imagination, conviction, speech or understanding. Nor is it speech *per se*, understanding *per se*. It cannot be spoken of and it cannot be grasped by understanding. It is not number or order, greatness or smallness, equality or inequality, similarity or dissimilarity. It is not immovable, moving or at rest. It has no power, it is not power, nor is it light. It does not live nor is it life. It is not a substance, nor is it eternity or time. It cannot be grasped by the understanding since it is neither knowledge nor truth. It is not kingship. It is not wisdom. It is neither one nor oneness, divinity nor goodness. Nor is it a spirit, in the sense in which we understand that term. It is not sonship or fatherhood and it is nothing known to us or to any other being. It falls neither within the predicate of nonbeing nor of being. Existing beings do not know it as it actually is and it does not know them as they are. There is no speaking of it, nor name and knowledge of it. Darkness and light, error and truth – it is none of these. It is beyond every assertion and denial. We make assertions and denials of what is next to it, but never of it, for it is beyond every assertion, being the perfect and unique cause of all things, and,

---

18 The imagery of divine darkness is important for Dionysius and also appears in Letter 1:

Darkness disappears in the light, the more so as there is more light ... However, think of this not in terms of deprivation but rather in terms of transcendence and then you will be able to say something truer than all truth, namely, that the unknowing regarding God escapes anyone possessing physical life and knowledge of beings: His transcendent darkness remains hidden from all light and concealed from all knowledge. (1065A)

and Letter 5:

The divine darkness is that 'unapproachable light' where God is said to live. And if it is invisible because of a superabundant clarity, if it cannot be approached because of the outpouring of its transcendent gift of light, yet it is here that is found everyone worthy to know God and to look upon him. (1073A)

by virtue of its preeminently simple and absolute nature, free of every limitation, beyond every limitation; it is also beyond every denial. (*MT* 1048AB)

Dionysius, thus, denies any kind of assertion of God, including negative statements which can have a metaphysical impact when attributed to an entity such as the One. As with Proclus, who denies all assertions and negations of the One, Dionysius denies positive and negative names of God. However, unlike Proclus, Dionysius appears to go a step further – he seems to pose an ineffable aspect to the highest principle, which he asserts, unlike Proclus, to be God's true nature. In this way, Dionysius seems to follow more closely the metaphysical position of Damascius, whose negative language in describing the One in his *Commentary on the Parmenides* and in his treatise *On First Principles* bears some parallel to Dionysius. Although Damascius seems not to have had much influence over Dionysius, there are certain philosophical tendencies associated with him which may have interested Dionysius.

While Proclus argues in his *Commentary on the Parmenides* that there does not exist a first beyond the primal One, Damascius posits the existence of an ineffable One coming before the One of the first hypothesis.[19] Damascius says of this ineffable One:

> That One is the principle of all things. And Plato also having returned to that principle did not need another principle in his arguments. For that ineffable is not a principle of arguments nor of knowledge; for it is not a principle of living beings nor of beings nor of henads, but of all without qualification, posited beyond all thought. Therefore he did not make any indication about that principle, but starting from the One, he made negations of all other things except the One itself. For ultimately he denied that it is one but he did not deny the One. Moreover he denied even the negation, but not the One, and he denied every name and thought and knowledge; and what else further could one say? He denied the whole and entire Being, yes, even the unified and the unitary and, if you wish, Infinity and the Limit, those two principles, but he did not in the least deny the one that is beyond all those. (Damascius, *De Princ.* I, p. 55, 9–25, trans. Steel (1999))

This passage is of interest because it denies similar categories of the One as Dionysius is careful to deny of God. Despite the obvious differences with respect to Dionysius omitting any mention of Platonic dialogues, the two passages also differ in so far as Dionysius denies the levels of the second hypostasis, including Being and Life, as well as the genera he attributed to God in the *Divine Names*, while Damascius denies names of the henadic realm – Henad, Limit and Infinity, and he is careful to separate the One Being from the One. It is possible that Damascius' efforts here differ from Dionysius' because Damascius is engaged in a debate concerning the topic of the second hypothesis of the *Parmenides* – particularly, whether it deals with the One or with One-Being. Debates concerning what can be said of the One in light of the first hypothesis of the *Parmenides* touch on the subject, although Proclus deduces that the first hypothesis tells us that the One is other than the listed negatives. The propositions about the One do not express anything about it, but rather are the negative ways in which we describe the One, and so should be treated

---

19 On this topic, see Steel (1999), 365ff.

in the same ways as positive statements are treated – that is to say, disregarded as limited. In this way, Dionysius' negative treatment of God in the *Divine Names* more closely resembles Damascius' description of the One, in so far as both try to express a purely negative, ineffable entity.

In his article 'Pseudo-Denys L'Aréopagite, Porphyre et Damascius', Salvatore Lilla outlines linguistic similarities between Dionysius and Damascius. Of particular interest is Damascius' use of the prefix *hyper-* to describe the unknowability of God.[20] Lilla also shows how both authors treat ignorance and silence as aspects of the first principle, rather than just characteristics of human intelligence with respect to the divine (*De princ.* §13, p. 39, 13–14 and §29, p. 84, 19–21). The more accurate language for Dionysius to discuss God as a negation of a negation becomes that of darkness and unknowing. At the beginning of the *Mystical Theology*, Dionysius recommends to Timothy that he must approach the 'ray of darkness' to seek God (*MT* 1025AB), and follows this with an image of a sculptor carving a statue, as one scraping aside material (including positive names of God), in order to find the immaterial God:

> For this would be really to see and to know: to praise the Transcendent One in a transcending way, namely through the denial of all beings. We would be like sculptors who set out to carve a statue. They remove every obstacle to the pure view of the hidden image, and simply by this act of clearing aside they show up the beauty which is hidden. (*MT* 1025AB)

This imagery, originally from Plato's *Phaedrus* 252Dff., seems to be borrowed from Plotinus' *Enneads* I, 6 (1) 9, 7–14, where Plotinus advises how to see into the beauty of the pure Soul in order to know its beauty, including how to fix imperfections in the Soul which is not purely beautiful:

> If you do not find yourself beautiful yet, as does the creator of a statue that is to be made beautiful; he cuts away here, he smooths there, he makes this line lighter, this other purer, until a lovely face has grown upon his work. So do you also: cut away all that is excessive, straighten all that is crooked, bring light to all that is overcast, labor to make all one glow of beauty and never cease chiselling your statue, until there shall shine out on you from it the godlike splendor of virtue, until you shall see the perfect goodness surely established in the stainless shrine. (trans. Gerson–Dillon)

The two passages differ in so far as Dionysius urges the catechumen to find God by sloughing away the material of creation, whereas Plotinus urges one to find the divine beauty of the Soul by attending to its imperfections, but the overall imagery is very similar.

Theoria and Mystical Contemplation

Analogy and connecting ranks of the universe allow all beings to hieratically participate in the divine. This section shows how the angels use *theoria* for ritual

---

20 Lilla (1997).

participation, for even with this higher brand of *theoria*, ritual is still necessary for eliciting *henosis*. This is seen both in the angelic ranks, where primary contemplation is described as an 'initiation' by Jesus, and in the human realm, where the hierarch enters into mystical contemplation by the angels when he is fully initiated into the sacraments. Moral excellence is necessary for proper *theoria* – but this excellence is only part of the structure of initiation. The need to perform liturgies that are experienced is the mandate of *henosis*. This section will show that *theoria* as mystical contemplation is performative in function, very much as in the Neoplatonic theurgical tradition. Because the mystical contemplation of the hierarchs mimics angelic contemplation, this section will begin with an examination of angelic *theoria*. First and foremost, angelic ranks (the angelic hierarchies) partake of a pure enlightenment because of their proximity to the One. Although all the angels are so called because they share a superior capacity to conform to the divine, ranks vary considerably in this power of divine conformity.[21] This distinction in power[22] means that those angels farther away from God rely on the first hierarchy of angelic beings for initiation into pure unification.[23] We in the ecclesiastical hierarchy also receive light mediated through the connective angels. Our *theoria*, however, differs from that of lower angelic orders in that it begins with material symbols and has a limited performative function: primarily, *theoria* serves to purify us for higher unification which is hyper-noetic and non-discursive.[24]

Based on the above-mentioned distinctions, angelic *theoria* is exhibited in nine different degrees according to the nine angelic orders.[25] Although the ranks differ in degree of participation in the divine, generally the angelic orders are all characterized by a theomimetic thinking process.[26] Just to expand on what was explained earlier, the three vertical ranks are divided again into three horizontal categories,[27] equal in power. The ranks closer to God act as the initiators of those less close and the last rank among the celestial beings are said to lack participation in the supreme powers.[28]

---

21 *CH* 196D.

22 This distinction in power relates to the Procline principle that 'in every sacred rank the higher orders have all the illumination and powers of those below them and the subordinate have none of those possessed by their superiors'. *CH* 196BC. Proclus, *ET* prop. 60: 'Whatever principle is the cause of a greater number of effects is superior to that which has a power limited to few objects and which gives rise to parts of those existences constituted by the other as wholes' (trans. Dodds).

23 *CH* 181A.

24 Dionysius uses the Procline term 'henad' to refer to angels only once in the corpus, *DN* 892D. In other places, it refers to divine unity as distinguished from the Trinity *CH* 212C; *DN* 588B, 589D, 637A. See Sheldon-Williams (1972), 65–71.

25 Roques in de Gandillac (1958), xx.

26 *CH* 180A. This passage is interesting because it will basically reappear in the *EH* when Dionysius speaks of the efficacy of the sacraments. The sacraments also become stamped into us for our own *theomimesis*.

27 *CH* 200D: 'The word of God has provided nine explanatory designations for the heavenly beings, and my own sacred initiator has divided these into three-fold groups.' Rorem, note 68: triadic arrangement is taken from Hierotheus, *DN* 3, n. 128.

28 *CH* 181A.

The first group is forever around God and is said to be directly united with him – this group consists of the seraphim, cherubim and thrones. The second group consists of authorities, dominions and powers; the third of angels, archangels and principalities: these last two groups contemplate divine light mediated through the first hierarchy.[29] This appears similar to Syrianus' division of the intelligible world – three triads: an intelligible, an intelligible-intellective and an intellective, the relations between and within which are set out at length in Proclus' *Platonic Theology*, Books III–VI.

The following description of the first angelic hierarchy in the *Celestial Hierarchy* is worth quoting in full:

> The first beings have their place beside the godhead to whom they owe their being … But, again, they are contemplative not because they are contemplating sensible or intellectual symbols nor that they are being elevated to the divine while contemplating composite sacred writing, but because they are filled to completion of light higher than material knowledge and as permitted by the contemplation of that which creates the most beautiful and is the primordial and superessential beauty manifested in three persons because they are judged worthy of communion with Jesus not by means of holy images shaped in such a way as to carry the similar impressions of divine operation, but truly living in first participation of knowledge of divinely operative light and because they have received in a higher degree the divine imitation and they have communion according to their ability in the primordial power in the virtues of divine works and love for mankind. (*CH* 208BC)

This passage describes perfect angelic activity as noetic contemplation, noetic communion with Jesus and knowledge of divine work – activity that culminates in angelic participation in *theourgia*[30] and *philanthropia*. Here, the angels of the first hierarchy have a superior kind of *theoria* as they possess a 'pure vision' in which they are enlightened by the simple and primordial light of God.[31] They do not rely on images or impressions from scripture but are instead granted a primary participation in Jesus.

So far, this description complies with traditional Platonic *theoria* of the Plotinian variety.[32] If one is willing to bear an extended analogy, it is interesting to compare the *nous* of the first angelic hierarchy to the highest part of the Plotinian human soul, which remains in the intelligible world while the lower part descends.[33] Just to summarize, this Plotinian higher intellect 'contemplates' the One transcendently without using discursive reasoning. The lower part of the Plotinian soul descends below and engages with the body, while a middle part serves as our normal level of consciousness. Our higher soul – permanently fixed in the intellect – becomes

---

29 Proclus, *ET*, prop. 28. Dodds explains this triadic configuration that 'two doubly disjunct terms AB and not-A not-B cannot be continuous, but must be linked by an immediate term, either A not-B or B-not A, which forms a triad with them'. Dodds (1992), xxii.

30 Theurgic lights occurs twice more: *DN* I, 4, 589D–592A and *Ep*. 9, 1, 1108A.

31 *CH* 212A. The notion of divine light and the power of enlightenment has its roots in mystery language and the *Chaldaean Oracles*. The Oracles describe the supreme heavenly father enthroned above the world whose vigour flows outwards by means of golden rays; the soul's ascent is described as an ascent towards that light. Lewy (1956), 15.

32 Cf. Plotinus, *Enn*. III, 8: 'On Nature and Contemplation'.

33 Cf. Steel (1976), 34–8.

conscious when it is reflected in our thinking through discursive reasoning. Thus, for Plotinus, we can reunite our middle part to our higher undescended intellect through discursive reasoning alone, without the help of magico-religious rites. In the Dionysian hierarchy, the highest angelic intellect remains permanently above, permanently engaged in pure contemplation with God in a manner similar to the Plotinian undescended intellect. And yet, Dionysius also describes these most perfect initiating beings as they are initiated:

> The very first of the heavenly beings ... begin by exchanging queries among themselves, showing their eagerness to learn and their desire to know how God operates. They do not simply go leaping beyond that outflow of enlightenment provided by God. (*CH* 209C)

Ecstasy

Progressing through the exercises of discursive thinking, the participant must strip himself of every rational process in order to mimic *theoria* as the mystical contemplation of the angels. This process involves the use of negative language[34] characteristic of the divine names,[35] but it also transcends this language.[36] The preferred language, then, is one best described as stripping or ecstatic language; the initiate must strip himself of all language, mind and being (the denial of all being). Without intellect, the participant will be able to engage in direct contemplation of God because the knower and known will be identical. The second half of the equation, ecstasy, has to do with the concepts of *eros* as a movement that breaks the soul out of its own intellect. The transcendent unification that takes place with these two actions is an angelic *theoria* described in initiation language.

With ecstasy, the soul is taken completely out of itself – just as God leaves himself for love of man during creation, so must man mimic God's mode of creation while he returns to God. Namely, an overwhelming love for God forces the soul out of itself, *eros* being 'a hunger for an unending, conceptual, and true communion with the spotless and sublime light, of clear and splendid beauty'.[37] This ecstatic

---

34 Negative theology, as first seen in the first hypothesis of the *Parmenides*, demands the negation even of one's negation. This results in a positive theology: theurgy alone, however, provides souls with the means to transform their obstacles into icons. Damascius showed the utter contradiction involved in making positive statements about the One, including those expressed in negative terms. He argued that the goal of negative theology was not to reach the purity of the One because there was no 'One' to reach. The word *hen* is merely a symbol for the Ineffable.

35 Lossky (1939), 204. Names are used to avoid other expressions susceptible to corrupting this notion of absolute inaccessibility.

36 Negative theology and mystical contemplation differ from one another in that negative theology rests on a discursive train of thought, while mystical contemplation is situated beyond discourse. Negative theology operates in reference to affirmative theology, which limits it and corrects its formulations.

37 *CH* 144A.

union is a radical rupture from the human realm of the intellect.[38] Dionysius builds upon the Plotinian tradition of *eros* as a moving force. Plotinus reinterprets Platonic *eros* in his description of the return to the One. In the *Enneads* (e.g. III, 5), it is a dynamic force that unites the intellect with the Divine Mind. The soul proceeds to unity by logical reasoning, part of which includes an ascetic turning away from this world. Once the philosopher has achieved this amount of otherworldliness he enters a noetic state in which he is able to enter the One, harnessing the part of the intellect that eternally remains with the One. In this state, the Intellect stripped of knowing enters into a drunken euphoria of loving (cf. VI, 7, 35).

Conclusion

Mystical union, according to Plotinus, takes place between the intellectual-principle of the soul and the One when it first intellectually grasps its own contents (it knows itself) and secondly, it advances to know its transcendent source. Here, the internal activity of self-reversion precedes intellectual motion toward the One. The soul prepares herself by turning away from all around her: now she is able to focus her vision solely on the One. With this vision there is no distinction between the seer and thing seen: the union is purely intellectual and without distinction.[39] This is a state of absorbed contemplation, happiness in which 'the soul knows beyond delusion that she is happy': it is the first stage of unity, referred to as 'intellect knowing'. After the soul has cognizance of the One, the Intellect transcends its newly acquired knowledge. The soul comes to the One, whom the soul loves, in a second state known as 'intellect loving'.[40] Here, the soul is stripped of its wisdom in the intoxication of the nectar; 'by this excess it is made simplex and is happy; and to be drunken is better for it than to be too staid for these revels'. Plotinus explains union with the One as a two-stage process. The process begins with soul leaving its physical self to return to its intellect as it resides in the Divine Intellect: the soul euphorically steps out of itself in complete contemplation of the One. In the second stage, the soul must transcend contemplation so that it ascends to the Supreme 'not as reason but as reason's better'.The final union is one of drunken love.

Dionysius uses Plotinian language to explain *eros* as a cosmic system of procession and return. His description differs in that it is further systematized and Christianized. As with Plotinus, however, Dionysius describes *unio mystica* with the language of negation and ecstasy. Likewise, there are two kinds of ecstasy. There is an ecstasy of procession, here Christianized: God himself loves so much that he steps out of himself to create the universe. And there is an ecstasy of return: man's ecstasy as he negates the sensible world, stepping out of his own rationality to unite with God.

---

38 Roques (1952), col. 1898. Ecstasy is above all union to God and divinization: the Dionysian divinization does not consist only in rejoining or liberating in its own purity the more noble part of the soul, nor similarly in regaining the hidden unity.

39 *Enn.* VI, 7, 34.

40 *Enn.* VI, 7, 35, 24ff.

Chapter 9

Conclusion

In the course of Letter 7, written to a certain Bishop Polycarp,[1] Dionysius presents us with a scenario which sheds an ironic light on what must have been a concern to him in real life, the possible unmasking of the extent of his borrowings from the Greeks:

> But you say that the sophist Apollophanes reviles me, that he is calling me a parricide, that he charges me with making unholy use of things Greek to attack the Greeks. It would be more correct to say to him in reply that it is the Greeks who make unholy use of godly things to attack God. They try to banish divine reverence by means of the very wisdom which God has given them. I am not talking here of the beliefs of the common people who in their materialistic and passion-bound way cling to the stories of the poets, and who 'serve the creature rather than the creator' (Rom 1.25). No, I am talking of Apollophanes himself who makes unholy use of godly things to attack God. This knowledge of true being (*ta onta*), which he rightly calls philosophy, and which the divine Paul described as the 'wisdom of God' (1 Cor 1.21–4; 2.7), should have led true philosophers to be uplifted to him who is the cause not only of all beings but also of the very knowledge which one can have of these beings. (*Ep.* 7, 1080AB)

Thus does Dionysius seek to turn the tables on his possible critics. The passage is of interest, as betraying in Dionysius' mind a certain degree of concern as to whether his great enterprise would succeed in evading detection.[2] In the event, he need not have worried. He went on to become, in his assumed persona, one of the pillars of the Eastern Orthodox, and to some degree also of the Western mediaeval, Church.

We in our turn can only marvel at the largeness of his conception. Let us recall the scenario to which we have committed ourselves. Emerging from the milieu of the Platonism of the Alexandrian or Athenian Schools (or both), some time towards the end of the fifth century AD, this extremely clever and well-educated young man, possibly of originally non-Christian birth and upbringing, experienced a conversion to Christianity – of an at least mildly Monophysite tendency, it would seem – probably towards the end of his studies. Instead of rejecting outright the elaborate philosophical system he had studied as the work of Satan, he conceived the magnificent idea of reclaiming it all for Christianity by posing as St Paul's first convert in Athens, and composing an interlocking series of works (with arch references to still

---

1   He may or may not be intended to be identical with the historical Polycarp of Smyrna, but if so, chronological plausibility is stretched to its limit, since Polycarp lived to AD 155 or later.

2   As we have seen in the introduction, certain odd remarks by his first commentator, John of Scythopolis, seem to give evidence also of a certain anxiety, or at least defensiveness, on this front.

others, unfortunately 'lost') which set out a whole system of Christian philosophy, including an elaborate exposition of sacramental theurgy, based upon what he had read and listened to in the Platonist schools of his time. As a Christian philosopher, he owes, certainly, much to the Cappadocian Fathers, and something also to Origen, but his synthesis is largely his own. As an exercise in intellectual *chuzpah*, it is rivalled, perhaps, only by that of Philo of Alexandria, nearly five centuries earlier, in proposing to reclaim the whole of the Pythagorean-Platonic philosophical tradition (including many formulations from Stoicism) for Moses.

What exactly Dionysius' philosophical influences were must, we think, remain somewhat uncertain, though further clarity may be hoped for from future research. We can be reasonably certain that he was well acquainted with the writings of Proclus, but can he also be shown to have been acquainted with those of Damascius? Further close study of his terminology, in comparison with that of Damascius, may well shed firther light on this question; but what are we to say of the works of Plotinus, Porphyry, Iamblichus, and even Syrianus? There is perhaps nothing of Iamblichus' defence and explanation of theurgy in the *De Mysteriis*, or of Syrianus' elaborate explication of the second hypothesis of the *Parmenides*, that he could not have learned of through Proclus; but what of the distinctive metaphysical position of Porphyry, dismissed out of hand by Proclus (without even naming him), and only glancingly alluded to by Damascius in his *De Principiis?* It is possible that Dionysius managed to read for himself such a work as Porphyry's *Commentary on the Parmenides*, but it is possible also that he picked up his Trinitarian theology directly from such a figure as Gregory of Nazianzus, who in turn would have contracted a debt to Porphyry which he would have left entirely unacknowledged. However that may be, it is one of the contentions of this book that it is Porphyry's innovations in metaphysics that provides the key to his doctrine of God as both a totally transcendent Monad and as a Triad of Father, Power (or Life) of the Father, and Son/Intellect.

It is from Iamblichus, as well as a theory of theurgy, that Dionysius might conceivably have adopted the idea of operating under a pseudonym – though Iamblichus' adoption the persona of the Egyptian high-priest Abammon in order to reply with suitable dignity in the *De Mysteriis* to Porphyry's troublesome questions on theurgy in his open letter to the (probably fictitious) Egyptian priest Anebo is a much more transparent literary manoeuvre than that adopted by Dionysius. What state of mind, we may ask, are we to attribute to Dionysius in embarking on this enterprise? Is it a question of conscious fraud, for however worthy a motive, or is it something more complex? A certain amount has been written, notably by Walter Burkert,[3] on the possible mentality that produced the vast and varied array of pseudo-Pythagorean writings during the last two or three centuries BC, and Kurt Aland, more or less contemporaneously, contributed a stimulating essay on the phenomenon of anonymity and pseudonymity in the Christian literature of the first two centuries AD.[4] Burkert argues that the majority of the Pythagorean fraudsters were motivated, not by any desire to enrich themselves (though a market in pseudo-Pythagorica did spring up in the first century BC through the antiquarian enthusiasms of King Juba of

---

3   Burkert (1961).
4   Aland (1961).

Mauretania), but rather by a conviction that Pythagoras and his immediate associates had in fact anticipated all later developments in Greek philosophy, at least in the Platonic, Aristotelian and Stoic traditions, but that they had been precluded from expounding them by reason of their vows of silence; so the pseudonymous authors were simply making up for this deficiency.[5]

As for the early Christians, in Aland's view we must postulate the addition of a further factor in the shape of a conviction, on the part of a number of post-apostolic figures, that one is possessed by the Spirit, and thus in a position to discern directly what a given apostolic figure, such as Paul, would have said on a certain subject, had he been moved by the Spirit to do so. There may be a degree of self-deception involved here, but no real desire to deceive others – rather, a desire to set the record straight.

This insightful analysis of Aland's may well be valid for pseudonymous writers of the first Christian centuries, but we would see Dionysius as adopting a position nearer to that of the Pythagorean pseudepigraphers, or indeed of Philo. If one comes to believe that all truth derives from Christ, then, if one is further persuaded that the Platonists have developed a series of valid insights into the truth, it stands to reason that they must have derived such truth as resides in them from the one source of Truth. It comes to seem reasonable, then, to claim back from them the insights that they have developed – a process characterized some centuries earlier, by Clement of Alexandria, as 'despoiling the Egyptians'. The only problem is to fix on a plausible vehicle for conveying this truth, and St Paul's first convert in Athens – especially as, being a member of the Areopagus, he might be assumed to be well-educated – must have seemed a reasonable candidate.

It is hard indeed to penetrate the state of mind of a man like Dionysius, but something like this must, surely, have been his justification for his actions. His more immediate motivation, of course, though tied in with his larger vision, was to defuse the Chalcedonian–Monophysite controversy by producing, from an impeccable source, a formula describing Christ's nature such as would satisfy both sides. In this latter aim he was not quite successful, but in the process found himself adopted, after some initial hesitation and suspicion, by the orthodox establishment, and consecrated, in that capacity, for over a thousand years as an inspired authority. He may thus be acknowledged to have perpetrated perhaps the most successful forgery in the history of ancient thought.

---

5   Philo of Alexandria, of course, as we have noted above, boldly carries this one stage further, by proposing to reclaim all of Pythagoras' insights, and thus all of (valid) Greek philosophy, for Moses.

Bibliography

Editions Cited of the Principal Texts

Damascius

Westerink, L.G. and J. Combès, *Damascius: Traité des premiers principes*, 3 vols (Paris, 1986–91).
——, *Damascius: Commentaire du Parménide de Platon*, 2 vols (Paris, 1997).

Iamblichus

Clarke, E.C., J.M. Dillon and J.P. Hershbell, *Iamblichus: On the Mysteries* (Atlanta, 2003).
Dillon, J.M., *Iamblichi Chalcidensis in Platonis Dialogos Commentariorum Fragmenta* (Leiden, 1973).
Finamore, J. and J. Dillon, *Iamblichus, De anima: Text, Translation, and Commentary* (Leiden, 2002).

Plotinus

Armstrong, A.H., *Plotinus: The Enneads*, 7 vols (Cambridge, MA, 1966–88).

Porphyry

Smith, A., *Porphyrii philosophi fragmenta* (Stuttgart, 1993).

Proclus

Cousin, V., *Procli Philosophi Platonici opera inedita* (Paris, 1864), pp. 603–1314 (*In Parmenidem*).
Diehl, E., *Procli Diadochi in Platonis Timaeum commentaria*, 3 vols (Leipzig, 1903–1906).
Dodds, E.R., *Proclus, The Elements of Theology: A Revised Text, with Translation, and Commentary* (Oxford, 1992).
Kroll, W., *Procli Diadochi in Platonis Rem publicam commentarii*, 2 vols (Leipzig, 1899–1901).
Morrow, G.R. and J.M. Dillon, *Proclus' Commentary on Plato's Parmenides* (Princeton, 1987).
Opsomer, J. and C. Steel, *Proclus: On the Existence of Evils* (Ithaca, 2002).
Pasquali, G., *Procli Diadochi in Platonis Cratylum commentaria* (Leipzig, 1908).

Saffrey, H.D. and L.G. Westerink, *Proclus: Théologie platonicienne*, 6 vols (Paris 1968–97).
Steel, C., *Trois Études sur la Providence, III, De l'existence du mal*, ed. and trans. D. Isaac, notes by C. Steel (Paris, 1982).

Pseudo-Dionysius

de Gandillac, M., *Oeuvres Complètes du Pseudo-Denys l'Aréopagite* (Paris, 1943).
——, *La hiérarchie céleste. Introduction par René Roques; étude et texte critiques par Günter Heil. Traduction et notes par Maurice de Gandillac* (Paris, 1958).
Rorem, P., *Pseudo-Dionysius: The Complete Works*, trans. C. Luibhéid; foreword, notes and translation collaboration by P. Rorem; preface by R. Roques; introductions by J. Pelikan, J. Leclercq and K. Froehlich (Mahwah, New Jersey, 1987).
Suchla B., G. Heil and A.M. Ritter, *Corpus Dionysiacum* (Berlin, 1990).
van den Daele, A., *Indices Pseudo-Dionysiani* (Louvain, 1941).

Other

Acta conciliorum oecumenicorum (Strasbourg, 1914–), 4–II: 172.
Athanasius, *Letter to Serapion*, trans. A. Robertson, Nicene and Post-Nicene Fathers of the Christian Church (repr. Grand Rapids, 1957).
Gregory of Nyssa, *The Great Catechism*, trans. W. Moore and H.A. Wilson, Nicene and Post-Nicene Fathers of the Christian Church (repr. Grand Rapids, 1972).
Tertullian, *On Baptism*, trans. C. Coxe, Nicene and Post-Nicene Fathers of the Christian Church (repr. Grand Rapids, 1973).

Secondary Literature

Aland, K., 'The Problem of Anonymity and Pseudonymity in Christian Literature of the First Two Centuries', *Journal of Theological Studies*, XII (1961), 39–49.
Boese H., *Procli Diadochi tria opuscula latine Guilelmo de Moerbeka vertente* (Berlin, 1960).
Brons, B., *Sekundäre Textparteien in Corpus Pseudo-Dionysiacum? Literarkritische Beobachtungen zu ausgewählten Textstellen* (Göttingen, 1975).
——, *Gott und Seienden. Untersuchungen zum Verhältnis von neuplatonischer Metaphysik und christlichen Tradition bei Dionysius Areopagita* (Göttingen, 1976).
Burkert, W., 'Hellenistische Pseudopythagorica', *Philologus*, 105 (1961), 28–43.
Corsini, E., *Il trattato de Divinis Nominibus dello Pseudo-Dionigi e i commenti neoplatonici al Parmenide* (Turin, 1962).
Coulter, J., *The Literary Microcosm: Theories of Interpretation of the Later Neoplatonists* (Leiden, 1976).
Dalamais, I., *Eastern Liturgies* (New York, 1960).

Dawson, D., 'Allegorical Reading and the Embodiment of the Soul in Origen', in *Christian Origins: Theology, Rhetoric and Community* ed. L. Ayres and G. Jones (London, 1998).

De Andia, Y., *L'Union à Dieu chez Denys l'Aréopagite* (Leiden, 1996).

Des Places, E., *Oracles Chaldaïques* (Paris, 1971).

Dillon, J., 'Iamblichus and the Origin of the Doctrine of Henads', *Phronesis* 17 (1972), 102–106.

——, 'Porphyry and Iamblichus in Proclus' *Commentary on the Parmenides*', in *Gonimos, Neoplatonic and Byzantine Studies* (Buffalo, 1988), 21–48, repr. in *The Great Tradition: Further Studies in the Development of Platonism and Early Christianity* (Aldershot, 1997), Ch. XVII.

——, 'The Magical Power of Names in Origen', in *The Golden Chain: Studies in the Development of Platonism and Christianity* (Aldershot, 1990).

——, 'Porphyry's Doctrine of the One', in *Sophies Maietores*, ed. M.-O. Goulet-Cazé, G. Madec and D. O'Brien (Paris, 1992), 356–66, repr. in *The Great Tradition*, Ch. XVI.

——, 'Iamblichus and the Henads Again', *The Divine Iamblichus: Philosopher and Man of Gods*, ed. H.J. Blumenthal and E.G. Clark (Bristol, 1993)

——, 'The Platonic Philosopher at Prayer', in *Metaphysik und Religion: Zur Signatur des spätantiken Denkens. Akten des internationalen Kongresses vom 13.–17. März in Würzburg, hrsg. von Th. Kobusch und M. Erler*, Beiträge zur Altertumskunde 160 (München-Leipzig, 2002).

——, 'What Price the Father of the Noetic Triad?', in *Studies on Porphyry*, ed. G. Karamanolis (London, 2006).

—— and L.P. Gerson, *Neoplatonic Philosophy: Introductory Readings* (Indianapolis, 2004).

Gersh, S., *From Iamblichus to Eriugena: An Investigation of the Prehistory and Evolution of the Pseudo-Dionysian Tradition* (Leiden, 1978).

Hadot, P., 'Etre, vie, pensée chez Plotin et avant Plotin', in *Les Sources de Plotin*, Entretiens Fondation Hardt, Vol. V (Genève, 1960).

——,'Fragments d' un commentaire de Porphyre sur la Parménide', *Revue des études grecques*, LXXIV (1961), 410–38.

——, *Porphyre et Victorinus* (Paris, 1968), Vol. II.

——, *Marius Victorinus. Recherches sur sa vie et ses oeuvres* (Paris, 1971), Vol. II.

Hathaway, R., *Hierarchy and the Definition of Order in the Letters of Pseudo-Dionysius. A Study in the Form and Meaning of the Pseudo-Dionysian Writings* (The Hague, 1969).

Honigmann E., *Pierre l'ibérien et les écrits du Pseudo-Denys l'Aréopagite* (Brussels, 1952).

Ivanka, E. von, 'Zum Problem des christlichen Neuplatonismus: I. Was heist eigentlich, "Christlicher Neuplatonismus?"', *Scholastik*, 31 (1956a), 31–40.

——, 'Zum Problem des christlichen Neuplatonismus II: Inwieweit ist Pseudo-Dionysius Areopagita Neuplatoniker?', *Scholastik*, 31 (1956b), 384–403.

Koch, H., 'Proklus als Quelle des Dionysius Areopagita in der Lehre vom Bösen', *Philologus*, 54 (1895), 438–54.

——, *Pseudo-Dionysius Areopagita in seinen Beziehungen zum Neuplatonismus und Mysterienwesen: eine litterarhistorische Untersuchung* (Mainz, 1900).

Labauche, L., *The Three Sacraments of Initiation: Baptism, Confirmation, and the Holy Eucharist* (New York, 1922).

Lamberton, R., *Homer the Theologian: Neoplatonist Allegorical Reading and the Growth of the Epic Tradition* (Berkeley, 1986).

Leeming, B., *Principles of Sacramental Theology* (London, 1960).

Lewy, H., *Chaldean Oracles and Theurgy: Mysticism, Magic and Platonism in the Later Roman Empire* (Cairo, 1956).

Lienhard, J.T., 'Ousia and Hypostasis: The Cappadocian Settlement and the Theology of "One Hypostasis"', in *The Trinity: An Interdisciplinary Symposium on the Trinity*, ed. S. Davis, D. Kendall, and G.O. Collins (Oxford, 1999).

Lilla, S., 'Terminologia trinitaria nello Pseudo-Dionigi l'Areopagita. Suoi antecedenti e sua influenza sugli scrittori successivi', *Augustinianum*, 13 (1973), 609–623.

——, 'Pseudo-Denys L'Aréopagite, Porphyre et Damascius', in *Denys l'Aréopagite et sa postérité en orient et en occident*, ed. Y. de Andia (Paris, 1997).

Lossky, V., 'La théologie négative dans la doctrine de Denys l'Aréopagite', *Revue des Sciences Philosophiques et Theologiques*, 28 (1939), 204–221.

—— and H.-C. Puech, 'La notion des "analogies" chez Denys le Pseudo-Aréopagite', *Archives d'Histoire Doctrinale et Littéraire du Moyen Age*, 5 (1930), 279–309.

Louth, A., 'Pagan Theurgy and Christian Sacramentalism in Denys the Areopagite', *Journal of Theological Studies*, n.s. 37 (1986), 38–43.

——, *Denys, the Areopagite* (London, 1989).

O'Meara, D.J., *Plotinus: An Introduction to the Enneads* (Oxford, 1993).

—— (ed.), *Neoplatonism and Christian Thought* (Norfolk, VA, 1982), 65–74.

Opsomer J., 'Proclus on Demiurgy and Procession: A Neoplatonic Reading of the Timaeus', in *Freedom and Necessity: Essays on Plato's Timaeus*, ed. M.R. Wright (Bristol, 2000).

Pépin, J., 'Hyparxis and hypostasis en Cappadoce', in F. Romano and D.P. Taormina (1994).

Powers, J., *Eucharistic Theology* (New York, 1967).

Prestige, G.L., *God in Patristic Thought* (London, 1952).

Puech, H.-C., 'La ténèbre mystique chez le Pseudo-Dionysius l'Aréopagite et dans la tradition patristique', *Études carmélites*, 23/2 (1938), 33–53.

Rist, J.M., 'Dionysius and Neoplatonism', in *Platonism and its Christian Heritage* (London, 1985).

Romano, F. and D.P. Taormina (eds), *Hyparxis e hypostasis nel neoplatonismo: atti del I Colloquio internazionale del Centro di ricerca sul neoplatonismo, Università degli studi di Catania* (Florence, 1994).

Roques, R. 'Contemplation, extase, et ténebre selon le Ps-Denys', in *Dictionnaire de Spiritualité Ascétique et Mystique, Doctrine et Historique*, Vol. 2 (Paris, 1952).

——, *L'univers dionysien: structure hiérarchique du monde selon le Pseudo-Denys*, (Paris, 1954).

Rorem, P., 'Iamblichus and the Anagogical Method in Pseudo-Dionysian Liturgical Theology', *Studia Patristica*, 18 (Oxford, 1979).

——, *Biblical and Liturgical Symbols within the Pseudo-Dionysian Synthesis* (Toronto, 1984).

——, *Pseudo-Dionysius: a Commentary on the Texts and an Introduction to Their Influence* (New York, 1993).

—— and J. Lamoreaux, *John of Scythopolis and the Dionysian Corpus: Annotating the Areopagite* (Oxford, 1998).

Saffrey, H.-D., 'New Objective Links between the Pseudo-Dionysius and Proclus', in D.J. O'Meara (1982), 64–74.

Sambursky, S. and S. Pines, 'The Concept of Time in Late Neoplatonism', *Proceedings of the Israel Academy of Sciences and Humanities* 2 (1968).

Shaw, G., 'Neoplatonic Theurgy and Dionysius the Areopagite', *Journal of Early Christian Studies*, 7.4 (1995), 573–99.

——, *Theurgy and the Soul: The Neoplatonism of Iamblichus* (University Park, 1995).

Sheldon-Williams, I.P., 'The Ps-Dionysius and the Holy Hierotheus', Texte und Untersuchungen, 93 (Berlin, 1966), 108–117.

——, 'Henads as Angels: Proclus and Pseudo-Dionysius', *Studia Patristica*, VIII 2 = TU 108 (Berlin, 1972), 65–71.

Sheppard, A., *Studies on the Fifth and Sixth Essays of Proclus' Commentary on the Republic* (Göttingen, 1980).

Sicherl, M., 'Ein neuplatonischer Hymnus unter den Gedichten Gregors von Nazianz', in *Gonimos: Neoplatonic and Byzantine Studies Presented to L.G. Westerink*, ed. J.M. Duffy and J.J. Peradotto (Buffalo, 1988).

Smith, A., *Porphyry's Place in the Neoplatonic Tradition: A Study of Post-Plotinian Neoplatonism* (The Hague, 1974).

——, 'Iamblichus' Views on the Relationship of Philosophy to Religion in the *De Mysteriis*', in *Divine Iamblichus: Philosopher and Man of Gods*, ed. H.J. Blumenthal and E.G. Clark (Bristol, 1993).

——, 'Hypostasis and Hyparxis in Porphyry', in F. Romano and D.P. Taormina (1994).

Steel, C., *The Changing Self: A Study on the Soul in Later Neoplatonism: Iamblichus, Damascius, and Priscianus* (Brussels, 1976).

——, 'Le *Sophiste* comme texte théologique dans l'interpretation de Proclus', in *On Proclus and His Influence in Medieval Philosophy* ed. E.P. Bos and P.A. Meijer (New York, 1992).

——, 'Hyparxis chez Proclus', in F. Romano and D.P. Taormina (1994).

——, 'Proclus et Denys: l'existence du mal', in *Denys l'Aréopagite et sa postérité en Orient et en Occident, Actes du Colloque International Paris, 21–24 septembre 1994*, ed. Y. de Andia (Paris, 1997).

——, '"Negatio Negationis": Proclus on the Final Lemma of the First Hypothesis of the Parmenides', in *Traditions of Platonism. Essays in Honour of John Dillon*, ed. J. Cleary (Aldershot, 1999).

Stiglmayer, J., 'Der Neuplatoniker Proclus als Vorlage des sogen. Dionysius Areopagita in der Lehre vom Uebel', *Historisches Jahrbuch*, 16 (1895), 253–73, 721–48.

——, 'Der sogenannte Dionysius Areopagita und Severus von Antiochien', *Scholastik*, 3 (1928), 1–27, 161–89.

Stone, D., *A History of the Doctrine of the Holy Eucharist* (London, 1909).

Struck, P., 'Pagan and Christian Theurgies', *Ancient World*, 32.2 (2001), 25–38.

——, *Birth of the Symbol: Ancient Readers at the Limits of Their Texts* (Princeton, 2004).

——, 'Divination and Literary Criticism?', in *Mantike: Studies in Ancient Divination*, ed. S.I. Johnston and P. Struck (Leiden, 2005).

Thorndike, L., *A History of Magic and Experimental Science* (New York, 1943).

Torjeson, K.J., *Hermeneutical Procedure and Theological Method in Origen's Exegesis* (Berlin, 1985).

Trouillard, J., 'L'activité onomastique selon Proclus', in *De Jamblique à Proclus*, Entretiens Fondation Hardt, Vol. XXI (Geneva, 1974).

Vanneste, J., *Le mystère de Dieu, Essai sur la structure rationnelle de la doctrine mystique du pseudo-Denys l'Aréopagite* (Paris, 1959).

von Balthasar H.U., *Herrlichkeit: Eine theologische Aesthetik*, Vol. II (Einsiedeln, 1962).

Völker, W., *Kontemplation und Exstase bei Pseudo-Dionysius Areopagita* (Wiesbaden, 1958).

Vorgrimler, H., *Sacramental Theology*, trans. L.M. Maloney (Collegeville, 1992).

Index

Aland, K. 132–3
Alexandria 2, 90, 97
Analogy/*analogia* 51, 65–7, 7–11, 91,125
de Andia, Y. 4, 36, 40, 41, 49, 118–19, 122
angels 6–9, 59–62, 67–8, 72–3, 81, 83, 86,
    89, 94, 106–107, 114, 125–8
Antioch 2, 3
Athanasius 2, 41, 109, 113

Basil of Caesarea 34, 37, 39, 40–42, 44,
    109–110
Being 6–7, 15, 20, 23–7, 29, 33–4, 38, 46,
    47–8, 58, 64–5,
Brons, B. 4, 8
Burkert,W. 132

Cappadocian Fathers 2, 34, 37, 39, 54, 132
Chalcedon, Council of 11–12
Chaldaean Oracles 13, 54
Christ, Jesus 5–6, 16, 20, 35, 38, 40, 49, 50,
    60, 91, 93, 100–102, 104, 111–12,
    114, 118, 126, 127
christology 4, 41, 49,
Corsini, E. 4, 22–4, 32,
Cyril of Alexandria 58, 2, 48

Damascius 2, 7, 10, 13, 34, 45, 46, 117, 125,
    128, 132
Dillon, J.M. 19, 21–3, 27, 29–30, 37, 44–7,
    53, 55–7, 63–4, 69, 72, 89, 91–2, 93,
    95, 97, 101, 102, 104, 125
Dionysius of Corinth 1
Dodds, E.R., 37–8, 65, 88, 94, 127

Engelhardt, J.G. 3
Eriugena 3

de Gandillac, M. 4, 126
Gersh, S. 4, 30, 54–5, 66
Good, The 6, 11, 12, 15, 17, 18, 21, 35, 43,
    47, 48, 52, 54, 55, 61, 67, 70–72,
    75–84
Gregory of Nazianzus 7, 34, 40, 109, 132
Gregory of Nyssa 36–7, 39–40, 42, 120

Hathaway, R. 4, 14, 87–9, 96
henad/henadic 12, 23, 24–5, 36–8, 40, 46,
    58, 61, 64–5, 72–3, 80, 88, 119, 121,
    124, 126
henosis 13, 36, 40, 63, 102, 118, 119, 126
hierarch 8–9, 59, 60, 63, 66, 68, 103,
    105–109, 111–13, 115, 117, 126
hierarchy/*hierarchia* 7, 8, 10, 13, 51, 56–7,
    58–9, 60, 62, 63–73, 81, 83, 86,
    93–4, 101–103, 106–107, 109–111,
    114, 117, 120, 126–8
Hierotheus 9, 59, 126
hierourgia 12, 99, 100–102, 111–12
Honigmann, E. 3
hyparxis 11, 41–5
Hypatius of Ephesus 2
hypostasis 26, 26, 38, 41–5, 47, 124

Iamblichus 9, 12, 15, 23, 25–7, 29, 33, 45,
    53, 57, 63–6, 72–3, 76, 89, 92–3, 97,
    99–105, 107, 110–13, 121, 132
Ignatius of Antioch 3
von Ivanka, E. 4

John of Scythopolis 3, 6, 49, 94, 131
Justinian, Emperor 3

Koch, H. 4, 17, 18, 39, 75

Life 6, 12, 15, 24–6, 34–5, 47–8, 61, 64, 77,
    124, 132
Lilla, S 4, 5, 16, 125
Lossky,V. 4, 51
Louth, A. 4, 99–100
Lubhéid, C. 15, 99, 118

Monad 6, 15, 23, 30, 34–5, 41, 53, 118–19,
    132
monê 12, 19, 29, 30, 34, 51, 118–19
monenergism 2, 5
monophysitism 2
monotheletism 2

One, the 6, 10, 12, 15–6, 18–35, 38, 42–3, 45–8, 52–6, 61–2, 64–5, 69–73, 77–8, 103, 106, 117–29
Origen 13, 82, 84, 90, 91, 93, 132
ousia 11, 12, 39, 41–6, 48–9, 86, 89–90, 107–108

Peter the Iberian 2
Philo of Alexandria 12–13, 17, 90, 120, 132–3
Plato 6, 11–12, 15, 17, 20–21, 27, 43, 47, 48, 56–7, 77, 108, 119, 124–5
    Cratylus 17
    Parmenides 12, 15–6, 21–2, 25, 27–9, 31, 33–5, 37–8, 42–3, 47, 58, 73, 121–2, 124, 128, 132
    Phaedrus 125
    Republic 15, 17–18
    Sophist 6, 15, 20, 27, 121
    Timaeus 63, 108
Plotinus 15–18, 24–5, 33–4, 38, 46, 48, 52, 55, 57, 71–2, 75, 81, 104–105, 122–3, 125, 127–9, 132
Polycarp 9–10, 131
Porphyry 5, 9–10, 15–6, 24–7, 33–5, 43, 45–9, 73, 101, 112, 132
prayer 6–7, 63, 102, 111, 113, 118
Priscianus 104–5
procession 6–7, 12, 29, 30, 31, 33–4, 36, 41, 47–8, 51, 54–6, 58, 77, 87, 91, 95, 103, 105, 119, 129
Proclus 2–4, 6–7, 9–10, 12–13, 15–16, 18–35, 38–9, 43–7, 51–9, 61–6, 69, 72–3, 75–96, 99–101, 105, 109–110, 117, 119, 121, 124, 126–7, 132

Rahner, K. 105
return 106, 109, 118–19, 122–3, 128–9
Rist, J.M. 100
Roques, R. 4, 41, 44, 49, 54, 57, 60, 62–3, 65, 68, 86, 126, 129
Rorem, P. 3–4, 9, 63, 99–100, 126, 136

sacrament 8, 12, 49, 57, 59–60, 63, 68, 85, 99–100, 103–114, 117–18, 120, 126
Saffrey, H.–D. 4, 6, 22, 94,
St. Paul 1, 4, 9–10, 39, 99–100, 122, 131, 133
Sambursky, S. 105
Severus of Antioch 2–4
Shaw, G. 99–100, 108
Sheppard, A. 88, 90, 96
Sicherl, M. 7
Smith, A. 5, 43, 100
Soul 24, 28, 43, 56–7, 61, 64–5, 69, 125, 127
soul 5, 7, 9, 24, 26, 30–1, 37, 56, 60, 63–4, 67, 71, 79–81, 83–4, 86–8, 92, 94, 106–107, 111, 114, 117–9, 121–3, 127–9
sphragis 99, 108–110
Spirit, Holy 32, 38, 41, 48, 110–13
Steel, C. 21, 28, 43, 75–7, 80–82, 121, 124, 127
Stiglmayr, J. 2–4, 75
Struck, P. 85, 87, 95, 97, 100, 112
symbol/*symbolon* 7–10, 13, 22, 49, 60, 85–92, 94–7, 99, 101–105, 107–109, 111, 113, 118, 126–7
Syrianus 9, 12, 15, 21–3, 25–8, 30, 33, 39, 57–9, 72–3, 85, 121–2, 127, 132
synthema 87, 92, 101, 103, 108, 112

Tertullian 113
theoria 85–6, 95, 101, 103, 125–8
theurgy/*theourgia* 10, 12, 63, 86, 95, 99–102, 105, 107–108, 110–12, 114–15, 128, 132

Vanneste, J. 4
Vorgrimler, H. 104

Wisdom 6, 12, 15, 25–6, 47–8